W9-DAU-643

A SHORT HISTORY OF RUSSIA

THE U.S.S.R. WORLD POSITION

A SHORT HISTORY
OF RUSSIA

D. M. STURLEY

Senior History Master, The Royal Grammar School, Guildford

HARPER COLOPHON BOOKS
Harper & Row, Publishers
New York

A SHORT HISTORY OF RUSSIA. © 1964 by D. M. Sturley.
All rights reserved. No part of this book may be used or
reproduced in any manner whatsoever without written
permission except in the case of brief quotations embodied in critical articles and reviews. For information
address Harper & Row, Publishers, Incorporated, 49
East 33rd Street, New York, N. Y. 10016.

First HARPER COLOPHON edition published 1966 by
Harper & Row, Publishers, Incorporated, New York.

This book was first published by Longmans, Green and
Company, Ltd., London, in 1964, and is here reprinted
by arrangement.

LIBRARY OF CONGRESS CATALOG CARD NUMBER: 66-19878

Contents

List of Maps

FOREWORD

It should not be necessary to urge the need for an understanding of Russian and American history as part of the general education of boys and girls growing up in the second half of the twentieth century, for their lives will be influenced, if not decided, by the relations between these two powers. The difficulty is to know where to fit it in. Until the G.C.E. authorities include it in their syllabuses the place seems to be either in the fourth or the sixth forms. This book has been written for the intelligent fourteen-to-sixteen-year-old and for the sixth-former in search of a simple introduction.

It has been found possible at Guildford to devise a short course of American and Russian history for able boys in the pre-G.C.E. O level year. This has served as a useful general outline for non-history specialists and as an introduction for those who might wish to pursue the subject further. It has also served as a complement to the normal fifth form work in the following year. The absence of a suitable text-book for the purpose is the sole justification for this work. It has been written almost entirely from secondary sources and the author's debt to the books he mentions will be at once apparent.

The plan has been to present a chronological narrative by reigns, with enough detail to keep the story going, but depending upon questions and suggestions for further reading to stimulate a wider interest. The books mentioned are, in general, only those easily obtainable, in English, from any good library.

The terms Russia and the Russians are used as a matter of convenience to designate the land more correctly known as the U.S.S.R. and the peoples living there.

Spellings of Russian names and terms can be confusing owing to the differences in the alphabet and the practices of transliteration. They should be pronounced phonetically.

Dates, too, can be confusing. Until 1699, the Russian calendar was reckoned from the beginning of the world, and the year began in September. Peter the Great adopted the Julian calendar (Old Style) which was in use in western Europe at the time, but this was inaccurate, since it was eleven days behind in the eighteenth century, twelve days in the nineteenth, and thirteen days in the twentieth centuries. Most of the other European countries changed to the Gregorian calendar (New Style) in the eighteenth century—England did so in 1752—

but the change was not made in Russia until 1918. The dates in this book are given according to the Gregorian calendar.

There is a useful pamphlet published by the Historical Association in its Teaching of History series: No. 4, *Russia—Notes on a Course for Modern Schools*, by P. D. Whiting. The Society for Cultural Relations with the U.S.S.R., 118 Tottenham Court Road, London, W.1., will loan illustrative material, and there is a film strip on the history of Russia published by *Common Ground*.

ACKNOWLEDGEMENTS

I was able to begin this book during a sabbatical term as a Schoolmaster Student at the University of Nottingham. I am grateful to the Surrey Education Committee and to the Headmaster of the Royal Grammar School, Guildford, who gave me leave, and to the Vice-Chancellor of Nottingham University and the Warden of Cripps Hall, whose hospitality I enjoyed.

I am deeply indebted to Dr J. L. H. Keep, who read the manuscript and made many useful suggestions, to Mr D. Floyd, who gave me much help and encouragement, and to Mr J. P. Cole, for help with the chapter on the geography of the U.S.S.R.

I also wish to thank Mrs G. Cotterill, who typed the manuscript, and my wife for her help in many ways.

Part One

CHAPTER I

THE GEOGRAPHIC BACKGROUND

The country that most people refer to as 'Russia' has, since 1922, been officially known as the Union of Soviet Socialist Republics. According to the Constitution it is a federal state formed on the basis of a voluntary union of equal Soviet Socialist Republics, at present fifteen in number, but it is the Russian Republic, and the Russian people, that dominate the others, and Russian is the official language.

The term Russia did not come into general use until the eighteenth century; before that time, although the rulers of Muscovy had made claims to all the Russian lands, i.e. wherever Russian people were settled, Muscovy consisted only of what is now known as the north-eastern part of European Russia. Modern Russia has developed out of the expansion of Muscovy, but there was an earlier Russian State centred on Kiev, the Kievan Rus, which flourished before the Tartar invasions.

A study of Russian history must begin with an appreciation of the geographical factors which, at all times, have influenced the course of events, the actions of the rulers, the economic development of the country, and the character and fortunes of the people.

First, take an atlas, or better still a globe, and consider the size of the country. Modern Russia extends through nearly 180 degrees of longitude halfway round the world. The total area is about eight and a half million square miles, which is approximately one-sixth of the total land area of the world. It covers half of Europe and one-third of Asia: it is three times as big as the United States, and about 180 times as big as England and Wales. From the Baltic to the Pacific it is 6,000 miles—the trains on the Trans-Siberian Railway take twelve days to make the journey—and it is an average of 2,000 miles from north to south.

The Soviet zone of Berlin is only 600 miles from London, the North Pole is less than 1,000 miles from the Russian mainland, and the United States is a mere thirty-six miles across the Bering Strait. There is access to the Arctic Ocean, the Baltic Sea, the Mediterranean via the

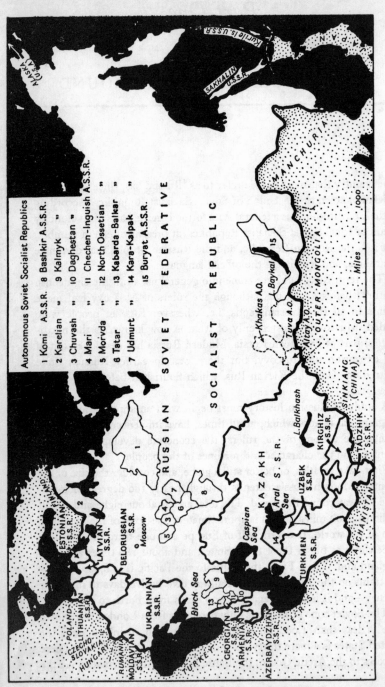

Autonomous Soviet Socialist Republics

1 Komi A.S.S.R.	8 Bashkir A.S.S.R.
2 Karelian "	9 Kalmyk "
3 Chuvash "	10 Daghestan "
4 Mari "	11 Chechen-Inguish A.S.S.R.
5 Mordva "	12 North Ossetian "
6 Tatar "	13 Kabarda-Balkar "
7 Udmurt "	14 Kara-Kalpak "
	15 Buryat A.S.S.R.

THE U.S.S.R. POLITICAL FRONTIERS AND ADMINISTRATIVE DIVISIONS

(See note bottom of p. 3.)

Black Sea, and the Pacific Ocean. Russia's neighbours are Canada (across the North Pole), Scandinavia, Poland, Rumania, Turkey, Persia, Afghanistan, China, Japan and the United States. Consider what problems, as well as what opportunities, of defence and diplomacy such a widespread variety of neighbouring states may give rise to.

This vast size is a source of strength and of weakness in many other ways. About a quarter of the total area lies north of the Arctic Circle; much of the rest is too dry, infertile or inaccessible to be of much use, and only about one million of the eight and a half million square miles are suitable for agriculture, although modern scientific developments and techniques may be able to increase this somewhat in time.

Russia forms the heartland of the Eurasian continent and is sufficiently favourably served with internal lines of communication to encourage dreams of world domination, but the distances are enormous, and the physical barriers in the south are sufficient to have brought these dreams to nothing in the past. Communications are costly and difficult to maintain, and this has contributed to the economic backwardness of Russia in the past, as it has to the problem of exercising the authority of the State, so that an autocratic, centralized form of government has been a natural growth, best suited to the physical conditions. The great amount of land in proportion to the relative shortage of labour to work it, and the existence of an open and moving frontier has led to the desire of the people, on the one hand, to move freely in internal colonization, while on the other, the governments and the landowners have attempted to restrict that freedom of movement, and this has contributed to the development of serfdom and the persistent peasant discontent which constitutes such an important part of Russian history.

Russia's intermediate position between Asia and Europe has made

The administrative units of the U.S.S.R. are based upon the different ethnic groups and the economic regions. It is a federal state of fifteen Union Republics of which the Russian Soviet Federal Socialist Republic is the largest in population and area. The other republics are known as S.S.R.s—Soviet Socialist Republics. There are also, often within the Union Republics, other administrative divisions with various degrees of government autonomy for smaller ethnic groups: these are the A.S.S.R.s—Autonomous Soviet Socialist Republics. In addition, there are Autonomous Oblasts (Regions) for peoples not numerous enough to form A.S.S.R.s and National Okrugs (administrative units forming part of an oblast) for the sparsely populated native areas in Siberia. In theory, promotion to a greater degree of autonomy follows development, so that a N.O. may become an A.O., an A.O. an A.S.S.R., and an A.S.S.R. may in time achieve the status of S.S.R. Changes are frequent according to political or economic development; for example, the Karelo-Finnish S.S.R. was downgraded to become the Karelian A.S.S.R. in 1956, and the Kalmyk A.S.S.R., which was formed from the Kalmyk A.O. in 1935, was removed from the map in 1943 and the entire population was deported. It was restored as an A.O. in 1957 and became an A.S.S.R. again in 1958.

her subject to influences from east and west, so that at times, there has been apparent a kind of dual personality and a blend of cultures. Sometimes Russia has been the defender of Europe against invasion from the east; sometimes Russia has seemed to be the greatest danger to Europe herself. All the invasions have left their mark on Russia: under the Mongols Russia was subject to Asiatic influences, but since the seventeenth century she has absorbed much from the west, while there has been a lasting influence from the early contacts with Byzantium. Sometimes Russia has been cut off almost entirely from Europe, sometimes she has been the intermediary for European influences on the Far East—Chinese Communism, for example—yet out of all this a distinct sense of unity and of Russian national feeling has evolved.

Now to look a little more closely at the major physical characteristics of this vast land. The most obvious feature is the absence of any significant physical barriers in what is essentially an enormous plain reaching from central Asia to north Germany. The Ural mountains running 2,000 miles from north to south, and conventionally separating Asia from Europe, are nowhere more than 8,000 feet high, with an average of 1,500 feet, and are easily passed in the central part. In the north there is the Arctic Ocean and in the south there are the mountains of the Carpathians, the Caucasus and of central Asia, but the freedom of movement that was possible throughout Russia from east to west has been a basic factor in her history. It has led to frequent invasions when the Russians were weak, but it has also helped them to survive by retreating, and to expand when they were strong.

In this great plain the most distinctive, and the most important features are the rivers. The size of the country and its relative flatness has made the rivers long and slow running. In European Russia they radiate out from a central watershed; in Siberia they flow south to north with tributaries running west to east and east to west, so that it is possible to travel by water and portages, or nowadays by connecting canals, to almost every part of Russia. These water roads hold the key to much Russian history: in early times, trade moved from northern Europe via the Baltic, the Neva River, Lake Ladoga and Lake Ilmen, then by portage either to the River Volga, thence to the Caspian Sea and Persia, India and the Far East, or to the Dvina River, then by portage to the River Dnieper, thence to the Black Sea, Constantinople and the Mediterranean. Kiev and Moscow owed their importance to their positions in relation to these waterways. There are 180,000 miles of navigable waterways in Russia: none of them flow towards the major trade routes of the world, and most of them are frozen for a considerable part of the year, but they have always been the chief means of communication, and their importance in the internal history of Russia has been vital, particularly in linking up the forest lands of the north and their timber, furs, honey, wax, etc., with the steppe lands of the south and their food and luxury goods. The early inhabitants moved via the rivers, Siberia was explored and colonized along the rivers, and today they are still important for transport as well as sources of hydro-electric power and for irrigation.

Because of the continental situation and the great extent from north to south there are considerable variations and extremes of climate. In general, rainfall diminishes from north-west to south-east, and drought and famine have often added to the hardships of the Russian peasants. Winters are long and severe: at Verkhoyansk in Siberia, the January mean temperature is −50°C (−58°F), and the July mean is 14°C (59°F)—a range of 64°C (117°F). About 17 per cent of the land is cold desert in the north and another 10 per cent is hot desert in the south. Agriculture is difficult and the life of the people is hard, for the climate has exercised a determining influence upon the formation of the soils and upon the vegetation.

Broadly speaking, Russia is divided latitudinally from west to east by distinct belts of soil, and these, in conjunction with the climatic zones, give rise to parallel zones of vegetation. Working south from the Arctic tundra in the north there is a great belt of coniferous forest covering almost half the country; this gives way to deciduous forest, which in turn opens out on to the grasslands of the steppes; further south there are desert regions beyond the Caspian, while Mediterranean-type vegetation is found around the Black Sea coast, and there are some subtropical areas, as well as some of alpine type in the Caucasus region. The size of Russia, and the variety of vegetation found there, has made the country almost self-sufficient and not dependent upon imports for food supplies.

Historically, the forest and the steppe zones have been both in rivalry with, and complementary to, the development of Russia; the settled or shifting forest culture and farming of the north have complemented the trading and nomadic activity of the south; the forests have offered security and refuge; the steppes have been the highways of invasion and the home of freedom; together, and linked by the rivers, they have made the wealth and the civilization of Russia what it is.

Certain constant themes in Russian history can therefore be related to the geographic conditions: the poverty of the soil and the severity of the climate help to account for economic backwardness, as they probably do for much in the character of the Russian people—their physical endurance, the importance placed upon the community rather

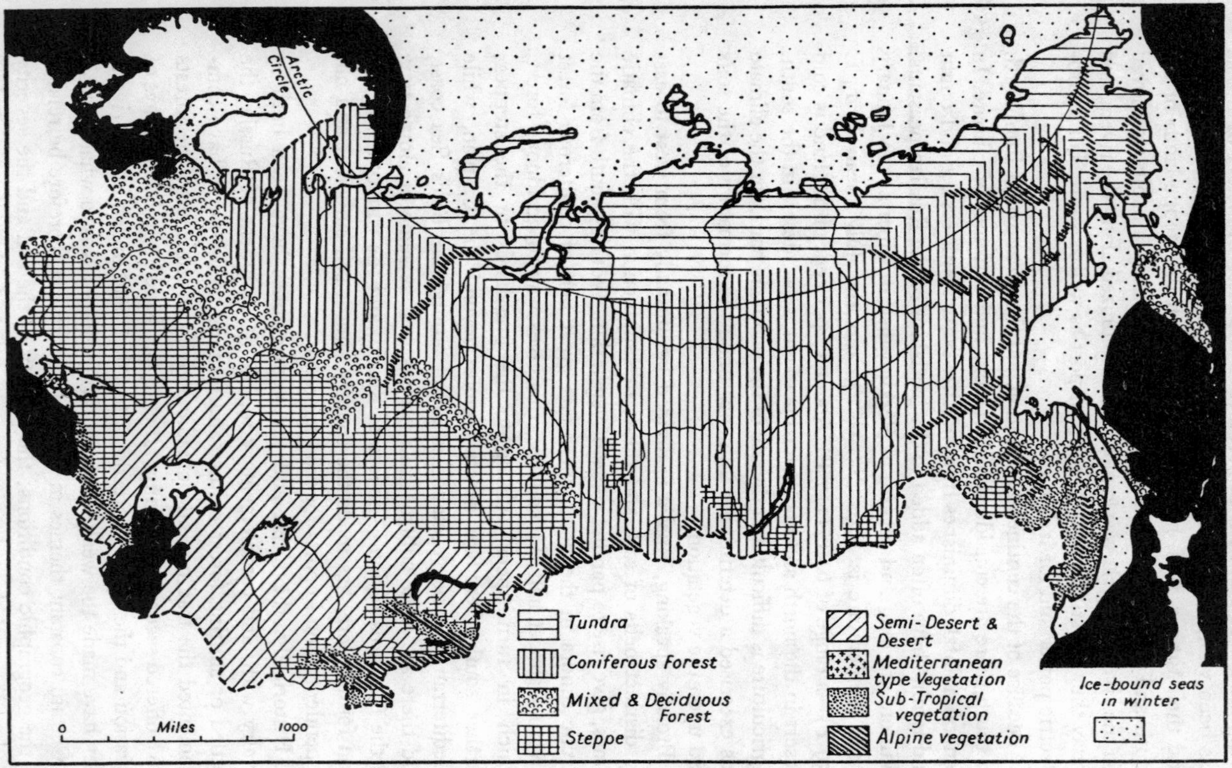

THE U.S.S.R. VEGETATION

Semi-Desert & Desert
Mediterranean type Vegetation
Sub-Tropical vegetation
Alpine vegetation

ice-bound seas in winter

Tundra
Coniferous Forest
Mixed & Deciduous Forest
Steppe

Arctic Circle

Miles
0   1000

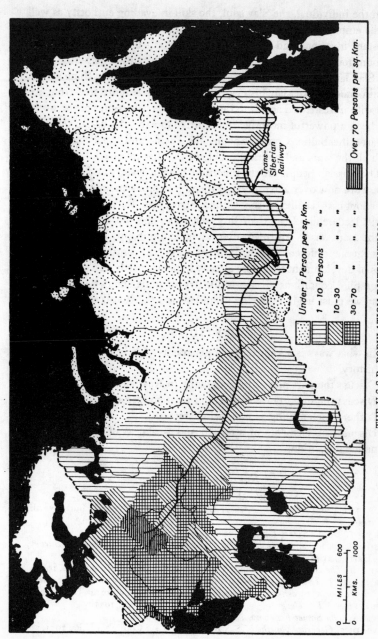

THE U.S.S.R. POPULATION DISTRIBUTION

Note how sparsely populated the U.S.S.R. is in general. In Siberia the population tends to be distributed narrowly along either side of the Trans-Siberian Railway.

than the individual, the Slav soul, the skill in evading authority as well as the emphasis on the need for it, and their devotion to the land. The constant invasions and the feeling of being cut off from Europe may account for the distrust of the foreigner, and the aim of gathering in all the Slav lands has been made feasible by geography. One thing stands out in modern Russian history. The lack of a seaport free from ice and with unrestricted access to the oceans and trade routes of the world has been a powerful incentive in the drive to expand Russian territory towards the Baltic, Constantinople, the Pacific and the Persian Gulf, with all the wars and political problems that has involved.

The Russian people are the inheritors of their history and geography. There are now over 200 million of them, numerous enough and powerful enough to challenge the United States and Europe in a bid for world leadership. Less than fifty years ago the old imperial Russia of the tsars was overthrown after a long and unhappy history, but the new Russia, different as it is, in many ways still continues the general lines of development that were already in being, partly as a result of the geographic conditions. If we would try to understand the Russia of today we must begin by trying to understand the Russia of yesterday.

QUESTIONS

1. In what ways is a knowledge of geography of help to the student of history?
2. Discuss the part played by geography in Russian history.
3. Discuss the importance of rivers in Russian history.
4. Is there such a thing as national character?
5. Discuss the elements of strength and weakness of Russia's international position.

Further Reading

COLE, J. P. *Geography of World Affairs*. Penguin, 1959.
COLE, J. P., and GERMAN, F. C. *A Geography of the U.S.S.R.* Butterworth, 1961.
GRAY, G. D. B. *Soviet Land*. A. and C. Black, 1947.
GREGORY, J. S., and SHAVE, D. W. *The U.S.S.R., a Geographical Survey*. Harrap, 1944.
JORRE, G. *The Soviet Union*, trans. E. D. Laborde. 2nd edn., Longmans, 1961.
KERNER, R. J. *The Urge to the Sea—the Course of Russian History. The role of rivers, portages, ostrogs, monasteries and furs*. Univ. California Press, 1942.
MIROV, N. T. *The Geography of Russia*. New York, Wiley, 1951.
NOVE, A. *The Soviet Economy*. Allen and Unwin, 1961.
SHABAD, T. *Geography of the U.S.S.R.* Oxford U.P.; Columbia U.P., 1951.

Atlases

GOODALL, G. *The Soviet Union in Maps*. G. Philip, 1949.

HORRABIN, J. F., and GREGORY, J. S. *Penguin Atlas of the U.S.S.R.* Penguin, 1945.

KISH, G. *Economic Atlas of the U.S.S.R.* Univ. Michigan Press, 1960.

MCEVEDY, C. *The Penguin Atlas of Medieval History*. Penguin, 1961.

Muir's Historical Atlas. G. Philip, 1961.

The Oxford Regional Economic Atlas of the U.S.S.R. Oxford U.P., 1956.

Shepherd's Historical Atlas. 8th edn. G. Philip, 1959.

SELLMAN, R. R. *A Student's Atlas of Modern History*. Arnold, 1952 and later editions.

STEMBRIDGE, J. H. *An Atlas of the U.S.S.R.* Oxford U.P., 1942.

MILES 0 500

FINNO-UGRIANS

VARANGIANS
9th. Century

TEUTONIC
KNIGHTS
& LITHUANIANS
13 Century

SLAVS
6th. Century

Boundary of Forest Zone
& Steppe Lands

BULGARS
5th. Century

AVARS 6th. Century

HUNS 4th. Century

TARTARS
13th. Century

MAGYARS
1st. Cent.

POLOVTSY
11th.-13th. Century

ALANS
SCYTHIANS
7th.-3rd. Cent. B.C.

PECHENEGS
9th.-10th. Century

GOTHS
2nd.-3rd. Century

SARMATIANS
3rd. B.C.-2nd. Century

MAGYARS
8th. Century

KHAZARS
7th.-10th. Cent.

GREEK COLONIES
7th. Century B.C.

TARTARS
13th. Century

EARLY INHABITANTS AND INVADERS OF RUSSIA

Note that most of the early invaders kept to the open steppe lands and that the
forest acted as a frontier for the Slav people. The Polovtsy were also known as
Cumans and as Kipchaks.

CHAPTER II

EARLY HISTORY: ORIGINS OF THE RUSSIANS AND THE FIRST RUSSIAN STATE

Russian is a Slav language and the Slav peoples are a group of the Indo-European family whose origins are obscure and controversial, but it is thought by some that they originated in the area between what is now known as Poland and the Ukraine. The primitive civilization in this area which archaeologists term the 'Lusatian culture' disappeared about 500 B.C. but a new culture evolved about the beginning of the Christian era which is referred to as the 'Wendish'. Other authorities place the home of the Slavs farther east in central Asia.

But wherever their original home was, the Slav people were always to suffer the fate of movement before, or absorption by, the successive invasions of other peoples across the steppes and the great European plain. Some of these peoples settled down to cultivate the soil, others remained nomads; some concentrated on trade, others on plundering it; some remained comparatively isolated, while others coalesced to form extensive, but temporary, empires.

The Greeks established trading colonies and cities on the northern shore of the Black Sea and referred to the inhabitants of southern Russia as the Scythians, although these were probably only the ruling group over the native inhabitants. The Scythians were replaced about 200 B.C. by the Sarmatians and somewhere in this area the Amazons were supposed to live. The Greeks bought slaves, cattle, hides, furs, fish, timber, wax, honey and grain from the Scythians and sold them textiles, wine, olive oil and luxury goods.

These early inhabitants of southern Russia were in turn overrun by the Alans from the east in the first century A.D., by the Goths from the west in the second and third centuries, by the Huns and Bulgars from the east in the fourth century, and the Avars from the sixth to the eighth century A.D.

Meanwhile the Slav peoples had themselves been on the move spreading out in all directions: south down the Danube and towards the Balkans; west towards the Elbe and the Oder rivers; and east towards central Russia, driving the more primitive Finno-Ugrian peoples north and east. By the ninth century the Slav peoples were scattered over a wide area of eastern Europe, divided among many tribes and at various stages of cultural development. On the basis of language they have been distinguished as follows:

(1) The West Slavs—the ancestors of the present Poles, Czechs and Slovaks.

(2) The South Slavs—the ancestors of the present Serbs, Croats, Slovenes and Bulgarians.

(3) The East Slavs—the ancestors of the present Russians, who in turn are distinguished as (a) the northern group or Great Russians; (b) The central group or Belorussians (White Russians); (c) The southern group or Little Russians (Ukrainians).

Thus the East Slavs were scattered over most of the area now known as Russia in Europe, living for the most part in small settled communities, occupied chiefly in farming, supplemented by hunting and trading. The agriculture was very primitive, with the crudest of ploughs, and produced barley, wheat, rye, oats, flax, hemp, beet, and beans as the chief crops, with the raising of cattle, sheep, horses, pigs and poultry supplemented by hunting, trapping and fishing for meat. In the forest steppe, agriculture was shifting, the people burning down the forest and moving on when the land was exhausted; in the open steppe the two or three field system was used. Spinning, weaving, pottery making and metal working were carried on and the forest supplied honey, furs and timber. Religion took various forms, chiefly animistic. Slave trading was common.

To the south-east of the Slavs a new empire grew up under a people of Turkic origin, the Khazars. From the seventh to the ninth century, the Khazars maintained a military and trading domination over southern Russia that brought a higher degree of civilization and prosperity to the Slavs in return for the tribute exacted from them. The trade routes from the Baltic to Constantinople and Persia via the great Russian rivers were fully exploited.

It was along these routes that the next invaders, the Varangians or Vikings, came. These Scandinavian colonizers began to appear on the Russian side of the Baltic coast during the sixth century and later began to penetrate further into Russia via the rivers. By the ninth century

Varangians were in effective control of the waterways. They were the Rus who have given the Russians their name.

Before the Scandinavians had established full control there was yet another invasion from the east. This time it was the Magyars who overran the Khazars and passed through southern Russia eventually to establish themselves in the plain of Hungary. Together with the Magyars came another group of people, the Pechenegs or Patzinaks. It was these fierce fighters who blocked the mouth of the Dnieper and the trade routes and according to tradition led the people of Novgorod to appeal to the Scandinavians for protection.

In 862 a band of Vikings led by Rurik accepted the offer and before long they had taken control of Novgorod which Rurik ruled until his death in about 879. Rurik had placed relatives in control of outlying districts of Novgorod and despatched two of his followers, Askold and Dir, down the Dnieper towards Constantinople. On the way they made themselves masters of Kiev and the surrounding district (865). They actually made an unsuccessful attack on the capital of the East Roman Empire.

Rurik was succeeded by Oleg, who seized power in Novgorod and set out to conquer the neighbouring area and in 882 captured Kiev after trapping and killing Askold and Dir. He was proclaimed prince, and making Kiev his capital, set out to conquer the surrounding Slav tribes and to exact tribute from them. This is traditionally regarded as the beginnings of the first Russian State.

Kievan Rus—the first Russian State

The site of Kiev is on a high bluff above the River Dnieper near its junction with the Desna. It is strategically situated to connect with the network of waterways between the Baltic and the Black Seas and just within the forest belt where it merges with the steppes. From earliest times it was able to benefit from the trade between north and south and its strength and prosperity were a source of attraction—to the Khazars and the Varangians for example. In time it drew to itself an association of towns and territories that looked to it for protection or that paid it tribute, and from the ninth to the thirteenth century, under its merchant princes, it achieved a European reputation. At the height of Kievan power there were probably seven to eight million people acknowledging the authority of the prince; and Kiev itself, with a population of 100,000 was one of the greatest cities of Europe.

The rulers of Kiev attempted to consolidate their power, to protect trade and to extend their territories. This involved much feuding with the numerous princes who were members of the ruling family, constant

Riga

Dvina

POLOTSK

Novgorod

Suzdal

Vladimir

Route of Varangians

Smolensk

KIEVAN

CHERNIGOV

STATE

VOLHYNIA

Kiev PEREYASLAVL

GALICIA

Dnieper

PECHENEGS

DEPENDENCIES

OF

NOVGOROD

VIAHTKA

Volga

POLOVTSY

River roads and
Trade routes ·············

Furs, honey, wax & slaves
sent to the south.

Silks, perfumes, spices &
precious metals sent north

Constantinople

0   MILES   300

KIEVAN RUS AT ITS GREATEST EXTENT, *c.* 1054. RIVER ROADS AND
TRADE ROUTES

warfare against the Pechenegs, and later the Polovtsy who replaced them in the east, and above all a succession of campaigns against, and trade treaties with, the Greeks of Constantinople.

Oleg was succeeded by Igor (912–945) and Igor by his wife Olga. She was followed by her son, Svyatoslav (960–972) who led expeditions to the north-east, the south-east and towards the Danube, where he planned to move his capital to benefit from the trade with eastern Europe. The Greeks, alarmed by his ambitions, encouraged the Pechenegs to attack him once more from the east. His death was followed by disputes between his sons until in 980 Vladimir seized power and ruled until 1015. Vladimir also engaged in ceaseless warfare, but he is chiefly remembered for the introduction of the Christian faith into Russia. Vladimir's death was followed by another period of quarrelling between sons until the reign of Yaroslav (1019–1054) under whom the Kievan Empire reached its height.

Yaroslav the Wise (1019–1054)

Yaroslav reunited Kiev, Novgorod and Tmutorokan and organized the Kievan Rus. He was a scholar who beautified Kiev with churches and palaces, founded schools and libraries and patronized art and music. The law was codified for the first time as the Russkaya Pravda. He successfully fought the Poles and the Greeks, and inflicted a decisive defeat on the Pechenegs in 1036. He had a European reputation, and married his daughters to the Kings of Hungary, France and Norway, and his sister to the King of Poland.

The Introduction of Christianity

Christian missionaries may have visited southern Russia in the first century A.D. but the Slavs were pagan, as were the successive waves of invaders and conquerors. The Greek missionaries Saint Cyril and Saint Methodius introduced Christianity to Moravia and invented the Slav alphabet in the ninth century. They were also active round the shores of the Black Sea. There was always contact with Constantinople and Christian ideas must have been well known by the traders passing up and down the great water roads of Russia.

There was a church in Kiev in the ninth century and Askold and his followers were baptized. There was a reversion to paganism when Kiev was taken by Oleg. In 957, almost a hundred years later, Olga, wife of Oleg's successor Igor, visited Constantinople and was baptized.

But it is Vladimir who is credited with the introduction of Christianity. The legend is that he took advice from the Jews, Muslims, Roman Catholics and Orthodox Greeks before deciding which faith

to adopt. In fact he wished to secure a marriage with Anne, sister of
the Emperor of Constantinople. In this way Russia adopted the Greek
Orthodox faith officially in 988. The first Metropolitan was appointed
at Kiev in 1037.

The Importance of the Adoption of the Greek Orthodox Faith

The traders and rulers of Kievan Rus had always looked to Constantinople: now to the economic and cultural link was added that of
religion. The permanent theme of Russian aspirations towards Constantinople had been established. From the beginning Vladimir was
determined to have an autonomous Church, free from external control,
over which the ruler could exert supreme authority. There were to be
no struggles between the Church and the State as there were in western
Europe, and in that sense there was to be no stimulus to the development of individual liberty which such a struggle might bring. On the
other hand a State Church could be a force for national unity, in
particular in the encouragement it could give to the development of
the language, music, the arts and architecture. In Russia the Church,
in time, came to be a civilizing body providing for education, training
in the art of administration and the framing of the law. By adopting
Christianity, Russia became the defender of that faith against pagan
and Muslim invaders of Europe from the east, and after the fall of
Constantinople in 1453, a claim could be made for Moscow to be the
third Rome.[1] But by adopting the Greek Orthodox version of Christianity Russia cut herself off from cultural contact with the West Slavs
and the rest of Europe that was Roman Catholic, and became more
closely associated with Byzantine influence.

The Decline of Kievan Rus

Kievan Rus was a commercial confederation rather than a truly national
state. There were separate provinces each with its main city and surrounding towns. The Grand Duke ruled over these first through
appointed governors, but the practice of dividing up the princely
territories at death among the ruling family soon led to each province
having its prince bound only by family loyalty to the others and more
usually leading to struggles for power between them.

The main provinces were: in the north, Polotsk, Smolensk, Novgorod, and Rostov–Suzdal; in the south, Kiev, Chernigov, Volhynia and
Galicia. Each prince had his 'druzhina' or private army, the senior
members of which, the boyars, formed his duma, or council. The

[1] See Appendix D.

towns had their 'veche', or common council which was often an oligarchy. Struggles for power occurred between these bodies also, so that, for example, it was the prince who came to exercise complete authority in Vladimir, in Galicia it was the boyars, and in Novgorod it was the veche—they chose their own prince and their own bishop. What kept them together was the common interest in trade along the great waterways and the need for defence from the east. It was the divisions and the struggles for power that led to the weakness of Kievan Rus before the Tartar invasions. Civil wars weakened the State economically, trade was hampered and Kiev itself was sacked by Andrew Bogolyubsky, Prince of Suzdal, in 1169. In the south the prosperity of Constantinople upon which the trade depended was greatly reduced by the advance of the Seljuk Turks and by the first and fourth crusades, 1096–1204.

The attacks of the Polovtsy who replaced the Pechenegs in south-east Russia were constant from the eleventh to the thirteenth centuries and these were followed by the Tartars who sacked Kiev in 1240, overran the whole of southern Russia, advanced into Hungary and Poland, and eventually set up their capital of Saray near the mouth of the Volga.

In the north-west a Germanic invasion was taking place into the Baltic lands under the Teutonic Order of Knights.

Deforestation around Kiev was making life and trade more difficult and as a result of economic decline, internal disorders and attacks from outside, considerable emigration began to take place. Some moved westwards into Galicia, others north and north-east to the protection of the forests and the expanding towns of Suzdal, Vladimir and Moscow. Andrew Bogolyubsky (1111–1174) encouraged emigration to his new capital of Vladimir.

Ruined by the Tartar invasions, Kiev eventually passed out of Russian history when it came under the control of the Lithuanians in 1321 and became part of Poland in 1386.

From Kiev to Muscovy

In the thirteenth century the Kievan Rus was overwhelmed by the Tartar invasions from the east and by a series of losses of territory to her neighbours in the west. Only Novgorod retained her freedom from invasion, but it was the principality of Moscow that was eventually, by a policy of accommodation with the Tartars, to form the nucleus of the second Russian State.

Novgorod

Novgorod had grown as a trading centre on the banks of the River Volkhov in earliest times. It served to connect Scandinavia and northern Russia with the great water road going south through Kiev to the Black Sea. It was too far north, amid the forests, marshes and poor clay soil, to be self-supporting in food and depended upon trade for its survival. At first this trade consisted largely of exchanging the furs and forest products of the north for the commodities of the south, but with the decline of Kiev trade grew with the western countries of the Hanseatic League. The city paid tribute to Kiev until 1019; from then on its independence was increased and maintained until it found it prudent to recognize the Tartar domination of the rest of Russia.

Novgorod the Great consisted of the city itself, which was governed by a merchant oligarchy through the veche, and the lands extending over most of north-east Russia to the Urals which paid tribute to it.

Alexander Nevsky

The most famous of the rulers of Novgorod was Alexander Nevsky (1220–1263). He is an almost legendary figure who ranks as one of the earliest Russian national heroes and was later canonized by the Orthodox Church.

His life most clearly illustrates the policy that was forced upon Russian princes at this time of collaborating with the Tartars in order to be free to deal with the even more pressing need to defend their states from invasion from the west.

In 1240 he defeated an army of Swedes who were invading his lands, not only for purposes of conquest, but as part of a crusade on behalf of the Roman Catholic against the Greek Orthodox Church. From this battle on the river Neva he took the name Nevsky, and gained his canonization. He next defeated an invasion of the German Knights in 1242 and of the Lithuanians in 1245. But even Alexander counselled submission to the Tartars who recognized him as Grand Prince of Vladimir in 1252.

The Tartar Invasions[1]

Early in the thirteenth century the tribes of Mongolia were united by Khan Temuchin (1162–1227) who renamed himself Jhengis Khan. In 1213 he made himself master of northern China, then turned west to conquer central Asia and Persia. Continuing to move west in what was

[1] The Chinese referred to Temuchin's people as Mongols and the Mongols called them Tatars. In Europe the Tatars were associated with Tartarus (Hell)—hence the spelling Tartars.

really a reconnaissance in force, his armies attacked the Polovtsy who had been so much trouble to the Kievan state for the previous 200 years. In spite of this the Polovtsy appealed to the princes of Kiev, Chernigov and Galicia for help. Their combined forces were defeated

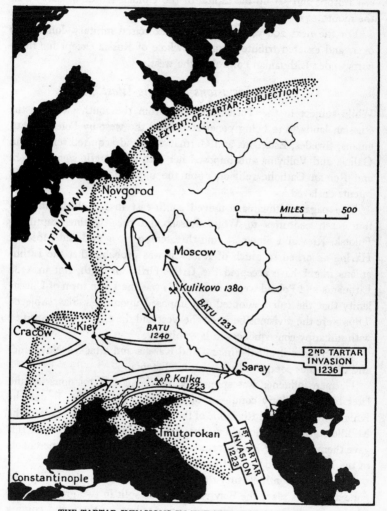

THE TARTAR INVASIONS IN THE THIRTEENTH CENTURY

by the Tartars on the River Kalka in 1223, but for the time being the Tartars went no further west.

Jhengis Khan was succeeded as khan by his grandson Batu (1227–1255) who defeated the Bulgars of the lower Volga region and then, aided by the divisions among the Kievan princes, rapidly overran most of Russia. Vladimir, Pereyaslav and Chernigov fell in 1238, Kiev in 1240, and then he swept on into Hungary and Poland. Only Novgorod retained for the time being her independence. Batu returned from eastern Europe and set up his capital of the Golden Horde at Saray near the mouth of the Volga.

For the next 200 years the Tartars exercised military domination over, and exacted tribute from, the whole of Russia except for those parts under Lithuanian control in the west.

The Invasions from the West

While subject to the Tartar invasions from the south and east the Russian lands were being penetrated from the west by Poles, Lithuanians, Swedes, Estonians and Germans. Poland acquired territory in Galicia and Volhynia and imposed her own aristocratic social system and Roman Catholic religion upon the population who were to all intents enslaved.

The pagan Lithuanians moved south-east in the thirteenth and fourteenth centuries to White Russia and the Ukraine, capturing Polotsk, Kiev and Smolensk and threatening Novgorod and Moscow. Having absorbed so much of Russia it was probable that the Lithuanians might have accepted the Greek Orthodox faith, but in 1386 Lithuania and Poland were united and it was the Latin form of Christianity that the rulers adopted and imposed upon their Slav subjects. Thus were the divisions between the west and the east Slavs intensified with unhappy consequences in later history.

The Swedes invaded Finland and Karelia and attacked Novgorod, and the Danes conquered what is now Estonia.

German influence was spread by merchants and missionaries and later by the military conquests of the Teutonic Knights. It was the Knights who founded Riga, one of the great ports for Baltic trade in the Middle Ages, and who in 1346 bought Estonia from the Danes; this gave them control of Russia's trade with the Baltic. German merchants of the Hanse were dominant in the trade of Novgorod.

By the fourteenth century the embryonic Russian state of Kiev had gone and in its place the Slav peoples were split in two groups: those who were subject to the Tartars, paying tribute to them and coming under Asiatic influences, but looking increasingly to Moscow and the Greek Church for national leadership; and those who had come under Polish–Lithuanian domination, accepting the Roman Catholic faith and coming under western European cultural influences.

The Decline of the Tartar Power

The Tartars exercised a savage military domination over their conquered territories but they did not attempt to colonize. The local princes were obliged to recognize the Great Khan and to pay heavy tribute: for the rest the Tartars were concerned only with punitive raids if the tribute was not forthcoming, with recruiting for their armies and with safeguarding trade. The Tartars had accepted the Muslim faith but made no attempt to enforce it on their captives. With the destruction of the state the Russian Church came to be one of the chief sources of national strength and resistance, gaining for it a power which it retained in succeeding centuries. Eventually, dynastic quarrels weakened the Tartar strength and encouraged Russian attempts to defy their conquerors, but from time to time such attempts met with savage retribution; the countryside was ravaged, the cities sacked, and the people carried off into slavery. It was the principality of Moscow that appeared as the leader of Russian resistance to the Tartars, and a Muscovite prince, Dimitry, who inflicted a defeat on the Tartars at Kulikovo in 1380.

In the late fourteenth century there came a revival of Mongol power under Tamerlane, or Timur (1336–1405). In a series of attacks between 1390 and 1394 he broke up the Golden Horde, occupied Moscow and defeated the Lithuanians, then turned to invade Persia and India before returning to Russia. The collapse of the Golden Horde made it easier for the princes of Muscovy to extend their territories following the death of Tamerlane.

The last invasion of the Tartars was halted by Ivan III (1462–1505) in 1480, but before then the princes of Russia had avoided paying tribute and were asserting their independence.

The Importance of the Tartar Invasions

Eventually a new Russian State centring in the principality of Moscow developed as the Tartar power declined, but the effects of 250 years of subjection to Asiatic masters blending with the inheritance of Byzantine traditions were lasting and are significant for an understanding of later Russian history.

Eastern methods of administration and tax collection were adopted; fashions in dress, and Asiatic customs such as the exclusion of women from all public life and their confinement to the terem remained until Peter the Great attempted to introduce western European ways of life in the late seventeenth century. The Tartar idea of service to the State was accepted and strengthened with the submission of all classes to the absolute rule of the prince, and Russia in general was cut off from western Europe, thus emphasizing the divisions between the East and the West Slavs that had already been made by the acceptance of the Greek faith by the East Slavs and which was to lead to bitter differences between the Russians and the Poles.

Economically too the Tartar invasions were disastrous: the total amount of material destruction was enormous. Not only Kiev and Moscow, but all the Russian cities, except Novgorod, were attacked and ransacked; thousands of Slavs were killed or driven into slavery, commerce and trade was destroyed with the towns, so too were the early forms of democratic self-government of the veches. Without a town life Russia became an agricultural country, economically backward, with an increasing tendency towards the growth of debt serfdom, and a centralized autocratic system of government, supported by a wealthy and privileged Church.

QUESTIONS

1. Give an account of the introduction of Christianity to Russia and indicate some of the consequences.
2. How do you account for the decline of Kievan Rus?
3. Give a brief account of the early history of Russia up to the sacking of Kiev by the Tartars (1240).
4. Discuss the importance of migrations and invasions in the early history of Russia.
5. Give an account of the Tartar invasions and assess their significance in the history of Russia.
6. Find out what you can and make notes on the following:
   The Scythians; Attila and the Huns; the Viking voyages; Yaroslav the Wise; Saints Cyril and Methodius; the Russkaya Pravda; the Greek Orthodox faith; the Seljuk Turks; the Teutonic Knights; the Golden Horde; Alexander Nevsky; the Fourth Crusade.

Further Reading

CHADWICK, N. K. The Beginnings of Russian History. New York, 1946.
DVORNICK, F. The Slavs: Their early history and civilization. Boston. American Academy of Arts and Sciences, 1956.
—— The Making of Central and Eastern Europe. London, The Polish Research Centre, 1949.
H. HOOKHAM. Tamburlaine the Conqueror. Hodder and Stoughton, 1962.
KENDRICK, T. D. A History of the Vikings. Methuen, 1930.
MONGAIT, A. L. Archaeology in the U.S.S.R., trans. Svirsky. Central Books, 1959. Also trans. by M. W. Thompson, Penguin Books, 1961.

PASZKIEWICZ, H. *The Origins of Russia*. Allen and Unwin, 1954.
RICE, T. T. *The Scythians*. Thames and Hudson, 1957.
VERNADSKY, G. *Ancient Russia*. Oxford U.P. for Yale U.P., 1943.
—— *Kievan Russia*. Oxford U.P., 1948.
—— *The Mongols and Russia*. Oxford U.P. for Yale U.P., 1953.
—— *The Origins of Russia*. Oxford U.P., 1959.
The Song of Igor's Campaign, trans. V. Nabokov. Weidenfeld and Nicolson, 1961.

CHAPTER III

THE RISE OF MUSCOVY

Moscow was founded as a frontier post for Suzdal by Dolgorouky and is first heard of in 1147. It remained of very minor importance, suitable only as an 'appanage'[1] for younger sons, and as such, Alexander Nevsky gave it to his son Daniel. The original fortress, surrounded by wooden walls in 1156, was known as the Kremlin.

The security of the fortress and the favourable geographic position which was exploited by a succession of able princes encouraged immigration and expansion, and by the time of Ivan IV (1533–1584) the foundations of modern Russia had been well established.

The map will show that Moscow is sited in a watershed area with the rivers of European Russia radiating out like the spokes of a wheel in all directions, and connecting by water roads with the Baltic, the White Sea, the Caspian and the Black Seas. It is favourably situated to benefit from trade going from east to west and from north to south: it is sufficiently far north to gain from the protection of the forest zone and yet to be in touch with the steppe lands.

Although the rulers of Moscow were obliged to recognize the authority of the Great Khan, and to pay heavy tribute to him (Moscow was destroyed once, and attacked by the Tartars on several occasions), in general they safeguarded their possessions from the worst effects of Tartar domination by a skilful and unscrupulous policy of collaboration. This enabled them to build up their own wealth and territories at the expense of their princely neighbours, until even Novgorod came under Muscovite control, and the Tartars were defeated.

In this process of consolidation and expansion the princes of Muscovy had the support of the Orthodox Church after the Metropolitan left Kiev in 1299 and made Moscow the centre of the Russian Church.

Prince Daniel, youngest son of Alexander Nevsky, and his son,

[1] It became the custom for the princes of the House of Rurik to divide their territories among their sons, and these 'appanages' were hereditary.

Yury, continued Alexander's policy of acting as the khan's collector of tribute, while using the opportunities this gave them to acquire further territories along the lines of the river routes from Moscow, so that by the fifteenth century, Daniel's inheritance of 500 square miles had grown to 15,000.

RUSSIA IN THE FOURTEENTH CENTURY

Two of the early rulers of Moscow are notable for their achievements: Ivan I and Dimitry IV.

Ivan I: Prince of Muscovy, 1305; Grand Prince, 1328–1340

Ivan I was known as 'Kalita', or Moneybags. He knew that money was essential, both to buy off the Tartars and to strengthen his own position. It was during his reign, that the Metropolitan of the Greek

Church moved to Moscow in 1326[1] and that Moscow became the capital and the centre of trade. Ivan also went a long way to ensuring that the principality was not split up among the ruling family, and his successors continued as hereditary princes of Moscow until the line died out in 1598.

Trade was not, however, the chief occupation of the princes of Moscow as it had been of the Varangians. Russia was to be a land of peasants and power was to be with the landowners not the merchants.

Dimitry IV: Grand Prince, 1363–1389

If Ivan built up the wealth and influence of Moscow, it was Dimitry who emphasized where national leadership was to be found. After successfully defending the country against the Lithuanians, he led the first successful attack against the Tartars and raised Russian prestige. The Battle of Kulikovo in 1380 showed that the Tartars were not invincible and even though they recovered, burning Moscow shortly after, and made a further attack on Moscow under Tamerlane in 1408, Dimitry of the Don, as he was now known, had shown what might be done.

From 1389 to 1584 Moscow enjoyed a relatively stable period of government with only five princes, who, free from the usual divisions and feuds of Russian history, were able to concentrate on the main problems of freeing Russia from Tartar rule, extending their own power and domains, and defending them in the west.

Ivan III: 'The Great' Grand Prince of Muscovy, 1462–1505

As in western Europe the late fifteenth century can be seen as a transitional period between medieval and modern times and it is this which gives the reign of Ivan III its significance.

It was Ivan III who first clearly asserted the ruler of Muscovy's claim to be Tsar of all the Russias. He refused to pay further tribute to the Tartars and established a strong monarchy, independent of the nobles and the people, and supreme over the Church. The appanage system of semi-independent principalities and the local self-government of the veches came to an end with their subjection to Moscow. The shift from towns and trade to landowning and agriculture as the economic basis of society led to the development of serfdom; and the gaining of freedom from subjection to the Tartars made it possible for the rulers to devote their attentions to territorial expansion and the gathering in of the Russian lands.

Patient, prudent, and thrifty, Ivan succeeded by cautious diplomacy

[1] Between 1299 and 1326 the Metropolitan was at Vladimir.

in trebling the territory belonging to Moscow, including all the lands of the once great city of Novgorod. First he set about taking into his own hands the appanages of his brothers and the lands that might have gone to other members of the family by the traditional division of estates: Yaroslavl, Riazan, Rostov and Tver. Novgorod capitulated to his demands in 1471 after he had skilfully played on the divisions within the city. It was eventually subjected completely to Moscow, its native aristocracy transported, and its economic life ruined.

Having asserted his supremacy over the Russian princes, Ivan turned to the enemies on the frontier. In the west he was able to exploit the dynastic quarrels between Lithuania and Poland in order to expand into Ukraine and Belorussia and to check the advance into Russian lands that had been proceeding there since the decline of Kiev. The acquisition of Novgorod was an essential first step in the conflict with Poland. In the east Ivan, benefiting from the struggles between the khanates, moved towards the Urals and claimed vague suzerainty over the Khanates of Astrakhan and Kazan, but not over the Tartars of the Crimea,[1] who remained to threaten southern Russia for another 300 years. Attempts were also made to open up communications with western Europe by sending ambassadors to Venice, Hungary and the Holy Roman Emperor, and a treaty was made with Denmark.

In many ways the most significant event of Ivan's reign was his marriage with Zoe, the daughter of the last Greek Emperor of Constantinople. In 1453 Constantinople was taken by the Turks and Zoe became a ward of the Pope. The marriage was suggested to Ivan as a means of bringing the Greek and Roman Churches together, but it had exactly the opposite effect. It took place in 1472, and from then on Ivan, encouraged by Zoe, assumed the role formerly exercised by the eastern emperors as protector of the Greek Orthodox faith, and Russia came increasingly under the influence of the inheritance from Byzantium. The double eagle of the Empire was adopted along with the elaborate court ceremonial, the exaltation of the majesty of the emperor, the administration of justice and the centralization of power.

The administration was in the hands of the Council of the boyars which consisted of the great hereditary landowners supplemented by talented men of humbler birth, jealous of their privileges and feuding and intriguing for more. There grew up a complicated system of ranking known as 'mestnichestvo', by which each noble's place at court was decided by his genealogy.

As the new lands were acquired some of them were handed over

[1] An independent khanate was set up in the Crimea in 1420 when the Golden Horde was in decline.

to army officers in return for the military services which they had performed, and were expected to continue rendering to the tsar. These estates were known as 'pomestie' and their landowners were 'pomeshchiki'. Since the pomeshchiki needed labour for their new lands the process of binding the peasantry still closer to the estates was stimulated and legal serfdom was brought a stage nearer.

While Russia was developing the forms of an autocratic State and her people were moving towards the economic slavery of serfdom, the rest of Europe was experiencing the tremendous intellectual experience of the Renaissance, but although Zoe imported Greek and Italian artists to enlarge the Kremlin and to build the Uspensky Cathedral, little of the spirit of that period found any response in Russia. To the Asiatic influences of the Tartar invasions were now added Byzantine intrigues, customs and ceremonial at the court, while the people remained brutalized and illiterate.

Ivan IV: 'Grozny',[1] 1530–1584

Ivan IV was one of the most remarkable of the Russian rulers and was held by recent Soviet historians to be a national hero comparable with Stalin. Like Stalin he achieved complete subjection to his personal authority through a reign of terror.

Ivan was a dual personality: the reign began well and ended in terror; he could be confiding and suspicious; merciful and brutal, religious and blasphemous; temperate and licentious; humble and arrogant; one thing remained constant—his determination to exercise his own will. His father died when Ivan was only three years old, and he became Grand Duke of Muscovy with his mother as regent. The regency was a most unhappy period for Ivan; he was ill-treated and humiliated while struggles for power went on among the boyars, who may have been responsible for his mother's death when he was seven years old. The struggle for power continued between the rival noble families of the Shuiskys and the Belskys. At the age of thirteen Ivan ordered the death of Andrew Shuisky for his offensive behaviour.[2] This early experience goes far to account for his determination to destroy the powers of the nobility later on. At the age of seventeen, already known for his willpower, his knowledge of theology, his joy in torturing animals, and his licentiousness, he had himself crowned as the first tsar of Russia (1547), ordered a parade of young girls from different parts of the realm, and chose Anastasia Romanov as his wife.

[1] The epithet 'Grozny' is often mistranslated as 'Terrible' although more correctly it means inspiring awe and relates to his regal qualities rather than to his cruel acts.
[2] He had lounged on the royal bed.

The reign began well; in spite of his brutal and vicious manners Ivan was well educated by the standards of the time; he had a good memory and was energetic and hard working. He chose able advisers from outside the ranks of the nobility such as the Metropolitan Macarius, the priest Sylvester and Alexis Adashev; these, together with his wife, seem to share the responsibility for the achievements of the first ten years of the reign.

In 1550 Ivan called a national assembly, where he confessed his youthful sins and promised to rule Russia justly in future. The assembly was called to hear petitions from the provinces drawing attention to abuses in the Government and these were followed by a series of reforms in the administration of justice, the legal code, the army, local government and in the Church.

Centralized absolutism at home and expansion abroad were the sources of Ivan's power. In 1552 he organized a successful expedition against the Tartars of Kazan, and four years later the Khanate of Astrakhan was also taken. The whole of the River Volga was now Russian and the way was open for expansion beyond the Urals into Siberia and towards the Caucasus. The Tartars remained in the Crimea and indeed, in 1571 they attacked and burned Moscow, but Ivan preferred to leave the south and concentrate on his frontiers in the west.

Ivan was determined to gain access to the west through Livonia, and in 1558 began a series of wars that lasted for twenty-four years. At first there was much success, but the determination of Poland-Lithuania, Sweden, Denmark and the Emperor to keep Russia out of the Baltic was so great that eventually all the Russian gains had to be returned.

Ivan not only wanted to break through the hold which foreigners had on Russian trade, but also to import skilled workmen from western European countries. These attempts were also foiled by the rivals on his western frontier who did not wish to see the techniques of their powerful neighbour improved.

After about 1560 there came a change in the nature of the reign. Ivan's wife died, he quarrelled with Sylvester and Alexis, and another of his counsellors, Kurbsky, deserted to the Lithuanians. Ivan felt he could trust no one—he went through a neurotic crisis, threatened to abdicate and, in 1564, instituted a reign of terror, the objects of which were to crush the boyars and to establish his own absolute rule.

He did this by means of the 'oprichnina'. The whole realm was split in two; the 'zemshchina' where the work of government was to be carried on ostensibly as before by the boyars, and the 'oprichnina' which was exclusively the property of the tsar. Here there was a separate administration with the 'oprichniki' or 'men apart', originally 1,000 in number, but later increased, a kind of military bodyguard and secret police responsible for carrying out the reign of terror against the boyars and all who might be considered as enemies of the State. Thus an élite within the service nobility was created, bound to the service of the tsar for the rewards that he could give and take away.

In 1566 Ivan summoned a Zemsky Sobor[1] to discuss the peace offer that had been made by Poland, and the decision was made to carry on with the war in the west. But in foreign affairs things went from bad to worse. Poland and Lithuania were united in 1568, and in 1575, one of the greatest soldiers of the period, Stephen Batory, became king. In the peace of 1582 Ivan was obliged to return his conquests in Lithuania and Livonia.

In the south the Tartars of the Crimea moved north and destroyed Moscow in 1571, and the Turks were attacking Astrakhan. Feeling that everyone was against him, Ivan's brutality became worse in his later years. The Metropolitan Philip was murdered for opposing him, his own son was struck down and killed in a fit of rage in 1581, other members of the family died, as well as many of the boyars, but one of his most savage acts was the destruction of Novgorod and the wholesale murder of families there in 1570 because they were suspected of negotiating with Poland.

There were, however, two significant developments in the later years of the reign of Ivan; one was the opening of diplomatic and trading relations with England, the other was the movement into Siberia.

In 1553 Willoughby and Chancellor set out with three small ships from England to attempt to discover a north-east passage to the Far East. Chancellor reached the White Sea and the site of what is now Archangel. From there he made his way to Moscow where he was granted trading privileges with Russia. For Ivan the Arctic route was a way to contact with the west that avoided his enemies in the Baltic; for the English it was a new means of opening up trade with Persia

[1] ZEMSKY SOBOR

The Zemsky Sobor (Assembly of the Land) consisted of representatives of the boyars, clergy, merchants, towns and districts, and was called to decide important matters of State policy. It evolved from informal consultations, but the first true Zemsky Sobor was called in 1566. It was something like the medieval estates in other European countries but it never developed along parliamentary lines, or as in England under the Tudors, as an instrument to curb the power and privileges of the nobility. At first it was an appointed body, but later its members were elected. The most important Zemsky Sobor, that of 1612, put an end to the Time of Troubles and elected Michael Romanov as tsar. The Zemsky Sobor was abolished by Peter I.

and India. The Muscovy Company was formed to handle this trade and it prospered, but Ivan wished to establish closer diplomatic relations with Queen Elizabeth, even a marriage with some kinswoman of Her Majesty, but this was an alliance that Elizabeth fought shy of.

The expansion into Siberia was largely the work of a private mercantile empire: that of the Stroganov family from Novgorod who were granted the land on the banks of the Kama river by Ivan, free of tax, on condition that they developed and protected it.

The Stroganov concession prospered and additional lands were acquired. In 1581, a cossack[1] called Yermak, was employed to lead an expedition east of the Urals. His small band, having the advantage of firearms, was extremely successful; he took the town of Sibir and moved further east establishing forts and trading posts in western Siberia.

The Achievements of Ivan IV

Ivan died in torment himself after terrorizing Russia for twenty years. He had given Russia the model of autocratic government and prevented the degeneration into aristocratic anarchy that occurred in Poland; he had persistently, if unsuccessfully, attempted to incorporate the Baltic lands into the Russian State so that it could have an outlet to the west; he had attempted to introduce western European artists and technicians to raise the cultural and economic standards of his country; he had added great areas of land in the east and the south-east, and the colonization of Siberia had begun.

Ivan had clear aims, many of which he succeeded in achieving, but what he did he also undid. The main lines of Russian policy; the expansion to the Baltic and to the east, the centralization of the administration and the movement towards autocracy were already in operation before his reign and were continued afterwards. It can be claimed that Ivan's reign did more harm than good and that he destroyed the very system he set up and created a legacy of trouble for his successors.

After the raid on Moscow by the Tartars of the Crimea, he modified the oprichnina leaving the defence of the south to the boyars who had formerly been responsible for that task. The extension of the pomestie especially in the central lands led to the further limitation of the freedom of the peasantry, and this with the oppression and destruction caused by oprichniki led to considerable depopulation, for there was greater freedom and more fertile soil in the new lands that had been acquired in the south-east. This depopulation to some extent accounted for the difficulty that Ivan had in maintaining and supplying his

[1] See chapter IV.

armies in the Livonian wars. Finally, the killing of his son led to the disputes over the succession that followed in the 'Time of Troubles'.

The Time of Troubles

The years 1584–1613, following the death of Ivan IV, are, with good reason, known as the 'Time of Troubles'; it was a revolutionary period when all the discontented elements in Russian society rose against the system imposed by Ivan in support of wild hopes and false pretenders and the situation was made worse by foreign intervention.

Ivan IV had broken the direct line of succession by killing his eldest son. He was succeeded by his second son, Feodor (1584–1598), who was an epileptic; pious, sickly and weak—'a sacristan, not a tsarevitch', while Dimitry, another son by his seventh wife, Maria, was removed to the town of Uglich. For a short time Feodor's uncle, Nikita Romanov, acted as regent but this power soon went to his brother-in-law, Boris Godunov. There was a plot to get rid of Boris by persuading Feodor to divorce his wife, Irene, but Boris foiled this and became regent in 1587.

The Regency of Boris Godunov

Boris meant well: he was able and shrewd, but he was not popular. He was successful against Sweden and the Crimean Tartars and tried to encourage colonization in Siberia, but faced with the problem of depopulation in the central provinces he issued a series of edicts limiting the freedom of movement of the peasants which helped to bring the imposition of legal serfdom a stage nearer. His greatest success was his handling of the visit of the Patriarch of Constantinople which resulted in the establishment of Moscow as a Patriarchate of the Orthodox Church. In 1591 Dimitry was found dead with his throat cut: whether Boris was implicated or not, it left the way clear for his accession when Feodor died in 1598. Maria, the mother of Dimitry had the best claim to the throne, but she preferred to enter a monastery as a nun, Martha.

The new Patriarch summoned a Zemsky Sobor to choose a new tsar. There were two possibilities: Boris or Feodor Romanov,—Boris, who had arranged things well, was chosen.

Tsar Boris Godunov, 1598–1605

After a show of reluctance Boris accepted the crown from the Patriarch, made sure of his position by exiling those boyars who might oppose him, and sent Feodor Romanov to a monastery where he became a monk as Philaret. Boris hoped to rule well and introduce western European ideas into the Government, but circumstances were against him. In the years 1601–1603 there was famine and efforts at relief did not prevent bands of hungry robbers roaming the countryside. Discontent was so great in all sections of society that a series of risings broke out under a number of pretenders to the throne.

The first of these was a monk, Gregory, who claimed to be Dimitry. He gained support from Poland where he adopted the Roman Catholic faith, and with a large but motley army, advanced on Moscow in 1604.

The Reign of the False Dimitry

Boris died while his army was facing that of the pretender Dimitry. He was succeeded by his son Feodor, but the anti-Godunov faction in Moscow supported the pretender for their own purposes and the mob was incited to rise and kill him and his mother.

The false Dimitry had the support of the Polish king, who hoped to benefit from the disorders in Russia, and of the Polish Church, which hoped to bring Russia within the fold of Roman Catholicism. But in addition to his Polish troops who followed him for what they hoped to gain from Russian property, the pretender was also supported by a general rising of the Russian people against the rule of Ivan IV and Boris Godunov. He entered Moscow and was acknowledged by the nun, Martha, as her true son.

Once in Moscow, Dimitry turned against the Poles, but became unpopular because of his behaviour, and because he insisted on marrying a Polish Roman Catholic princess. Once again the boyars aroused the mob, and Dimitry was murdered in 1606.

Tsar Vasily Shuisky, 1606–1610

The leader of the plot against Dimitry was Vasily Shuisky who exposed the body of the true Dimitry in an attempt to discredit the pretender and his supporters. Vasily was proclaimed tsar but he was immediately faced with a series of risings and a number of Dimitrys. The State disintegrated into civil war and was wide open to foreign intervention.

In 1606 occurred what the Soviet historians regard as one of the early class wars when a runaway slave, Ivan Bolotnikov, led a rising of peasants and serfs in a violent campaign of burning, robbing and murder. This was checked by Vasily, only to be followed by other risings supporting a second and a third Dimitry. Besieged in Moscow by the rebels Vasily appealed to the Swedes in 1608 for help. This they were willing to give in return for the lands that had been taken from them by Godunov. Seizing the opportunity of the civil wars the Polish king, Sigismund, invaded Russia because, he claimed, of the Swedish intervention, and besieged Smolensk in 1609.

In 1610 there was another rising in Moscow. Vasily was deposed and sent to a monastery. The Government, such as it was, was now in the hands of the boyars and they asked Ladislaus, son of the King of Poland, to become tsar, on condition that he ruled with their aid and consent.

The Russian Revival

It was really King Sigismund's plan to get the throne for himself and to unite the Russian and Polish thrones, but he underestimated the strength of Russian adherence to the orthodox faith. With the absence of all State authority in the Time of Troubles it was the Russian Church which provided the national leadership, and the Poles under the influence of the Jesuit leadership in the Counter Reformation were seeking to bring the Orthodox Church to accept the authority of Rome. With the Poles in control of Moscow, Smolensk, and the cities of the south-west, and the Swedes in Novgorod and the north-west, and the rest of the country in chaos, there came a national revival and a popular rising against the Poles initiated by the Patriarch Hermogenes in 1611. This almost succeeded in ousting the pro-Polish government from Moscow but the temporary unity did not last. Still urged on by Hermogenes, there came a second anti-Polish rising, this time organized by the patriotic citizens of Nizhny-Novgorod. There, a fund was raised by the mayor, Kuzma Minin, to provide for an army which was led by Prince Dimitry Pozharsky. Other cities joined with Nizhny-Novgorod and gave supplies for Pozharsky who moved to Moscow (still surrounded by the army of the Thief[1] and with a Polish garrison inside), and took it in 1612. A provisional Government had been established earlier and this summoned representatives from each city to choose a tsar. The lot fell upon Michael Romanov, son of the monk, Philaret.

The Importance of the Time of Troubles

Twenty-five years of anarchy and civil war had caused great material destruction and loss of life. The boyar class, in particular, was ruined, while it was the lesser nobility and the city merchants who eventually benefited from the social revolution that had taken place. For the peasants and serfs who had revolted in hopes of gaining economic freedom, the result was the intensification of serfdom, and Russia was doomed to backwardness for another 300 years. But perhaps what was most important was that the opportunity of uniting the Slav peoples was lost for ever.

[1] Nearly all the rebel leaders were known as Thieves or Brigands.

QUESTIONS

1. Give an account of the rise of Muscovy to the death of Ivan IV, 1584.
2. To what extent does Ivan III deserve the title 'The Great'?
3. Give an account of the reign of Ivan IV and assess his achievements.
4. Discuss the early activities of the Russians in Siberia.
5. Give an account of the Time of Troubles and assess its significance in Russian history.
6. Find out what you can and make notes on the following:

   The Kremlin; The cossacks; Tamerlane; the capture of Constantinople by the Turks in 1453; the 'oprichnina'; Willoughby and Chancellor; Anthony Jenkinson; the Stroganovs; the Streltsy; Boris Godunov.

Further Reading

FENNEL, J. L. I. Ed., *The Correspondence between Prince A. M. Kurbsky and Tsar Ivan IV*. Cambridge U.P., 1955.

—— *Ivan the Great of Moscow*. Macmillan, 1961.

GREY, I. 'Ivan the Terrible and Elizabeth of England', *History Today*, Sept. 1962.

HAKLUYT, R. *The Principal Navigations, Voyages, Traffiques, and Discoveries of the English Nation*, Vol. II. Traylen, 1927–8 and Everyman, 1962.

KLYUCHEVSKY, V. O. *History of Russia*, Vol. II, trans. C. J. Hogarth. Dent, 1931.

KOSLOW, J. *Ivan the Terrible*. W. H. Allen, 1961.

WALISZEWSKI, K. *Ivan the Terrible*, trans. Lady Mary Loyd. Evans, London and Philadelphia, 1904.

WIPPER, R. *Ivan Grozny*. Collet, 1948.

Films

Ivan the Terrible by S. M. Eisenstein.
Alexander Nevsky by S. M. Eisenstein.

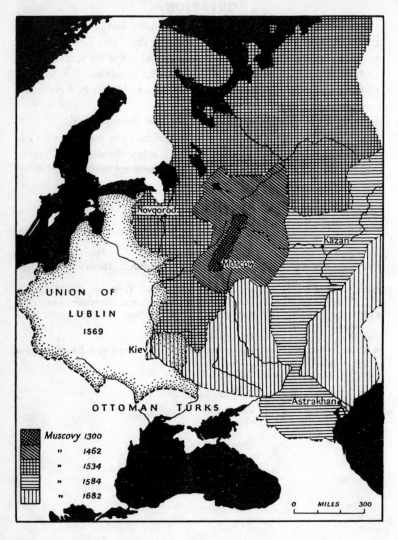

Novgorod

Moscow

UNION OF
LUBLIN
1569

Kazan

Kiev

OTTOMAN TURKS

Astrakhan

Muscovy 1300
"   1462
"   1534
"   1584
"   1682

0   MILES   300

THE EXPANSION OF MUSCOVY TO 1682 AND THE UNION OF LUBLIN, 1569

CHAPTER IV

THE CONDITION OF RUSSIA
IN THE SEVENTEENTH CENTURY

By the seventeenth century the Russian State was in being and the accession of Michael Romanov gave a direct line of succession until the revolution of 1917. It is convenient at this stage to attempt a general review of the condition of the Russian State and society, the machinery of administration, the life of the people and the part played by the Church.

Thanks to the work of Ivan III and Ivan IV the autocratic rule of the tsar had been established, the Church had formulated the idea of Moscow as the third Rome,[1] the need for defence against the Poles, Swedes and Lithuanians in the west, and of the Turks in the south, had stimulated a national consciousness, and the beginnings of expansion outwards had intensified the need for Government control over the new lands. Realization of the technical and cultural isolation of Russia had encouraged the first tentative attempts at seeking western European skills and knowledge to improve the standards of life and production. But whatever the rulers attempted to do, the permanent influences of geography and of previous history were at work, almost inexorably, to determine the general lines of development.

The country that Michael Romanov came to rule after the Time of Troubles was ruined economically and there was brutal poverty and high taxation. The people—about nine million of them—were ignorant and morally and culturally, as well as economically, backward, at a time when the rest of Europe, stimulated by the effects of the Renaissance, the great discoveries and the scientific revolution, was moving rapidly towards higher standards of living and efficiency in the organization of the State.

There was some provision for elementary education here and there, but none for higher education, and the first attempt to found a

[1] See Appendix D.

university at Moscow in 1649 came to nothing. The first printing press had been set up in Moscow in the 1550s to print religious books, but there was little native Russian literature until the eighteenth century.

The State

The need for defence on the frontiers made Russia a military state. The peoples on the frontiers, such as the cossacks, were military colonists who enjoyed relative freedom because of their distance from the centre and as a reward for their military duties. Within the frontiers, everything was, of necessity, subordinated to the needs of the State. The tsar exercised autocratic centralized control over his lands supported by a State Church and a service nobility that was bound to him in return for the land that was his only means of payment for their services of rendering men and supplies for military and State purposes. Since the land was of no use without labour the peasantry came to be tied to the land and were considered as part of it. The towns too, came under the same control; the townsmen were graded in rank, as were the nobility, and rendered service to the State.

The Machinery of Government

1. THE TSAR, although he sometimes sought advice, made all the decisions. Under Ivan IV and the oprichniki this reached the stage when every whim was law and the Church exalted the divine right of the monarch, while the Tartar and Byzantine influences developed a servile etiquette and procedure at court which magnified the authority of the monarchy, and, for the people, created the image of a semi-divine Little Father that remained until 1917.

2. THE 'MINISTRIES' evolved as and when they became necessary in a haphazard way out of the household offices of the early principalities. These 'prikazy' or commands, which were often overlapping in their activities, numbered thirty in 1600, and later grew to fifty: thirteen for the Palace, fifteen for war, ten for economic questions and only twelve for the affairs of the people. It was a complicated and clumsy bureaucratic machine with endless opportunities for intrigue, bribery and corruption.

3. THE DUMA or Council of the boyars consisted of the nobles of varying grades assisted by a number of non-noble clerks. This had traditionally claimed the right to share the work of government (legislation was preceded by the formula, 'The sovereign has instructed and the boyars have given their consent'), but Ivan IV had been determined to limit its powers. The tsar always made the decisions, but the large number of minors and weak rulers, and the determination of the boyars

to maintain and increase their power and privileges, resulted in a series of intrigues between the rival families, and a succession of poisonings, murders and coups d'état that make much of Russian history seem to be nothing but a succession of palace plots and conspiracies.

4.   THE ZEMSKY SOBOR was an embryonic national assembly that never succeeded in taking root and developing any kind of representative or parliamentary government in Russia. There had been an early form of limited general assembly in the reign of Ivan III in 1471, but the first Zemsky Sobor was summoned by Ivan IV in 1566 (see chapter III). It was necessary for Ivan to rely on classes other than the boyars, so he called representatives of the higher clergy, the Boyars' Council, high military and civil officials and merchants and the lesser gentry together on a number of occasions. The Zemsky Sobor played an important part in the Time of Troubles and was much used by the early Romanovs, but once the authority of the tsars had been restored the assembly lost its usefulness for them and the last was called in 1698.[1] The strength of the autocracy and the rigidity of the class divisions prevented any real development of a united representative assembly.

5.   LOCAL GOVERNMENT was in the hands of governors appointed from the court, but by the reforms of Ivan IV some districts were permitted to elect elders for the administration of justice and for the collection of taxes. Both the old system of governors and of local councils existed side by side. In the villages the landowner exercised almost complete authority amounting to power over life and death. Beneath this the village people were organized in the communal mir, with elected elders in the village assembly who were responsible for the allocation of the common lands, etc.

6.   TAXATION was heavy and became heavier on those who paid, that is, the peasantry and the townsmen. At first taxation was chiefly direct in the form of a land tax paid by the village community as a whole, but this later became a tax on each household. Indirect taxation tended to increase, particularly through the granting of monopolies, for example, on tobacco, and the tax on salt. Taxes were farmed, and extortion and corruption were rife. In time the burden of taxation was so great that the impoverished peasantry were forced into debt serfdom or into selling themselves into serfdom. The only alternative was flight. Such wealth as they might have was hoarded and not put to economic use.

[1] The last true Sobor was in 1653. Later assemblies were not really representative of all the land.

7. THE ARMY. Half the income of the State was expended on military matters. The service nobility were expected to perform military duties in return for the land they held. There were also some permanent regiments, the streltsy[1], and considerable use was made of mercenaries and cossacks. There was some artillery, but the chief strength of the Russian armies lay in the size of the population. For the peasant, service was for life, and he could be forcibly drafted as a punishment. If he was married, his wife could marry again after three years, and his children went to a military orphanage.

The Church

The alliance between the Church and the State which had been in effect since the introduction of Christianity was mutually profitable; so profitable in fact, that by the sixteenth century the Church and the monasteries owned vast estates and enjoyed very considerable privileges, such as freedom from taxation and their own courts, while the ruler in turn had been exalted almost to a degree of divine authority. It was the Church alone that had preserved the national consciousness during the Tartar invasions, for it was the only unifying force that was permitted to survive the destruction and national humiliation. Similarly it was the Church that gave the national lead in the Time of Troubles, that assumed the role of head of the Greek Orthodox faith after the fall of Constantinople to the Turks, that consistently refused to acknowledge the claims to supremacy of the Pope, and that gave strength to the resistance to the Polish attempts to take over the Russian State.

In addition to the political services which the Church rendered to the State the monasteries were the main centres of what literary life there was, they were in the forefront of the colonizing activity in the newly acquired lands, and they were often the most effective fortresses in time of need.

In 1439 a Council met at Florence to discuss the unification of the Greek Orthodox and Roman Catholic Churches, and because the Emperor at Constantinople needed help against the Turks he agreed to recognize the supremacy of the Pope. Although the Russians were represented they refused to have anything to do with this betrayal of the faith and in 1448 a Russian Metropolitan was chosen in Moscow by a council of Russian bishops.

Later attempts by the Poles to enforce a union of the faiths in those

[1] The streltsy regiments were formed in the reign of Ivan IV. They were conscripted for life from the townspeople and officered by sons of boyars. They were armed with muskets and their original function was to act as a bodyguard for the tsar. They were garrisoned in tax-free quarters in the towns and were permitted to engage in trade and industry in peacetime.

parts of south-west Russia under their control in the late sixteenth century were a failure and brought bitter opposition by the cossacks to Polish expansion, especially in the revolts led by Bohdan Khmelnitsky. Thus the Russian Church had the dual effect of strengthening national unity while cutting Russia off more completely from western Europe.

In the sixteenth century there came a series of protests against the wealth of the Church and the ignorance of the clergy. The demand for reform was encouraged by those who hoped to gain from the secularization of Church lands. A small group, known as the Trans-Volga Elders, protested at the great wealth of the Church and urged that it should be given up with a return to Christian humility and poverty. The majority of the clergy, on the contrary, claimed that the wealth was necessary to do the work of the Church and followed the lead of Joseph of Volokolamsk. The rulers favoured the Elders because they wished to secularize the Church land in order to extend their grants to the pomeshchicki, but it was the Josephites who upheld the close link between the Church and the State, and it was they who succeeded in crushing the heresy of the Judaizers as those connected with the reformers were known, at a Church Council of 1503. The Josephites promised unqualified support for the tsars if they would stop the secularization of Church lands.

Ivan IV continued the work of Church reform that had been postponed in the reign of Ivan III. Church Councils were summoned between 1547 and 1554 to consider such issues as ritual, morals, law, social institutions, but little genuine reform was achieved except the setting up of the first printing press in Russia to provide books for the better education of the clergy and the *Stoglav* or Church manual of 1551. One of the few martyrs in the Russian Church was the Metropolitan, Philip, who dared to protest against the actions of Ivan IV and paid the penalty for his temerity.

In the seventeenth century there came a schism that was to have lasting effects. Early attempts at reform within the Church had not come to much, and the maintenance of its privileges, and the increase of its wealth, continued, as did the ignorance, obscurantism and bigotry of most of the clergy. The use of the vernacular in the services meant that few priests had the knowledge of Greek and Latin to detect or appreciate errors in the translations that were revealed by Greek scholars such as Dionysius who was set to correct the texts in the early seventeenth century. The reward for his efforts was to be accused of heresy and to be thrown into prison.

The work of reform was next taken up by the Patriarch Nikon who was born a peasant in 1605, became a priest and then a monk, was be-friended by the Tsar Alexis, became an abbot, then Archbishop of Novgorod, and finally Patriarch of Moscow in 1652. He shared much of the work of government and proposed certain reforms designed to ensure that the Ukrainian Church, soon to be incorporated in the Russian State, should remain under the Moscow Patriarchate.

The reforms were matters of form rather than of substance, such as the correct spelling of Jesus, the use of three rather than two fingers in the blessing, the administration of the sacraments and the wearing of beards, but they aroused violent opposition which was made worse by Nikon's arrogant manner and his use of Greek, rather than Russian, advisers.

In 1654 a Church Assembly was held, the books were corrected and a new liturgy was issued. Nikon's only answer to mounting opposition to the reforms was punishment of the offenders, but he became more unpopular and lost the support of the tsar when he made claims for the supremacy of the Church over the State, until in despair, he retired to a monastery and was eventually deposed in 1666.

The corrected books remained, but the opposition continued. Those who insisted on retaining the old forms became known as the 'Raskolniki' or Old Believers. They held to their beliefs through much persecution, especially in the time of Peter I, and they were to be found involved in many of the revolts of later times. The most renowned revolt occurred when a group of 'Raskolniki' sought refuge with the monks of the Solovetsky monastery and withstood a siege lasting for seven years from 1668 to 1676. In time, the 'Raskolniki' split into sects which suffered a history of persecution and expulsion lasting to the twentieth century.

Thus religious consciousness was intensified by the schism; religious persecution became a feature of Russian life, many useful members of society were lost through emigration, and internal unity became more precarious. Another important result was that it tended to accentuate the gulf between the privileged classes and the rest of society by adding religious to social and economic differences, while it is probably also true that it led to a loss of zeal on the part of the official Church, thus weakening it and preparing the way for Peter I's subordination of the Church to the State. In the nineteenth century between ten and twenty million of the population were Old Believers, a minority too large to be persecuted, and some of the restrictions on them were eased until all restriction disappeared in 1917.

The Organization of the Russian Orthodox Church

The Greek Orthodox Church was organized in patriarchates: at Constantinople, Jerusalem, Antioch and Alexandria. Each patriarchate was divided into metropolitanates and bishoprics, and the bishoprics into parishes. In Russia the clergy were divided into regular and secular, with marked class distinction. The regular clergy were those who had taken monastic vows and were called the black clergy, and only these could reach the higher ranks of the Church hierarchy. The secular clergy were known as white clergy and ministered to the spiritual needs of the people as parish priests. These married, and their positions were often hereditary. Generally speaking they were barely literate and little better off socially and economically than the peasants they ministered.

The Patriarch of Constantinople created a metropolitanate at Kiev in 1037 when Christianity was introduced to Russia, but with the decline of Kiev the metropolitan moved first to Vladimir and then to Moscow in 1326. After the Council of Florence in 1439 Moscow decided to break with the Patriarch of Constantinople and future metropolitans were chosen by a Council of Bishops. At the same time the Patriarch of Constantinople appointed a new metropolitan at Kiev. After the fall of Constantinople to the Turks in 1453 Moscow regarded itself as the true centre of the Greek Orthodox Faith and the third Rome.[1] In 1589 the Metropolitanate of Moscow was raised to the status of a patriarchate: thus while still a part of the Greek Orthodox Church it was now a fully national church and was known as the Russian Orthodox Church. The Patriarchate was abolished by Peter the Great in 1721 who replaced it by the Most Holy Synod. A Church Council restored the Patriarchate in 1917 after the fall of the monarchy, but after the death of the Patriarch Tikhon in 1925 the Soviet authorities refused to allow the election of a new patriarch until 1943.

The Greek Orthodox Faith is based on the Old and the New Testaments, on the writings of the Fathers, and on the decisions of the first seven General Councils of the Church, but differences arose on matters of interpretation and dogma between the eastern and western branches centred at Constantinople and Rome.

In particular they differed on the essential nature of the Godhead and the doctrine of the Godhead in relation with manhood in the incarnation. The break came in the dispute over the *Filioque* clause defining the procession of the Holy Ghost. In the Apostles' Creed, the Eastern Church held that the Holy Ghost proceeded from the Father, while the Western Church added that the Holy Ghost proceeded from

[1] See Appendix D.

the Father and the Son. In 1054, Pope Leo IX excommunicated Michael Cerularius and his adherents in Constantinople for refusing to accept this addition.

The Eastern Church could never accept the claims to primacy of the Bishop of Rome nor the monarchical organization of the Western Church. The Orthodox Church is more like an oligarchy, or federation of bishops, each one supreme head of his own autocephalous church.

Some practices and dogmas, and indeed the architecture which expresses them, are quite different from those of the Roman Catholic Church. The emphasis in the Orthodox Church is on worship rather than on specific creeds: there are differences in the administration of the sacraments and in the confession; the laity partake both of the bread, which is leavened, and of the wine; the congregation stands throughout the service and does not take part in the liturgy; no graven images, only two-dimensional pictures and ikons are allowed; the secular clergy are permitted, indeed expected, to marry.[1]

The Condition of the People

In the seventeenth century the realization that Russia could not meet her western neighbours on equal terms, either militarily, economically or culturally, without adopting western skills and knowledge, led to a great increase in the number of professional men—doctors, engineers, merchants, army and navy officers—either being invited or making their own way to Russia from western Europe. There were about 18,000 foreigners in Russia in the reign of Feodor III. Numbers of Greek theologians and scholars were also prominent in the work of reforming the Church. By the end of the seventeenth century western European styles of dress, architecture, furniture, etc., as well as manners and etiquette were being adopted by certain sections of society. These influences, although important, were of course confined to a small section of the population—the court nobility and richer merchants. Yet even here there were acute divisions between those who were opposed to all importations as defiling the Slav soul, and others who wished, by adopting western European customs and techniques, to raise Russia to the cultural and material level of her western neighbours.

For the rest of the people there was frightful poverty, hardship and oppression. As the upper sections of society were beginning to enjoy higher and more civilized standards the great majority of the Russian people were being bound more closely into serfdom and the human

[1] For more information on the Greek Orthodox Faith see (a) Concise Encyclopaedia of Living Faiths, ed. R. C. Zaehner; (b) N. Zernov, Eastern Christendom; (c) T. Ware. The Orthodox Church, Penguin, 1963.

wretchedness which that entailed. To the devastations of invasion and civil war were added regular outbreaks of plague, famine and drought. Crushing taxation and the tyranny of the landowner ground the peasant at first into debt and then into serfdom or slavery. Evasion became the peasants' natural reaction to all authority, and drunkenness, flight or rebellion, his only means of expressing his discontent.

Punishments were savage. Torture was in general use, and tsars like Ivan IV and Peter I were quite prepared to administer it themselves. Beatings, beheadings and hangings were freely carried out; poisoning, flaying alive, the breaking of limbs and cutting off of ears, tongues and noses, were common variations, while exile to the rigours of life in Siberia was among the kindest of the punishments. When Ivan IV destroyed Novgorod thousands of people were killed by being thrown in the river and having men in boats to push them under, while the atrocities committed by both sides in the various peasant risings of the seventeenth and eighteenth centuries were appalling even by Russian standards.

The Development of Serfdom

Serfdom was common throughout Europe in the Middle Ages but changing social, economic, political and military conditions led in time to the freeing of personal obligations and the evolution of different links between the various orders of society. In Russia, on the contrary, serfdom was intensified and extended and was not abolished until 1861.

Until very recent times more than 95 per cent of the Russian people were peasants working in agriculture, yet the vast size of Russia and the nomadic instinct of the peasantry meant that there was always a shortage of labour for this vital activity. As the Russian rulers began to extend their possessions the need to ensure the productivity of the estates led to measures to retain the labour of the peasantry.

The Grand Prince of Moscow, Ivan III (1462–1505) instituted the system known as 'pomestie' whereby confiscated lands were distributed to army officers in return for certain services which they were obliged to render to him. Since the new owners of the estates could not render their services without peasants to work the land they sought means of ensuring an adequate labour force by limiting freedom of movement. The owner could offer protection or capital in the form of seeds or livestock to the peasant in need of it in return for payment by service. In this way debt serfdom evolved. Once the peasant had paid his debt he was free to move. In 1497 this freedom to move was limited to once a year in November. If the debt was not paid off he must work for another year.

By the sixteenth century the old common lands were fast disappearing and most of central Muscovy consisted of private estates either owned by the Crown, the Church, the hereditary nobility or by the pomeshchiki (the pomestie owners). The process had been hastened by the establishment of the oprichnina by Ivan Grozny in 1565. Wars, famines and harsh taxation made the labour shortage more pressing, so that landowners were obliged to get as much as possible out of those peasants they had while competing with other landowners for the available supply; indeed they sometimes resorted to kidnapping. As the landowners became increasingly influential at court and in the Government they were able to use their political power to extend their privileges and to strengthen the legal bonds which tied the peasantry to their estates. Flight was the only way out for the peasant and many did run away to join the cossacks or to go east of the Urals, but others were too poor, or too closely bound to be able to do so. Nevertheless almost half the villages in the central provinces had been abandoned in 1600. In 1597 owners were ordered to return to their former masters all runaway peasants who had settled on their estates in the past five years.

In 1649, at a time when it was disappearing from western Europe, serfdom was legally established by abolishing the time limit, so that runaway serfs were now liable to be returned no matter how long since they had escaped. Yet serfs were still a minority of the population: the extension of the system was to come later. In Catherine II's reign, 56 per cent were serfs: just before their liberation in 1861, nearly 90 per cent.

There were two kinds of private serf: the domestic serfs who held no land and were little more than household slaves, and the field serfs who held some land and a house which they paid for either by working on the owner's land, usually three days per week, or by rendering services of some kind (barshchina). Others paid for their land in money or in kind (obrok). The distribution of serfdom was not uniform; it tended to be most prevalent in the more fertile agricultural areas where labour was most necessary and less so in the north and in Siberia.

From the seventeenth century there came a series of edicts extending serfdom; at first limiting and eventually prohibiting the peasants' freedom of movement and introducing the system to areas where it had been previously unknown, for example, to the Ukraine. As manufacturing industry developed it was extended there also and a growing class of industrial serfs was created. In 1736 there was an edict binding workmen and their families to the factory or the mine for ever.

The lot of the peasant got worse as the privileges of the landowners increased. They could be bought, sold, hired out or gambled away; indeed bred and treated like the stock of the estate. Serfs were advertised as follows in the eighteenth century.

1. To be sold: a barber, and in addition to that, four bedsteads, an eiderdown, and other domestic chattels.
2. To be sold: banqueting tablecloths and also two trained girls and a peasant.
3. To be sold: a girl of sixteen of good behaviour and a second-hand slightly used carriage.

Passports were needed to move from place to place: beatings were common, while male serfs who had offended could be sent to join the army, which in effect meant banishment from their families for life.

The only alternative to a life of grinding oppression and poverty was drunkenness or rebellion. Serf mutinies and peasant risings were a constant feature of Russian history.

Peter the Great tried to create a new nobility. His idea was that of a state in which service should be due from all. Thus members of the upper classes must serve in either the army, the navy or the civil administration. They were graded in fourteen ranks the first eight of which carried entry into the nobility. As the bureaucracy grew so the number of serf owners increased. But as their numbers increased so did their efforts to increase their privileges and decrease their obligations of service. The Empress Anne reduced the period of service from life to twenty-five years and permitted retirement at the age of forty-five, while some nobles were exempted from all service. She also permitted the division of estates, which Peter had forbidden. The powers of the dvorianstvo, the hereditary serf-owning aristocracy, were still further increased by Peter III by his edict of 1762 releasing the nobility from all service, and by Catherine II in 1785, with her Charter to the Nobility.

The Cossacks

The cossacks were not a separate race; the term really describes a way of life—that of the free wanderer, horseman, or masterless man. The open steppes were a frontier land marking the division between the Russian State and the lands occupied by the Tartars and the Turks. Here runaway serfs, adventurers, outcasts and refugees of all kinds banded together and followed a life of hunting, fishing, robbing and slave raiding; a life that looked upon farming with contempt and where there were no landlords and men were free. There was much mingling of races, especially with the Tartars: what they had in common was a love of fighting, a devotion to the Greek Orthodox faith, and a hatred of Poles, Turks, Roman Catholics and Jews.

In the sixteenth century the cossacks had become organized in two democratic military republics; the first centred around their 'sech', or headquarters, on an island in the River Dnieper, and known as the Zaporozhye Cossacks (za porog = below the rapids); the second, farther east with their sech on the River Don.

Life in the sech was extremely democratic; property was communal, the leader or ataman was elected and loot was shared. Life was tough and exciting and the cossack was rarely out of the saddle. So long as there was fighting to be done and plunder to gain the cossack bands were ready to fight on behalf of the State or against it. Under Stephen Batory, the Poles claimed suzerainty over the Zaporozhye Cossacks and to some extent utilized them as frontier troops in the Ukraine (lit. borderland), but with the attempt to enforce the Uniate faith the cossacks became the bitter enemies of the Poles. Ivan the Great claimed suzerainty over all the Russias, but it was Ivan the Terrible who succeeded in making it effective in the south. Even so the Don Cossacks frequently attacked southern Russia, sometimes in alliance with the Tartars, and in the Time of Troubles most of the support for the successive false Dimitrys came from them. Eventually it was the cossacks who surrounded Moscow in the hope of imposing their own form of democratic government on Russia, and it was they who were instrumental in the election of Michael Romanov as tsar in 1613.

In time new cossack communities were created; there were eleven in all by the nineteenth century, covering about 230,000 square miles and numbering about eight million people. By then, however, social hierarchies had been established and the senior officers had estates of their own. They enjoyed certain privileges in return for military service: all men did compulsory military service for twenty years from the age of eighteen, and the communities which had formerly been the champions of freedom now provided the most effective military support for the tsarist governments.

The Part Played by the Cossacks in Russian History

From the sixteenth century on the cossacks played a turbulent and important part in all Russian history; sometimes taking the lead in risings and rebellions against the State, sometimes carrying out the work of the State in their ruthless and effective way.

They inherited the tradition of freedom that had formerly been known in Kievan Rus and upheld it against the early tsars; they created a great fighting tradition, and in spite of their attacks on Russia they also served to defend it against the Turks; they offered refuge to all fleeing from Polish and Muscovite oppression, and their exploits were celebrated in popular song and literature.

It was the cossacks under their ataman Yermak who on behalf of the Stroganovs, but ultimately for Russia, conquered Siberia and pioneered the expansion of Russia beyond the Urals. It was as the leaders and supporters of popular revolts against tsarist rule that they were most prominent in the seventeenth and eighteenth centuries—they were dominant in the Time of Troubles, there were the revolts of Stenka Razin in 1667–1671, Bulavin in 1707, Mazeppa in 1708 and Pugachev in 1773–1774, but in the nineteenth century they became the military police of the tsars, helping to crush revolts until 1917.

Lithuania, Poland and the Ukraine

The southern regions of old Kievan Rus had been severed from the rest of Russia by constant wars with Lithuania and Poland, and in 1321, Kiev itself was taken by Lithuania. The Lithuanian tribes had united under Prince Mindovg against the German invaders in the thirteenth century and had made Novogrudok their capital. Later, under Prince Gedimin they had set up a strong state in south-west Russia centred on Vilna. In 1386 a personal union had been established between Lithuania and Poland and from then on it was the Polish influence, particularly the Roman Catholic faith and the Polish feudal system, that predominated in the two regions.

In 1569 at the Diet of Lublin Poland and Lithuania were united in a single state. The southern half of Lithuania (south-west Russia) became part of Poland while the northern half became a separate principality in permanent union. In the transferred territories the Poles set about introducing their landowning system and the Roman Catholic faith. These regions had been almost deserted as a result of the Tartar invasions but with the decline of Tartar power settlers began to move back. The growing demand for wheat in western Europe in the sixteenth century encouraged the Polish nobility to acquire great areas of the fertile steppe-lands and to encourage immigration. But the imposition of serfdom and the attempts to enforce the Uniate Church upon the Greek Orthodox people caused great opposition and the consequent flight of the peasantry to the cossack lands. The result was constant border warfare between the cossacks and the Poles.

The Acquisition of Little Russia

In time senior cossacks departed from their early ideals and began to acquire large estates and they became as interested in maintaining the peasantry on the land as the landowners elsewhere. One of these was Bohdan Khmelnitsky who led a force of cossacks against the Poles in 1648 and made himself master of much of south-west Russia. At first he was very successful but later, fearing defeat by the Poles, he appealed to Tsar Alexis to take Little Russia under his protection. Alexis referred the matter to a Zemsky Sobor in 1653 which agreed, after much debate, and in 1654 Little Russia (the Ukraine) was annexed to Moscow.

This of course meant war with Poland, as well as civil war in the Ukraine, but the cossacks were crushed in 1659, and the war with Poland ended in 1667 with the Peace of Andrusovo, when the Ukraine was divided between Russia and Poland, and Kiev became Russian once more. See map p. 36.

Russia thus gained the fertile steppe lands east of the Dnieper, and the traditional freedom of the cossacks disappeared as serfdom was introduced to the new lands. The acquisition of Little Russia also brought Russia into the conflict with the Turks and the Poles which was to remain a feature of Russian foreign affairs for the next 300 years.

Expansion into Siberia

The term Siberia applies to all Russia east of the Urals: it consists largely of Arctic tundra in the north and a great belt of taiga (dense coniferous forest) with open steppe and desert in the south.

The early inhabitants were thinly scattered and primitive nomadic tribes who gained a living by hunting and fishing. The steppe lands in the south were crossed by the traditional caravan routes linking the trade of China and Europe. This area was overrun by the Mongols in the thirteenth century and the whole of Russia came under Asiatic influence. The Siberian Khanate was established with its centre at Sibir on the River Irtysh in the fifteenth century.

The prelude to Russian expansion eastwards was the acquisition of Kazan and Astrakhan at the expense of the declining Tartar khanates in the reign of Ivan IV, although traders from Novgorod had been active in Siberia since the eleventh century. The stimulus came from private enterprise rather than from the State, and the acquisition of Siberia came about through a constant process of emigration and settlement by the Russian people rather than by a deliberate policy of conquest, although armed bands of adventurers were always in the forefront, followed by unscrupulous traders with the settlers behind them. This enormous territory of about five million square miles was added to Russia by the activities of small and disorderly bands of freebooters, never more than a few dozen in number, but possessing the great advantage over the natives of a knowledge of firearms.

Once the movement east had begun, the absence of serious physical obstacles meant that the continent was crossed fairly rapidly, but the hostility of the tribes in the south and south-east always forced the explorers and settlers to the north where the climate was most severe, the winters long, and where the land was subject to flooding in the spring. Although most of this area consists of taiga, movement was easy because of the rivers. There are three great rivers running south to north across Siberia: the Ob, the Yenisei, and the Lena; their tributaries give a network of waterways flowing east and west. The cossacks who were in the forefront of the penetration of Siberia were as much at home in boats as they were in the saddle. There are easy portages between the rivers: for example it is only five miles from the Ob to the Yenisei basin, and only ten miles from the Yenisei to Lake Baikal and the Lena basin.

In 1555, the Khan of Sibir was obliged to pay tribute to Ivan IV, and in 1558 Ivan granted his charter to the wealthy merchant family of the Stroganovs which exempted them from taxation for twenty years in return for developing the production of salt and minerals and for cultivating and protecting the land in and beyond the Urals. The enterprise prospered and in 1581 the cossack Yermak, who was escaping from justice, was employed to lead an expedition into Siberia. He was extremely successful, roaming far and wide, establishing trading posts and forts, capturing the town of Sibir in 1582, and returning loaded with loot to gain a pardon from the tsar.

Yermak was followed by a succession of cossack adventurers in the seventeenth century, including Poyarkov, Khabarov, Stepanov and Atlasov, who continued the work of plundering, trading and establishing settlements. Tobolsk was founded on the Ob in 1587, Tomsk in 1604, Krasnoyarsk in 1628, Yakutsk in 1632; the River Amur and the mouth of the Kolyma in the Arctic were reached in 1644; Okhotsk was founded in 1648 and the Bering Strait reached the same year; Irkutsk was established in 1651, and Kamchatka explored and claimed in 1697.

Later the Bering Strait was crossed and trading posts were established down the west coast of North America from Alaska to California.

The Government lagged behind the adventurers, but a Siberian Department was established in Moscow in 1637, and Tobolsk became the administrative centre in 1670.

The chief concern was to extract tribute from the subjugated tribes, but trade developed, and diplomatic relations became necessary with China. In 1689 the Treaty of Nerchinsk was signed. The Jesuit missionaries acting for the Chinese Emperor were able to secure both banks of the Amur and control over Mongolia for China, while Russia was confined to the less attractive areas further north. This treaty was supplemented in 1727 by the Treaty of Kyakhta which lasted for more than a hundred years, chiefly perhaps because after the great surge to the east in the seventeenth century the attentions of the rulers of Russia were confined to expansion in the west in the eighteenth century, and large scale colonization of Siberia did not come about until the nineteenth century, although it was already in use as a place of exile for religious and political prisoners and refugees.

QUESTIONS

1. How was Russia governed in the seventeenth century?
2. Discuss the significance of Nikon's Church reforms and the results of the schism in the Russian Church in the seventeenth century.
3. Outline the development of relations between the Church and the State in Russia.
4. Give an account of the development of serfdom in Russia to the end of the seventeenth century.
5. Who were the cossacks, and what part did they play in Russian history?
6. Give an account of Russian expansion into Siberia in the seventeenth century.
7. Find out what you can, and make notes on the following: Nil Sorsky; The Uniate Church; the Patriarch Nikon; the Raskolniki; life in the sech; Stenka Razin; K. Bulavin; the Stroganovs; the Russians in North America; Yermak; Bohdan Khmelnitsky; the Diet of Lublin, 1569; the Peace of Andrusovo.

Further Reading

Cambridge History of Poland, 1697–1935. Cambridge U.P., 1941.

FIELD, C. The Great Cossack (Stenka Razin). Jenkins, 1947.

GOGOL, N. Taras Bulba, trans. O. Gorcharkov. Collet, 1958. Also, trans. D. Magarshak, John Lehman, 1949, and in Everyman, 1963.

HINDUS, M. The Cossacks. Collins, 1946.

KERNER, R. J. The Urge to the Sea, The Course of Russian History. Berkeley, 1942.

SEMENOV, Y. N. The Conquest of Siberia, trans. E. W. Dickes. Routledge, 1944.

VERNADSKY, G. Bohdan, Hetman of the Ukraine. New Haven, 1961.

WARE, T. The Orthodox Church. Penguin, 1963.

ZERNOV, N. Eastern Christendom. Weidenfeld and Nicolson, 1961.

THE HOUSE OF ROMANOV

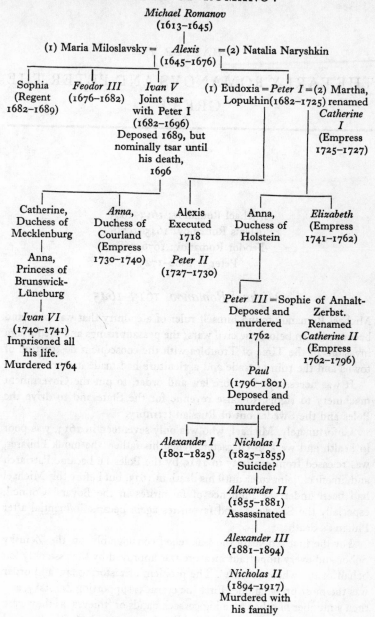

Michael Romanov
(1613–1645)

(1) Maria Miloslavsky = Alexis = (2) Natalia Naryshkin
(1645–1676)

Sophia
(Regent
1682–1689)

Feodor III
(1676–1682)

Ivan V
Joint tsar
with Peter I
(1682–1696)
Deposed 1689, but
nominally tsar until
his death,
1696

(1) Eudoxia = Peter I = (2) Martha,
Lopukhin (1682–1725) renamed
Catherine
I
(Empress
1725–1727)

Catherine,
Duchess of
Mecklenburg

Anna,
Princess of
Brunswick-
Lüneburg

Ivan VI
(1740–1741)
Imprisoned all
his life.
Murdered 1764

Anna,
Duchess of
Courland
(Empress
1730–1740)

Alexis
Executed
1718

Peter II
(1727–1730)

Anna,
Duchess of
Holstein

Elizabeth
(Empress
1741–1762)

Peter III = Sophie of Anhalt-
Deposed and   Zerbst.
murdered   Renamed
1762   Catherine II
(Empress
1762–1796)

Paul
(1796–1801)
Deposed and
murdered

Alexander I
(1801–1825)

Nicholas I
(1825–1855)
Suicide?

Alexander II
(1855–1881)
Assassinated

Alexander III
(1881–1894)

Nicholas II
(1894–1917)
Murdered with
his family

CHAPTER V

THE EARLY ROMANOVS AND PETER THE GREAT

Michael Romanov: 1613–1645
Alexis Romanov: 1645–1676
Feodor Romanov: 1676–1682
Peter I: 1682–1725

Michael Romanov, 1613–1645

Michael Romanov found himself ruler of a country that was poor and backward even before the civil wars; the peasant risings and the foreign invasions of the Time of Troubles with the consequent destruction of towns and the ruin of trade and agriculture had made it more so.

It was necessary to restore law and order, to put the Government machinery to rights, to raise revenue for the State and to drive the Poles and the Swedes out of Russian territory.

Unfortunately, Michael, who was only seventeen in 1613, was poor in health and weak in character. When his father, the monk Philaret, was released from captivity in 1619 by the Poles he became Patriarch and, in effect, joint ruler until his death in 1633, but before this Michael had been under the influence of favourites in the Boyars' Council, especially the Saltykovs, and favourites again became influential after Philaret's death.

For the first ten years the tsar relied considerably on the Zemsky Sobor and every important measure was approved by the assembly 'on behalf of the whole country'. The problem of restoring law and order was the most pressing one. First the cossacks supporting Zarutsky, and then a number of other roaming cossack bands or 'thieves' as they were known, were dealt with. Meanwhile the war against Sweden and Poland continued. A peace was negotiated with Sweden at Stolbovo in 1617 whereby Novgorod was restored to Russia, but the Swedes kept both sides of the Gulf of Finland, thus barring Russia from access to the Baltic. In 1618 a truce was arranged with Poland.

The Rule of Philaret

From 1619 it was really Philaret who ruled and he did so capably.

Philaret proposed certain administrative and financial reforms, such as limiting the power of the 'voevodas' (the military officials who had replaced the elected elders created by Ivan IV), and the revision of the taxation system, but these efforts came to nothing. The landowning system was reorganized by allotting lands only to those who were efficiently performing their services to the State, and the peasants were more firmly bound to the soil to prevent them spoiling the scheme by running away. An attempt was made to transfer direct taxation from the land to the household thus making each peasant liable for payment.

Surrounded by enemies the tsar had to have an army and that meant raising the revenue, which in turn meant increasing the burdens on the people. One way of increasing revenue was to encourage trade. Foreign merchants, especially English and Dutch, were granted special privileges to persuade them to trade with Russia, but under these conditions the greater part of the profits went to the foreign merchants rather than to the native Russians.

War with Poland broke out again in 1632 but the Russians were unsuccessful in their attempts to regain Smolensk, although when peace was made in 1634 the Polish king gave up his claims to the Russian throne.

In 1637 the cossacks in a private war with the Turks captured the fortress of Azov and offered it to Michael in return for help but the tsar did not feel able to face the war with Turkey that acceptance would bring and had to say 'no', so the cossacks left it to the Turks after destroying it.

Alexis, 1645–1676

Alexis was only sixteen years old when he succeeded his father in 1645 and for a time he came under the influence of a group of boyars led by his tutor, Morozov. The abuses and oppression of these men was such that in 1648 rioting broke out in Moscow and other cities. This seems to have opened the tsar's eyes to what had been going on. He appointed an able man, Odoevsky, in place of Morozov, and called a boyars' duma to discuss the restoration of law and order.

The result was a codification of the laws which was submitted to a Zemsky Sobor in 1648 and published as the Ulozhenie in 1649. The most important result was that the nobility were permitted to reclaim runaway peasants without any limit of time, in other words, serfdom had at last become legal.

The new code did not succeed in restoring law and order, for the next year there was rebellion in Pskov and Novgorod ostensibly over the terms of the Treaty of Stolbovo, and in 1662 there was more rioting in Moscow, partly because of famine following an outbreak of plague, and partly because of attempts by the Government to substitute copper for silver coins at the same value. But the most serious rising was that of Stenka Razin, 1667–1671.

Stenka Razin

So many people fled to the cossack lands that the established cossacks refused to share their rights and supplies with them. These late arrivals were called 'naked' because of their lack of possessions and they became little more than servants to the cossacks who would not permit them to cultivate the land. These dissatisfied fugitives formed the bands of rebels who were organized by Stenka Razin in 1667 to go on a plundering expedition down the Volga to the Caspian Sea and from there to the Persian settlements. In 1669 they returned to the River Don loaded with loot. Razin was joined by thousands of discontented persons in the south and planned an expedition against the tsar and the boyars. The rebellion had become widespread by 1670 and Razin was preaching a class war of the oppressed peasantry against the nobles and the merchants: 'There shall be no serfs any more, but all shall be free and equal.' In 1671 Razin was betrayed, captured, tortured, and quartered alive, but peasant resistance continued for years after in spite of savage punitive measures by the tsar's troops, and Stenka Razin and his exploits were celebrated in popular stories and songs, as Robin Hood has been in England.

The suppression of Razin's revolt was the beginning of the reabsorption into the Russian State of the lands of the Don Cossacks.

Alexis had to contend not only with serious discontent and revolts against the social and economic system but also with increasing divisions over religion due to the personality and the activities of his patriarch, Nikon, and opposition to the growth of western European influences and all things 'German'.[1]

In foreign affairs the wars against Poland and Lithuania for control over the Ukraine were continued from 1654–1667. Alexis, thanks to the work of a very able minister, Ordin-Nashchokin, was able to benefit from the growing weakness of Poland and to reconquer

[1] All foreigners tended to be referred to as German. See chapter IV.

Smolensk and Kiev. By the Treaty of Andrusovo, 1667, Russia gained that part of the Ukraine on the left bank of the Dnieper while Poland retained the right bank. War with Poland had inevitably involved wars with Sweden, 1656–1658, and with Turkey, but these were indecisive.

Alexis was one of the few tsars to be a likeable human being: he had ability and humanity and attempted to rule well but perhaps lacked the ruthless resolution that was needed to bully Russia into order as Peter I was to attempt to do. His reign, with its class warfare, peasant discontent, the divisions within society, and a change in foreign policy benefiting from the weakness of Poland and the acquisition of southern Russia indicates the beginnings of modern Russian history.

Peter I: the Great, 1682–1725

In the reign of Peter the Great Russia became a major European power. The main lines of Russian domestic and foreign policies had already been indicated by Peter's predecessors in the seventeenth century, but it was his forceful application of those principles as much as his success in achieving them that makes his reign so remarkable.

Personality and Character

Peter was a giant of a man—nearly seven feet tall, and with a nervous and restless energy that gave his activities a demonic quality which could make him a wonderful companion to his friends and an oafish or fiendishly cruel monster to his enemies, real or imagined. He had little understanding of people or of politics: his talents were largely practical—he was good with his hands and delighted in making things, especially boats, with as much noise as possible, and in drilling soldiers. He was quite free of affectation and mixed more easily with workmen than he did with the court which he distrusted and despised. He boasted that he had become proficient in fifteen trades, including dentistry, and liked practical jokes that were often cruel. His manners were coarse, his youth dissolute, and he had no understanding or respect for the manners of polite society. His early life was hard and dangerous and goes far to explain Peter, the man.

Early Life and Education

Tsar Alexis died in 1676 leaving two sons by his first wife, Maria Miloslavsky; Feodor, aged fourteen, who was sickly and partly paralysed and who became Tsar Feodor III, 1676–1682; and Ivan, aged ten, also sickly and blind, and feeble-minded as well. He became joint tsar as Ivan V, 1682–1696 with Peter, the extremely healthy son of Alexis's second wife, Natalia Naryshkin.

Peter's early life was dominated by the struggle between the Milo-slavsky and the Naryshkin families for power at court.

With the accession of Tsar Feodor III in 1676, Peter and his mother were driven from the court by the Miloslavsky faction. On the death of Feodor in 1682 Ivan should have succeeded him, but the Nary-shkins and the boyars opposed to the Miloslavsky faction, proclaimed Peter as tsar. Sophia, Ivan's sister, with her lover Golitsyn organized a revolt of the streltsy and after three days' rioting in which a number of Peter's relatives were murdered in front of him, Ivan and Peter were proclaimed as joint tsars with Sophia as regent, 1682–1689.

The Regency of Sophia, 1682–1689

Sophia and Golitsyn are credited with having plans for reforms, includ-ing the liberation of the serfs, but the most striking event was a treaty with China, the Treaty of Nerchinsk, 1689, for during the course of the seventeenth century Siberia had been traversed to the Pacific. In 1686 there was a peace with Poland whereby Russia was confirmed in the possession of Kiev in return for assistance to the Poles against the Turks. As a result Golitsyn sent two unsuccessful expeditions to the Crimea and this was used as an excuse for the overthrow of Sophia when it was known that she was planning to get herself made tsaritsa.

Peter's coup d'état, 1689

In 1689, matters came to a head between the Miloslavskys and the Naryshkins. Suspecting a plot against his life Peter was obliged to escape in his nightshirt to refuge and was able to muster enough support to arrest Golitsyn, send Sophia away to a convent and execute some of their supporters. Ivan still continued as joint tsar, but in fact the country was ruled by Peter's mother until her death in 1694, and the joint rule ended with the death of Ivan in 1696.

Peter took little interest in these early events; he was content to leave the work of government in the hands of his mother and her friends. Nevertheless these childhood experiences left their mark: Peter always had a nervous twitch after 1689, and he went out of his way to disregard the court, the boyars, and the higher ranks of the clergy.

The Regency of Natalia, 1689–1694

Natalia ruled with the aid of the patriarch's and her own friends while Peter continued to amuse himself as he had always done—playing and carousing with his friends in the back streets, and picking up all the technical information he could from the foreign craftsmen and tech-nicians in the German quarter. In 1689 his mother married him to his first wife, Eudoxia, but he left her almost immediately for companions of his own choosing.

Peter's Education

Peter had little formal education. He was well cared for in the reign of Feodor and learned to read and write, although not to spell. When he was banished from court by Sophia this formal education ceased and for the rest he was self-taught, acquiring a knowledge of mathematics, artillery, navigation, boat building and other crafts from foreign workers in Moscow, especially Lefort a Swiss, Gordon a Scottish soldier, and from Dutch and German seamen. In particular he loved to drill his companions as soldiers, to make fortresses and to play games of Mars and Neptune. In time this play came to develop into the real thing with full time regiments and fleets of boats.

With the death of his mother in 1694 Peter, aged twenty-two, was obliged to turn himself seriously to the work of government.

Peter's Aims

Although Peter had shown little inclination for the work of government and his education had not been such as to seem to have prepared him for such a task he set out to raise Russia from her backwardness and to create a new and greater Russia. The strength and power of the countries of western Europe were based upon their technical skills and knowledge; these Russia must have so that she could build up her own strength and be independent of foreign aid. To gain unrestricted communications with Europe it was essential for Russia to gain an outlet on the Baltic and if possible on the Black Sea. To do this a policy of war and expansion based on the development of Russian manufacturing industries was required. It was not a carefully thought out policy: to a great extent the wars were forced upon him by his neighbours, and his domestic reforms were forced upon him by the wars, but he adopted the policy ruthlessly as it developed.

The Grand Embassy: Peter's European Tour, 1697-1698

In 1697 Peter set out with a large following on a tour of Europe, with the objects of mustering European support for Russia's claims to Constantinople and for an alliance against the Turks. This came to nothing, but the other main object, to acquire as much knowledge as possible of western industrial techniques, especially of shipbuilding, and to recruit foreign workmen, was much more fruitful. The party travelled through Riga, East Prussia, Holland, England and back to Holland, Vienna and Poland. Peter worked as a carpenter in the shipyards at Saardam, Amsterdam and Deptford, and visited factories, museums, hospitals and the House of Commons. Everywhere the party went people marvelled at the intelligence and the disgusting manners of the Russians. At Deptford Peter stayed in John Evelyn's house which was badly damaged by the guests, as was a fine holly hedge through which it amused Peter to wheel his friends in a wheelbarrow. The party was in Vienna preparing to go to Venice when news reached them that the streltsy were in revolt again, and Peter hurried home.

The revolt of the Streltsy, 1698

Peter distrusted the streltsy for their reactionary ideas, and they had been ordered from Moscow to Azov after the detection of a plot against him in 1697. They mutinied, and had been crushed by the time Peter returned, but Peter was not satisfied, and began his own investigations. He suspected that Sophia was involved; she was denounced and ordered to become a nun. As for the streltsy, wholesale torture and execution was visited upon thousands of them and the regiments were disbanded.

Domestic Policy

On his return from Europe Peter determined to introduce western customs and methods to Russia.

He began immediately with a series of relatively minor, but symbolic actions, such as ordering his court to wear European dress and the men to shave their beards. The old calendar which was reckoned from the beginning of the world, and in which the year began in September, was replaced by the calendar in use in the rest of Europe. Thus New Year's day, 7208, became 1 September 1699. These changes shocked the Old Believers, for long beards and coats were fundamental signs of the orthodox faith. Attempts were also made to introduce western manners and social customs: women were emanicipated from the terem and encouraged to show themselves in public at compulsory dances, concerts, and theatres, and other public occasions. The alphabet was simplified, and the first Russian newspaper, *The Moscow News*, was started. Schools, hospitals, and a medical college were set up and in 1725 an Academy of Sciences was founded.

Much of this was superficial in that it only introduced a veneer of westernization to a limited section of Russian society. Throughout his reign Peter's main concern was with foreign wars, and everything in the State was subordinated to military needs. There was never any clearly thought out policy of westernization. The reforms were hastily improvized remedies for immediate problems, and in some respects the reforms created more confusion than existed before. But there was a tendency to think of the purpose of legislation and the good of the State. Except within the Church and the army, no fundamental changes were made in Russian society; indeed the traditional characteristics including serfdom, were emphasized and the autocracy strengthened.

The Government

Peter dispensed with the Boyars Duma and relied upon the advice of his chosen friends. In 1711 he created a Senate which carried out his commands and which acted as a supreme court of justice. In 1722 the office of Procurator-General was established to act as a link between the tsar and the Senate and to exercise general supervision over it. In addition to this there was a secret service to watch over the general activities and interests of the Government. In 1718 the former administrative departments were reorganized into colleges and there were attempts at making the provincial governments more uniform. But although the names were changed the general characteristics of Government were not altered: it was still a highly centralized bureaucracy with elected officials at the bottom of the administrative machine and appointed officials at the top.

The Army

The beginnings of a regular army had already been made, but Peter reformed and recreated it. The service nobility were transferred to regular service, which was for life. All had to work their way up from the bottom, and a new 'Table of Ranks' was drawn up in 1722 which created a regular system of promotion through fourteen ranks. The sons of the gentry were forced to study such subjects as mathematics, engineering and languages, in order to make them more efficient officers. The higher nobility were permitted to enter the two new guards regiments: the Preobrazhensky and the Semenovsky, formed from his childhood companions. There was compulsory military service except for the families of the clergy. At the end of the reign the army consisted of 200,000 regulars and 75,000 cossacks. The navy had forty-eight large ships, 800 smaller vessels, and 28,000 seamen. The army was used for administrative purposes such as raising levies and the poll tax and the country was divided into regimental regions for this purpose.

The Church

Peter was unpopular with the Church, both because of his private and his public acts. In particular the 'Raskolniki' and some of the followers of Nikon were opposed to what he had done. This brought him into conflict with the patriarch and the bishops, and when Patriarch Adrian died in 1700 Peter was in no hurry to appoint another. In 1721 the Patriarchate was abolished and a synod of the higher clergy, which was in effect a Government department, was put in its place. Those living on Church lands were subjected to military service and the powers of the Church courts were limited. To complete the subjection of the Church to the State the monasteries were brought under stricter control in 1724.

Economic Affairs

There were attempts to encourage the growth of manufacturing industry, particularly of those industries which would be useful in war such as iron making, silver and copper production, the cloth and leather trades. There were surveys of the mineral resources of the Urals and of southern Russia, nobles were urged to invest their capital, State factories were set up and then handed over to private enterprise, new methods in agriculture were recommended, and canals, roads and bridges were built. Trade and commerce could only flourish in towns and this Peter tried to foster by granting more freedom to the town governments. He wanted to build up a vigorous and independent merchant class such as he had seen in western Europe; skilled workmen were recruited from abroad, idle persons were conscripted, and peasants were drafted to the factories. Foreign trade quadrupled and a favourable balance was created.

Taxation

Probably half the Government revenue went on military expenditure, and taxation had to be increased to meet the cost of the wars. Direct and indirect taxation was intensified, the former by shifting the onus of payment from the household to the individual 'soul', the latter by imposing new taxes on everything taxable from beards and baths to paper for legal documents. In addition to money taxes the people were also obliged to pay in kind in the form of labour, wagons, horses, etc., when called upon to do so.

Peter had little understanding of financial matters except that money was necessary. All the costs of the wars had to be met from taxation since no one had the capital or would take the risk of lending money to the Russian State. A special department was set up to think of new taxes. Church lands were confiscated, monopolies were granted for a variety of commodities ranging from salt and tobacco to oak coffins, the coinage was debased and the army was used to enforce collection. There was much corruption among officials; possibly only one-third to one-half of the taxation that was raised ever reached the treasury, and there was much evasion by the peasants.

St Petersburg

Determined to have his window to the west, Peter spent much of his time when not engaged on military campaigns on the construction of his new port, fortress and court centre of St Petersburg. It became almost an obsession with him, and the Russian people were taxed and driven by forced labour to work on it. It remains the most obvious symbol of his driving will and determination to overcome all obstacles.

In the early stages of the Great Northern War the Russians captured the Swedish fortress of Nyenschanz. Here Peter built the fortress of St Peter and St Paul and began the construction of his city. It was not a good site; it was subject to flooding in spring and was frozen in the winter and the low-lying marshes were unhealthy and unsuitable for building. Yet Peter persevered, disregarding the loss of life, the cost, the hostility of those who were forced to live and work there and the jealousy and rivalry of the old Muscovy represented by the city of Moscow.

Risings and Opposition

He was extremely unpopular with large sections of Russian society and there was a number of serious risings that hampered his foreign campaigns. There were revolts of the streltsy before and during his first foreign journey; there was the support for his son Alexis against his father, and there was open rebellion in the south and south-east at the most crucial period of the Great Northern War. These rebellions gave expression to the discontent arising from the ruinous taxation, the forced labour to build ships, towns and canals, the levies for the army, the reorganization of the nobility and the hostility of the Church, and those who opposed the general programme of westernization.

In 1705 there was a rising in Astrakhan, the Bashkirs were in arms from 1705 to 1711, and in 1707 the most serious rising, that of the Don Cossacks, under Bulavin, necessitated the employment of a large army before it was crushed in the usual merciless fashion.

Family Life and the Problem of the Succession

Peter did not spare himself in the task of creating a new Russia under his own firm personal control, yet he was unsuccessful in securing that his work would be continued after his death. His first wife, to whom he had been married by his mother, he forced to enter a nunnery in 1698, and their son, Alexis, was given to his aunts to be brought up.

Peter took a girl of humble birth, who had been taken prisoner in Livonia, as his mistress. The alliance was not popular with the Russian nobility, but Catherine was a good companion for Peter: she travelled with him, and cared for and comforted him. They were privately married in 1707, publicly married in 1712, and in 1724, Catherine was crowned Empress. She ruled after Peter as Catherine I.

At first Peter's hopes for the succession were centred on Alexis, but the relationship between them was never satisfactory, and developed into open hostility. Alexis was lazy and interested in none of the things that his father tried to force him into doing. Peter despaired of making him a suitable successor to himself and tried to force him into resigning his claim to the throne or entering a monastery. By 1716 the tension between father and son was such that Alexis fled and sought refuge with the Emperor of Austria. He was enticed back to Moscow where a great investigation was begun into his activities. There was little evidence of any treasonable plotting, but Alexis was the hope of all those who suffered under Peter, and wished for change at his death. Alexis died after being tortured, and his associates were imprisoned and executed.

In 1722 Peter issued a law stating that the ruling tsar could name his own successor but he died without indicating who it was to be and it was Catherine who followed him.

He established the precedent of marrying Russian princes and princesses to foreigners and using these personal links in the further-ance of his westernizing ambitions and foreign policy. Alexis was married to Charlotte of Wolfenbüttel; a niece, Anna, to the Duke of Courland; another niece, Catherine, to the Duke of Mecklenburg; and a daughter, Anna, betrothed to the Duke of Holstein.

These German alliances and the failure to produce a male heir were to have important consequences for the history of Russia in the eighteenth century.

Foreign Policy

Peter was engaged in warfare with his neighbours for most of his reign and it was this constant preoccupation with military and naval affairs that to a great extent influenced the course of domestic events within Russia. He was menaced by the Turks in the south, Poland in the west and Sweden in the north-west. Behind these were the other powers of Europe who were concerned to check the growing strength and west-ward movement of Russia while pursuing their own interests in the Baltic area and in north Germany.

At the beginning of the eighteenth century there were two large-scale wars going on almost independently in Europe: the War of the

Spanish Succession involving Britain, France, Holland, Austria and Spain, and the Great Northern War involving Sweden, Russia, Poland, Denmark and Prussia. The Baltic area was extremely important in an age of maritime expansion because of the naval stores that were produced there, as well as the furs, fish, grain and minerals for which it was noted. During the seventeenth century, Sweden under a remarkable succession of kings had gained control of most of the Baltic coastline and had been in constant conflict with Denmark, Poland and the Empire as a result. Peter's hopes of gaining an outlet on the Baltic could only be achieved at the expense of Sweden.

The Azov Campaign

His first adventure was against the Turks on the northern shore of the Black Sea.

At the beginning of his reign Russia was in alliance with Poland and Austria against the Turks, and in spite of the failure of Golitsyn's campaigns in the Crimea war was renewed. Peter determined to take Azov, the heavily fortified Turkish base, but although a land attack down the Dnieper valley was successful, the attempt on the fortress failed because the Turks were able to keep it supplied from the sea. He saw that control of the sea was needed so he set about constructing a fleet and the next year succeeded in taking the fortress. He then chose a site at Taganrog and began the work of building a naval harbour and enforcing colonization of the surrounding region. He now conceived the idea of constructing a large navy and forming a great coalition of European powers to drive the Turks out of Europe. So after celebrating his victories in Moscow and initiating a great programme of ship construction, he set out on his grand embassy to Europe in 1697.

The Great Northern War

In the late seventeenth century the power of Sweden seemed to be in decline and the new King, Charles XII was only a boy of fifteen in 1697. Led by Poland, Sweden's other rivals in the Baltic, Denmark and Russia conspired to seize the opportunity of benefiting from her apparent weakness. Peter did not want to fight a war on two fronts and his ally, Austria, made peace with the Turks in order to give more attention to the problem of the Spanish succession, so he sought to make peace with the Turks also. The moment Peter knew of the Peace of Constantinople in 1700 he declared war on Sweden.

Thus began twenty-one years of warfare, which resulted in the defeat of Sweden and the emergence of Russia as a major European power. But before that came about, Peter had much to learn and the Russian people had much to suffer.

Unfortunately for the allies Charles XII proved to be a military genius, and somehow Sweden kept him supplied. In 1700 Russian troops were sent into the Baltic provinces and besieged Narva, an

LATER INVASIONS OF RUSSIA

important port and fortress. Charles first defeated the Danes and then moved to Narva to deal with the Russians. Although outnumbered three to one, Charles inflicted an ignominious defeat upon the Russians, and then instead of consolidating his victory by advancing into Russia he turned to deal with Poland, thus giving Peter an opportunity to learn from his mistakes and reconstruct his army—an opportunity that was taken. His policy was to keep Sweden occupied by supporting the Poles, to reorganize his army, and consolidate his position in the Baltic provinces.

While the army reforms were being forced through at home, Peter maintained one army in Poland and with another he took Nöteborg, which was renamed Schlüssellburg (1702), Nyenschanz where he built Kronstadt and St Petersburg (1703), and Dorpat and Narva (1704).

In 1707 Poland gave up the struggle and Charles was free to turn against Russia and just at this time when Peter was faced with a Swedish invasion, there were serious risings in Russia.

Mazeppa

There had been a rising of the Don Cossacks in 1707 which had been crushed in 1708 when there was more trouble in the Ukraine. Mazeppa (1644?–1709) was of noble birth and had been educated at the court of John Casimir, King of Poland, but he had fled to join the cossacks after an intrigue with the wife of a nobleman, who, it is said, flogged him, and bound him naked to the back of his horse. He joined Doroshenko the leader of the Dnieper Cossacks and became ataman in 1687, after visiting Moscow and gaining the favours of Golitsyn. He was thought very highly of by Peter, who was grateful for his help in the Azov campaign and in the early stages of the Great Northern War, but Mazeppa began to have doubts about the outcome of the war and threw in his lot with Charles XII. Fortunately for Peter, the Ukrainians were not willing to follow Mazeppa, and the Ukraine was occupied by Menshikov.

In 1708 Charles moved successfully towards Moscow from Poland, but instead of taking Smolensk on the way as was expected, he turned south into the Ukraine to join with Mazeppa. This meant that he outpaced the supplies he was expecting from Livonia, and at the Battle of Lesnaya, the Swedish general, Lewenhaupt, who was in charge of the relieving army, was defeated. There was no Ukrainian revolt in support of Charles and he was defeated at the siege of Poltava in 1709.

The Importance of Poltava

Charles and Mazeppa escaped and fled to Turkey, but for the time being Peter was free to pursue his campaigns in the Baltic. The prestige for Russia of defeating the greatest military leader and nation in northern Europe was great. It gave Peter a new confidence, and Russia a new importance in the diplomatic affairs of Europe. Peter also thought that he could now deal with the Turks.

The Second Turkish Campaign

Charles persuaded the Sultan to declare war on Russia in 1710. No doubt Peter would have preferred to remain free to wage his war in the Baltic provinces but he thought this an opportunity to extend Russian claims against the Turks by moving towards the Danube in alliance with Poland, Moldavia and Wallachia. In a bid to get support he offered a general protectorate over all Greek Orthodox Christians in the Turkish Empire—a claim that was to play an important part in the development of the Eastern Question and the Crimean War in the nineteenth century. Unfortunately for Peter his hurriedly mustered and badly equipped army was met by a greatly superior army at Stanileshte on the River Pruth. He could only capitulate and by the terms of the settlement, confirmed in the Treaty of Adrianople in 1713, Peter had to give up Azov, his Black Sea fleet and all that he had won from the Turks in 1700. He was also bound not to interfere in Poland and to allow Charles XII to return to Sweden. Thus his ambitions in southern Russia had come to nothing after vast expense in men, materials and money.

Meanwhile he concentrated on trying to get a decision in his favour in the war in the north. Russian naval power was making itself felt in the Baltic and in the north his successes were altering the whole balance of power. The result was that his allies began to get less co-operative and he began to face the active opposition of England and Holland, much alarmed at the threat that Russian naval strength meant to their Baltic trade. In 1717 Peter visited France in a vain attempt to persuade the Government that Russia had now replaced Sweden as the surest ally of France in the north.

Negotiations for peace between Sweden and Russia began in 1718, but the death of Charles XII in that year brought a change of Swedish policy. Sweden made peace with her enemies in order to be able to continue the war against Russia alone. Britain came to the aid of Sweden, but could not prevent Peter's fleet from raiding the Swedish coast. Eventually peace was made at Nystadt in 1721.

The Peace of Nystadt

Russia obtained Livonia, including the port of Riga; Estonia, including Reval and Narva; Ingermanland and part of Karelia with Viborg. Russia restored Finland to Sweden and agreed to pay two million thalers. Thus Peter had secured for Russia the Baltic coast from Viborg to Riga and had secured his window to the west. In the victory celebrations Peter assumed the title of 'Emperor of all the Russias' and the Senate conferred on him the titles of 'The Great' and 'Father of his country'. The Baltic provinces were not colonized by Russian land-owners but continued under their German gentry, who in later years contributed many of the more efficient and least corruptible of the higher servants to the Russian administration.

Persia, Central Asia and the Far East

The Great Northern War occupied most of Peter's attention but it did not prevent him from considering the extension of Russia's interests in other directions. There was an increase of trade with China after the Treaty of Nerchinsk, 1689, and Peter sought to extend his influence and improve his relations in the Far East. Kamchatka was conquered, and the Kurile Islands annexed, and Bering was sent to discover whether Asia and America were in fact separated by sea.

In Central Asia there were expeditions to Khiva and Bukhara in 1714, and in 1723 an abortive expedition was sent to Madagascar in an attempt to open up contacts with India by sea.

A mission was sent to Persia in 1715 which resulted in a commercial treaty in 1717 and also revealed the weakness of Persia at that time. As soon as the Great Northern War was ended Peter made war on Persia with the aim of forestalling the Turks by getting control of the Caspian Sea and the silk trade. Derbent and Baku were occupied, and by the peace that was made in 1723, Russia gained control of the southern and western shores of the Caspian Sea. This brought the danger of conflict with Turkey that was only avoided with the assistance of the French at Constantinople and an agreement that left Russia in control of the Caspian while Turkey secured Georgia.

Peter's Achievement

Peter's place in Russian history is a matter of some controversy: the extent to which he was a revolutionary or merely the continuer of traditional lines of development; whether he had any clear plan in domestic and foreign policy or whether his foreign campaigns and domestic reforms were forced upon him by circumstances; whether he even understood what he was doing—these are all open for discussion, but the evidence of his achievement seems clear enough.

In foreign policy his work was based on the creation of a strong army and navy which meant the development of industries at home to supply them, and a drive towards the coasts of the Baltic, Black and Caspian Seas, and the Pacific Ocean. He failed in the south towards Turkey and the Black Sea but succeeded elsewhere. He created an army of 200,000 men and an effective naval force in the Baltic which altered the balance of power in northern Europe in Russia's favour and made Russia a European power. He introduced a veneer of European manners into Russian society but also split it between reformers and conservatives; a split symbolized by the rivalry between St Petersburg and Moscow. The bureaucracy and the autocracy had been strengthened and the Government reorganized, though the Russian people

were no better off. The nobility were reorganized, the Church subjugated, the peasantry made more wretched, and serfdom intensified.
Factories and mines had been developed and the amount of land under
cultivation increased, but all benefits had gone to the State, not the
people. There was jubilation at Peter's death and a cartoon showed the
mice enjoying the funeral of the cat.

Certain other features of Peter's reign were significant: he had
worked for an alliance with France which came to nothing until the
late nineteenth century; he sought to keep Poland and Sweden weak;
he began the policy of marriage alliances with the German states which
led to foreign influences and rulers in the eighteenth century, and the
creation of the guards who provided the instrument for a series of
Palace revolutions after his death.

QUESTIONS

1. He began few things and finished less. Is this a fair judgment on
   Peter I?
2. To what extent does Peter deserve the title Great?
3. Give a brief account of the rule of the early Romanovs to 1689.
4. How successful was Peter the Great in his policy of westernization?
5. Give an account of either (a) Peter the Great's domestic policy; or
   (b) his foreign policy.
6. What is the significance of the Great Northern War in European
   history?
7. Find out what you can, and make notes on: Philaret; the Ulozhenie;
   Stenka Razin; Peter's social reforms; Peter's journeys abroad; the
   building of St Petersburg; Mazeppa; the Azov campaign; the Battle
   of Narva; the Battle of Poltava; Doroshenko; the Peace of Nystadt;
   Vitus Bering.

Further Reading

LORD ACTON. *Lectures on Modern History*. Macmillan, 1950 and Collins Fontana
Library, 1962.
FIELD, C. *The Great Cossack (Stenka Razin)*. Jenkins, 1947.
GREY, I. *Peter the Great, Emperor of all Russia*. Hodder and Stoughton, 1962.
KLYUCHEVSKY, V. *Peter the Great*, trans. L. Archibald. Macmillan, 1958.
MARSDEN, C. *Palmyra of the North*. Faber. 1942.
PUSHKIN, A. S. 'Peter the Great's Negro', in *The Captain's Daughter and
other Great Stories*, trans. T. Keane. New York, Random House, 1936 and
Everyman, trans. N. Duddington.
SUMNER, B. H. *Peter the Great and the Emergence of Russia*. English Universi-
ties Press, 1951.

CHAPTER VI

RUSSIA IN THE EIGHTEENTH CENTURY
from Peter I to Catherine II

Peter I: 1682–1725
Catherine I (Peter's widow): 1725–1727
Peter II (Peter I's grandson): 1727–1730
Anna (daughter of Peter I's half-brother, Ivan): 1730–1740
Ivan VI (son of Anna's niece): 1740–1741
Elizabeth (daughter of Peter I by Catherine I): 1741–1762
Peter III (grandson of Peter I): 1762
Catherine II (wife of Peter III): 1762–1796

The period between the death of Peter I and the accession of Catherine II covers a series of Palace revolutions and struggles for power between groups of nobles with the backing of the guards regiments. Peter had failed to define the succession and the system of government which he had created could not work without the strength of his will to direct it. During this time the Russian crown became the object of the intrigues not only of the Russian nobility, but also of the Baltic German advisers and of the ambassadors of the other European powers. Political power at home was exercised by a succession of favourites, while the weakness of the rulers enabled the nobility to extend their privileges while the burdens on the peasantry increased to provide for the extravagance of the court. Abroad, Russia became involved in European affairs during the wars of the Polish and Austrian Successions and the Seven Years' War, largely to serve the purposes of the other powers concerned. It was Catherine II who took up Peter the Great's policies where he had left off and added her particular character to them.

Class Structure and Extension of Privileges

Peter I had created a new nobility and had forced the old to accept the same obligations of service to the State. His enforced westernization had antagonized the conservative and traditional forces among the nobility and the Church, and began that division within Russian society that marked the Slavophils and the westernizers in the nineteenth century; and he intensified the struggles for power between the rival noble factions. After his death, 'westernization' continued, although at a more moderate pace, and German advisers and French ideas and customs became increasingly influential. French became almost the official court language, and French fashions, particularly in dress and architecture, transformed the appearance of St Petersburg and its high society.

The nobility, those at court and the service gentry throughout the country, extended their privileges and became still more cut off from the life of the majority of the population. In 1736 the dvorianstvo (the service nobility) obtained reductions in their obligations for military service, and in 1762 they were freed from all obligations to the State and became, as in France, a parasitical, leisured class of tax-free, hereditary nobility whose privileges were obtained at the expense of increased burdens on the peasantry in the form of higher taxes, increased duties, and a general intensification and extension of serfdom.

Growth of Population and Extension of Territory

The population at the beginning of the eighteenth century was about thirteen million: by the end of the century it had increased, through natural increase and foreign conquest, from thirty-six to forty million. About 95 per cent of this was rural and only 5 per cent lived in towns. More than half were serfs and serfdom was extended to the newly conquered lands in the south where it had not existed before. The middle class remained negligible in numbers and influence in spite of Peter the Great's efforts to encourage them.

Exploration of Siberia and the Far East continued but there was little attempt at development there, and most effort was concentrated on the new lands in the south and the west.

Economic Developments

In spite of Peter the Great's efforts to force industrialization, agriculture remained the major economic activity, and the forest, with its furs, salt and timber was the chief source of wealth. Nevertheless, agricultural methods were still very primitive because of the lack of capital and the communal organization. The ignorance of the peasantry and the lack of incentive to introduce improvements kept production low; shifting agriculture was still practised in central Muscovy, and the sickle and the wooden plough were in common use. The chief crop

THE EXPANSION OF RUSSIA IN THE EIGHTEENTH CENTURY

was rye, although Peter had tried to encourage the growth of flax and hemp for industrial purposes.

In manufacturing industry there had been some development, and Russia became an important exporter of iron in the eighteenth century. By 1725, there were more than 200 industrial undertakings, some of them quite large scale, but many of them also still dependent upon the domestic system and on seasonal labour. Many of the factories had been founded by the State and were granted to the nobility who ran them as private enterprises. Much of the production was for the Government, and there was little internal trade. Labour was always short: skilled workers had to be imported from abroad, while a new class of factory serfs was established by forced drafts from the countryside.

Trade is dependent upon communications, and something was done to improve the roads, but water transport received most attention. The canal linking the Volga and the Neva was built in 1708. Nevertheless transport costs remained very high and were a limitation on trade.

Foreign trade increased throughout the eighteenth century with a favourable balance of trade: exports increased threefold in the first half of the century and tenfold by its end, but imports were chiefly of a luxury character for the pleasure of the nobility rather than for the benefit of the country as a whole.

The revenue was never adequate in spite of punitive taxation. The extravagance of the court, the peculation of ministers and officials, and the general financial incompetence meant that the State was always on the verge of bankruptcy. No real accounts of revenue and expenditure were kept and smuggling on a great scale complicated matters further. In 1742 there was a 'mistake' of one million roubles, while arrears of revenue were three million roubles in 1742 and eight million roubles in 1761.

CATHERINE I, 1725–1727

When Peter I died there was doubt as to his successor:[1] it might be the Lithuanian servant girl who had become his second wife; his grandson, Peter, by his first wife; or his daughter, Anna, by his second wife. The problem was solved by a former lover of the empress, Menshikov, who brought out the guards and declared Catherine as tsarina, with himself as the power behind the throne. Catherine had neither the wish

[1] The order of succession had followed the rule of male primogeniture since the election of Michael Romanov by the Zemsky Sobor in 1613. Peter I decreed that the reigning monarch should nominate his successor, who would not necessarily be his eldest son. Unfortunately Peter died without naming his successor and there was doubt as to whom he had intended to follow him. The rule of primogeniture was restored by Paul.

nor the ability to rule and Menshikov was arrogant, ambitious and avaricious. Catherine's extravagance brought protests and Menshikov was forced to meet the opposition of the nobles by creating a Privy Council of six to let them share the work of government.

In order to strengthen his position Menshikov proposed to marry his daughter, aged sixteen, to the young Peter, aged twelve, who, when Catherine died in 1727, succeeded as Peter II, with Menshikov still in control.

The most important event of the reign was the treaty with Austria in August 1726, whereby each promised military aid to the other if attacked, and mutual support against the Turks. This alliance determined Russian policy for the first half of the eighteenth century.

PETER II, 1727–1730

Menshikov's triumph was shortlived, for his rivals among the nobility succeeded in turning Peter against him and he and his family were exiled.

Peter disliked St Petersburg and transferred the Government to Moscow, but he was more interested in hunting than in the business of being tsar, and the Dolgoruky family and the conservatives gained control. They proposed to marry Peter to one of their daughters, but he died of smallpox in 1730, on the day arranged for the wedding, without designating his successor: this time the nobles chose as tsarina, Anna of Courland, the daughter of Tsar Ivan V (Peter the Great's half-brother).

ANNA (OR ANNE), 1730–1741

Anna was thirty-seven in 1730; poorly educated and extravagant, 'dull, fat, coarse and spiteful', yet she was the most autocratic of Peter the Great's successors, and attempted to continue his policy without inheriting his ability. She preferred her native Courlanders, whom she thought she could trust, to the Russian nobility whom she knew she could not. Thus began a period when Russian affairs were partly controlled by foreigners.

Before nominating Anna, the Supreme Privy Council had imposed certain conditions, and these she accepted only to reject them by a coup once she was on the throne. Among the conditions were the following: that without the consent of the Council she was not to marry; she could not name her successor; she was not to declare war nor to make peace; she was not to raise taxes, to create boyars or to make senior military appointments; and in general she was to be a puppet for the great nobles. Anna had the support of the other nobles in her resistance to the demands of the boyars, and she made the restored Senate, which replaced the Council, subordinate to a 'cabinet' while continuing to rely on the advice of Baltic German ministers; particularly of her lover, Biren; the Löwenwolde brothers; Münnich and Osterman. The Old Russian party was overthrown, the Government returned to St Petersburg, and two new guards regiments, the Izmailovsky and the Cavalry, officered by Germans, were created to counter the influence of the Russian nobility in the Preobrazhensky and the Semenovsky regiments.

The Rule of Biren

For ten years, Russia suffered in order that Anna might be amused and that Biren might become rich. To natural disasters such as storms, famines and plagues, were added heavy and extortionate taxation to meet the extravagance of the court, and a brutal campaign of terror was imposed upon opponents of the régime, with spies and informers everywhere, executions and wholesale exile to Siberia.

The gentry were able to extend their privileges while evading their duties; their period of service was reduced to twenty-five years in 1736, and second sons were excused duty to enable them to manage their estates; in addition a Cadet Corps was created that permitted sons of the nobility to enter service as officers instead of working their way up from the ranks.

Foreign affairs were rather more successfully handled by Osterman, with Münnich as Commander-in-Chief. The Persian conquests of Peter the Great were handed back, but in the War of the Polish Succession, 1733–1738, when all the neighbours of Poland intervened to secure the election of a king of their own choosing, the French candidate, Stanislaus Leszczinski, was eventually driven out by a Russian army, and Augustus III, the Russian candidate, was elected in 1734.

There was also war with Turkey, 1735–1739, when Münnich invaded the Crimea, captured Ochakov, and defeated the Turks. The Treaty of Belgrade, 1739, gave Russia extra territory in the steppe lands but not access to the Black Sea coast. The Crimean campaign was notable for the fighting qualities of the Russian soldier, the attempt to muster support from the Balkan Christians for a united move against the Turks, and the incompetence and corruption of the supply services.

IVAN VI, 1740–1741

Anna named the six-week-old son of her niece, also called Anna, as her successor, with Biren, whom she had created Duke of Courland, as regent. Ivan's mother was anxious to be regent herself and she intrigued with Münnich to replace Biren. This was not difficult, for Biren was hated by Russians and Germans alike, and within a month he had been kidnapped and sent off to Siberia.

The Grand Duchess Anna now acted as regent for her son, with Münnich as the power behind the throne, but she was indolent and self-indulgent, and the struggles for power within Russia continued against the background of the wider European conflicts of the time. The regent favoured the alliance with Austria while Osterman, who replaced Münnich, supported Prussia; this was difficult when Prussia and Austria came to blows in the War of the Austrian Succession in 1740. Meanwhile, France was anxious to reduce German influence at the Russian court and to break up the Austrian alliance.

Elizabeth's coup d'état, December 1741

Elizabeth was thirty-two, and as the daughter of Peter the Great, she seemed to offer hopes of a return to the firmness of his policies and an end of the German influences at the court. Encouraged by France, Sweden, who hoped to recover some of the territories lost to Peter the Great, declared war on Russia, ostensibly in support of Elizabeth's claim to the throne. Meanwhile at the Russian court, La Chetardie, the French Ambassador, the Swedish Ambassador, and Lestocq the court physician who was in French pay, encouraged Elizabeth to make a bid for the throne.

Before the guard could leave for the front where they had been ordered, Elizabeth went to the headquarters of the Preobrazhensky regiment, which had also been provided with French money, and they acclaimed her as empress. The baby Emperor, Ivan, was arrested in the middle of the night and imprisoned for the rest of his life; his mother and family were sent to the provinces; and Münnich and Osterman joined Biren in exile.

ELIZABETH, 1741-1762

'The Empress had keen intelligence, was of a gay disposition, and indulged in excessive pleasures. I think she was kind at heart: she had great high-mindedness and much vanity; she wanted to shine and was fond of admiration. I believe that the beauty of her body and her natural laziness did much damage to her character.' So thought Catherine II who had studied Elizabeth well. The new Empress never again showed as much energy and determination as she did at the time of the coup d'état. 'She developed a fondness for power without a corresponding fondness for work', wrote Platonov. Her illnesses may excuse her some of the charge of laziness, but she was also ignorant, coarse, capricious, and superstitious. She was known for her untidiness and extravagance; at her death she left 15,000 dresses, 5,000 pairs of shoes and piles of unpaid bills. She was also immoral, and her lovers ranged from the illiterate cossack shepherd and choirboy, Alexis Razumovsky, whom she married and raised to great wealth, to Ivan Shuvalov, a patron of art and letters who did much for education and founded Moscow University in 1755. Elizabeth encouraged the arts, even if at extravagant cost: the Winter Palace was built by the architect Rastrelli for ten million roubles; the theatre was established and French fashions and the French language were adopted by the court and nobility. Elizabeth was more able than she is sometimes allowed to have been; she knew how to pick able men to advise her, and she did her best for Russia.

Domestic Affairs

The coup d'état was followed by a manifesto which declared that Elizabeth had assumed her rightful place as empress. She proposed to continue her father's programme; the terror of Anna's reign was mitigated, surviving nobles were allowed to return from exile, and 'Birenism' was ended. The work of government was carried on by favourites; some of them able men, including Prince Trubetskoy, President of a restored and strengthened Senate; A. P. Bestuzhev-Riumin, who was in control of foreign affairs until 1756; Peter and Ivan Shuvalov; and, until their expulsion, La Chetardie and Lestocq were influential.

The support of the nobility was sought by extending their privileges until they had almost complete control over local administration and over the fate of their serfs. They were granted the exclusive right to own serfs; they could force free peasants into serfdom in the new lands; they could exile serfs and arrange their marriages; a State bank was created with favourable rates of interest to enable them to improve their estates, and the length of compulsory service was effectively reduced by enabling them to register for service in infancy and to count service from the date of registration.

There was some development in education and the arts: French culture was dominant and members of the court corresponded with the Philosophes, including Voltaire. Schools were established for the nobility and a university was founded in Moscow in 1755. Peter the Great's Academy of Science became active, and expeditions were sponsored to Siberia and Kamchatka. Historical studies were begun, and one of the most remarkable of Russian scholars, Lomonosov (1712–1765) gained a European reputation.

But if the nobility received much attention the rest of Russian society did not. The revision of the legal code was begun and capital punishment was abolished; internal tariffs and duties were dispensed with, and some efforts were made to remedy the financial situation through reform of the coinage and of the taxation system; but the burden remained on the peasantry who could only flee or rise in rebellion in protest.

The Problem of the Succession

Elizabeth sought to forestall probable conflicts over the succession by choosing as her heir the son of her sister Anna who had married the Duke of Holstein. Charles Peter was already being prepared to succeed to the Swedish throne when in 1742, at the age of fourteen, he was called to Russia as Peter, and obliged to forsake the Lutheran faith for the Russian Orthodox. Elizabeth also chose his wife—the fifteen-year-old Sophie (renamed Catherine) of Anhalt-Zerbst, to whom he was married in 1745.

Foreign Affairs

Domestic events tended to be overshadowed by international affairs which were in the capable hands of Bestuzhev-Riumin from 1741–1758. Catherine II said of him that he was 'infinitely more feared than loved, he was a great intriguer, suspicious, firm and intrepid in his principles, occasionally tyrannical, an implacable enemy, but the true friend of his friends, whom he abandoned only when they turned their backs on him; he was certainly difficult to get on with and often petty'.

His career as Chancellor was influenced by intrigues at court, the international situation and his own prejudices. He had gained a varied diplomatic experience as one of Peter the Great's young men, and had taken part in the negotiations over the Treaty of Utrecht in 1712. He had also served with the Elector of Hanover, later George I of England, and with Anna, Duchess of Courland.

Bestuzhev saw the growth of Prussia as the chief threat to Russian security and he was opposed to the strength of French influence in the lands surrounding Russia: Sweden, Poland and Turkey. Consequently he sought to counter the Franco-Prussian threat by cultivating an alliance between Russia, Austria, Britain and Saxony. Unfortunately, Elizabeth was not disposed to favour either Britain or Austria, and he had to counter the constant intrigues not only of the French and Prussian ministers but also of the rival court factions, in particular that of the Shuvalov family. The marriage of the Grand Duke Peter with Catherine was seen as an attempt to increase Prussian influence at the Russian court and for this reason Bestuzhev was opposed to it.

The Swedish War, 1741–1743

Sweden had been urged into war by France to facilitate Elizabeth's coup d'état, but the Russian troops were successful and occupied most of Finland. In spite of French efforts to save their accomplice, Russia was able to take part of southern Finland from Sweden at the Peace of Abo, 1743. Bestuzhev was able to show Elizabeth evidence of the intrigues of La Chetardie and he was expelled; so, too, was Catherine's mother who had been an ineffectual Prussian agent at the court. Bestuzhev was promoted to Chancellor and rewarded with lands and a palace.

The War of the Austrian Succession, 1740–1748

Without taking a direct part in the war, Bestuzhev was able to add to Russia's prestige and influence in European affairs. He secured a defensive alliance with Austria in 1745, and an agreement with England in 1747 for the protection of Hanover. The possibility of a Russian army as close to the French frontier as this hastened the Treaty of Aix-la-Chapelle which ended the war.

The Fall of Bestuzhev

Bestuzhev had succeeded: France had been humiliated and Prussia was isolated; but further conflict between Prussia and Austria seemed likely, and if that happened, Russia must support Austria. Since France and Austria were traditional enemies, and since Britain and France were in conflict, it followed that Russia must ally with Britain against France.

In 1755 a new British Ambassador, Sir Charles Hanbury Williams, arrived in Russia with instructions to work for an understanding to prevent Prussian designs on Hanover. Bestuzhev was able to secure an agreement to maintain a Russian army on the Prussian frontier in return for an annual English subsidy of £100,000, to be doubled in time of war (1755). This alarmed Frederick of Prussia, who turned the tables on Bestuzhev by negotiating the Convention of Westminster with Britain which guaranteed the neutrality of Hanover (1756). This double dealing by Britain weakened Bestuzhev's position and drove France into alliance with Austria by the Treaty of Versailles, 1756. This diplomatic revolution was the background to the Seven Years War which broke out when Prussia attacked Austria in 1756. Logically, Russia should now join Austria and France against Prussia, but Bestuzhev could not overcome his hostility to France, and it was Elizabeth, encouraged by the Shuvalovs, who brought Russia into the Seven Years War on the side of Austria in December 1756.

Surprisingly, the Russian troops under General Apraxin defeated the Prussians at Gross Jägersdorf, but they failed to consolidate their victory and withdrew. It was alleged by his enemies that Bestuzhev had withdrawn the troops in order to use them in a coup d'état while Elizabeth was ill. Certainly he had been trying to ensure his continuance in power after Elizabeth's death by intriguing with the Grand Duchess Catherine, but he was too anti-Prussian for the charge of deliberately withdrawing the army to be true. Nevertheless Apraxin was executed and Bestuzhev was dismissed, 1758, although Elizabeth resisted the demands of his enemies that he should be tortured to extract a confession.

The Seven Years War, 1756–1763

Elizabeth took charge of foreign policy during the war and pursued it with vigour. She kept her reluctant allies in the war and insisted on the campaign which took Russian armies into Berlin and almost brought Frederick to defeat. He was only saved by the death of Elizabeth and the accession of Peter in January 1762.

QUESTIONS

1. Give an account of the main events in Russia from the death of Peter I to the accession of Catherine II.
2. Discuss the part played by Russia in: (a) the War of the Polish Succession; (b) the War of the Austrian Succession; (c) the Seven Years War.
3. To what extent was Peter I responsible for events in Russia after his death?
4. Discuss the development of western influences in Russia after the death of Peter I.
5. Discuss either (a) the extension of the powers of the nobility; or (b) the condition of the peasantry in eighteenth-century Russia.
6. Find out what you can, and make notes on the following: Prince A. Menshikov; Count A. Osterman; Count B. Münnich; Ernst von Biren; A. Bestuzhev; La Chetardie; M. Lomonosov; V. Bering.

Further Reading

The Cambridge Modern History (new edition).
BAIN, NISBET R. *The Pupils of Peter the Great: a history of the Russian Court and Empire, 1697–1740.* Westminster, 1897.
—— *The Daughter of Peter the Great.* Westminster, 1899.
MAROGER, D., ed. *The Memoirs of Catherine the Great,* trans. M. Budberg. Hamish Hamilton, 1955.
PUTNAM, P., ed. *Seven Britons in Imperial Russia.* Oxford U.P., 1952.

CHAPTER VII

PETER III AND
CATHERINE II (THE GREAT)

Peter III: 1762
Catherine II (The Great): 1762–1796

Peter I had decreed that the sovereign had the right to name his successor, and in 1744, the Empress Elizabeth chose her nephew, Charles Peter of Holstein as her heir. He was brought to Russia, made a Grand Duke, admitted to the Orthodox Church, and rechristened Peter Feodorovich. Peter was a sickly looking youth of sixteen who never responded to the attempts to Russianize him. He mocked his tutors, adhered to his Lutheran faith rather than his religion by adoption, and at all times preferred the interests of his native Holstein to those of Russia. Most important of all, he hero-worshipped Frederick II of Prussia—and this at a time when Frederick's ambitions represented the greatest threat to Russian security.

Elizabeth also chose the girl who was to become Peter's wife: Sophie Auguste Frederika, daughter of the Governor of Stettin and of Joanna of Holstein-Gottorp. She too was brought to Russia, admitted to the Orthodox Church, rechristened Catherine Alexandrovna, and married to Peter in 1745.

The marriage was not a success. Bestuzhev, the Russian Chancellor was opposed to the growth of Prussian influence which it seemed to represent, and he did all he could to make things unpleasant for the young couple. There was a real danger that having been designated Elizabeth's successors they would become the objects of intrigues and court factions against Bestuzhev and Elizabeth. For this reason they were closely watched and supervised.

Catherine and Peter soon became aware of their incompatibility. He seemed to have little interest in his future responsibilities: she, on the other hand, had her ambitions aroused. 'I myself felt little more than indifference towards him, though I was not indifferent to the Russian crown', she wrote in her memoirs. While Peter played at soldiers and acquired an ugly mistress, Catherine learned to ride and dance, to read everything she could, and began a series of handsome lovers. When a son, Paul, was born in 1754, the paternity of the child was by no means certain; indeed Catherine's personal life was notoriously immoral. She was passionate and sensual; one estimate gives her fifty-five lovers, and she died after a night of love at the age of sixty-seven.

Peter's opponents, particularly his wife, made him out to be a greedy, drunken, loutish oaf, who never grew up, and who was cruel to animals. Certainly he was unstable, and the prospects for the next reign were not very promising. Princess Dashkov says that he 'was not wicked, but his incompetence and lack of education, as well as inclination and natural bent, all combined to make him a good Prussian corporal and not the sovereign of a great empire'. On the other hand, of Catherine she said, 'I really believe there has never been anyone in the world, and certainly never any sovereign, to equal her in the sheer magic of personality, in the resources of the mind, in versatility, and above all in the charm with which she displayed these gifts'.

Unlike her husband, Catherine set out to identify herself completely with her country of adoption. Her intelligence, ambition, and strength of mind, drew the intriguers around her with plots to replace Peter by the infant Paul, with Catherine as regent after Elizabeth's death. Peter in turn, was planning to divorce Catherine and marry his mistress, Elizabeth Vorontsov, but when the empress died, Peter succeeded her with Catherine still as his wife.

Peter III

Peter began his reign by making peace with his hero, Frederick II of Prussia, thus saving him from probable defeat in the Seven Years War. Russia was in a strong position, and Frederick's situation was desperate, yet the peace restored to Prussia all the lands held by Russia and provided for an alliance. Frederick was saved and Europe was amazed.

In the next few months Peter granted amnesties to political exiles, extended religious freedom, abolished the secret police, reduced the salt tax, introduced Prussian uniforms to the army, reformed the law, secularized Church property and freed the nobility from their obligations of service to the State. Although some of these things were welcomed—the nobles in particular rejoiced in their freedom—Peter had succeeded in antagonizing large sections of the army, the clergy and those factions at court who resented the subjugation of Russian to Prussian interests.

Catherine's coup d'état, 1762

The first plans for a coup d'état were foiled by Elizabeth's death. In the early months of Peter's reign Catherine dissembled her intentions and exploited his mistakes. The chief conspirators were Nikita Panin, tutor to Paul; Princess Dashkov; and the five brothers Orlov, of whom Gregory was Catherine's current lover. The Orlovs were in touch with the guards regiments on whom the success of the coup depended. News of the conspiracy reached Peter and it became necessary to act without delay. Early in the morning of 9 July Catherine put herself at the head of three regiments of guards, issued a manifesto, and had herself proclaimed empress with her son Paul as her heir. Peter, who had been reviewing his soldiers was taken and forced to abdicate. On the 16th he was dead—in a drunken scuffle according to Orlov; poisoned or more brutally murdered according to others.

Thus began one of the most splendid reigns in Russian history, for Catherine, a foreign usurper, made herself more Russian than the Russians; she was determined to reign and rule; she was a master of diplomacy, and in the age of enlightened despotism she achieved for Russia a role of European pre-eminence.

CATHERINE II (THE GREAT), 1762–1796

Catherine studied Russia and the art of government: she was ambitious, talented and cultured; she loved power and she lived life to the full extent of her considerable abilities. Her diplomacy was as immoral as her private life, but she raised Russia to greatness, and there is little evidence that she let her private life interfere with the affairs of State. She worked up to fifteen hours a day, travelled about her dominions to see for herself, and kept up a correspondence with Voltaire, Grimm, Diderot and D'Alembert. She was an enthusiastic patron of the arts and was interested in architecture, sculpture, painting and engraving, although she was completely unmusical. She had literary tastes, and in addition to her correspondence with the Philosophes, she wrote plays, histories, and some very frank memoirs. In religion she was really atheistic for she had been successively instructed as a Roman Catholic, a Calvinist, a Lutheran, and as a Russian Orthodox, but she was punctilious in her observance of the orthodox faith, for she knew how important it was to keep up appearances. She was ruthless in disposing of her husband and of the former Tsar Ivan who had been in prison since 1742 and was murdered in 1764, but in her own epitaph she wished to be remembered as one who 'desired nothing but the best for her country and tried to procure for her subjects happiness, liberty and wealth.

She forgave easily and hated no one. Tolerant, undemanding, of a gay disposition, she had a republican spirit and a kind heart. She made good friends.'

Domestic Policy

Catherine wished to continue the work of Peter I. She saw clearly what was wrong with Russian society, and her contact with the Philosophes and her wide reading prompted her to put her ideas into practice, but she could only work within the limits imposed by the Russian situation. She wished to recover the authority of the Crown and to impose reforms, but she had to keep on the right side of the nobility who could be plotting against her and who represented the chief obstacles to reform.

She was, after all, a foreign usurper, and there were others with a better claim to the throne: her son, Paul, was the true successor to Peter III, but he was kept from the throne; until 1764 there was the unfortunate Ivan; there were many false claimants, including a 'Princess Tarakanova', who said she was a daughter of the Empress Elizabeth, as well as several who claimed to be Peter III; there were, in addition, all those members of the Old Russian party who were opposed to alien influences at the court, and there was, in fact, a number of plots and risings against Catherine throughout her reign. She could not feel really safe until after the crushing of Pugachev's rebellion in 1775.

The Men in Catherine's Life

Only four of Catherine's numerous lovers were important politically: Saltykov, who was probably the father of Paul; Gregory Orlov, whom she truly loved and who gave her three children; Stanislaus Poniatowski, whom she made King of Poland in 1764; and Potemkin, to whom she may have been married in 1774. In her declining years, her final lover, Plato Zubov, also exercised some influence at court.

Orlov led the conspiracy that put Catherine on the throne and he was suitably promoted and rewarded in return. He was interested in the problem of serfdom and on the whole was probably a good influence on Catherine's early policies. Poniatowski as King of Poland was intended to ensure that Russia had an obedient satellite on her western frontier, for he owed everything to Catherine, but his loyalty to his new kingdom proved to be more compelling than it was to his old mistress. Potemkin was the most remarkable of the men about the Empress. Catherine herself referred to him as 'one of the greatest, most bizarre, and most entertaining eccentrics of this iron age'.

Gregory Alexandrovitch Potemkin, 1739–1791

His father was a colonel and small landowner and Gregory was brought up by his uncle, a high civil servant in Moscow. Precocious and moody, Gregory had unpredictable spasms of energy and melancholia. After a brilliant career at the university he was expelled for laziness; he was fascinated by theology yet he was immoral; he was temperamental, ambitious and a great showman. He joined the guards as a private in 1755, became one of the young bloods about town, and was determined to make his mark at court. He took part in Catherine's coup d'état and was rewarded by cash and promotion. He became a great entertainer and joined Catherine's intimate circle where he aroused the jealousy of the Orlovs and lost an eye in a fight. Catherine took him under her wing, but his ambition could not be satisfied at court for he wanted military glory and promotion.

By 1772 Catherine needed a strong arm to lean on and she was in love with Potemkin although he was ten years younger than herself. She showered gifts, appointments and decorations upon her lover and there were two years of tempestuous romance, but as Catherine said, 'The essence of our disagreement is always the question of power and never that of love'. Having acquired wealth and power Potemkin set about using it. His special interest lay in the newly acquired southern provinces where he had dreams of empire, and in 1787 he stage-managed the great expedition to the south. For this he was rewarded and made Prince of Taurida.[1]

Although Catherine took other lovers, Potemkin was not dismissed and retained his influence at court until his death, even giving prior approval to the fifteen young men who succeeded him as the empress's favourites.

The Maintenance of the Autocracy

Apart from her favourites, Catherine was able to choose men who served her well, among them Count Nikita Panin (1718–1783), a scholar whom she called her 'encyclopaedia'. He had served under Bestuzhev in Elizabeth's reign and was appointed governor to the Grand Duke Paul in 1760. From 1762 to 1780 he was the chief influence on the direction of foreign policy. His great dream was the Northern Accord, an alliance of Russia, Prussia, Poland, Sweden and perhaps Britain, against France and Austria. Panin was succeeded by Count Bezborodko who switched the main aim of Russian foreign policy towards the 'Greek Project', an ambitious scheme to partition the

[1] The medieval name for the Crimea.

Turkish Empire and create a Greek Empire to be ruled from Constantinople by Catherine's grandson, named Constantine with that in mind.

Other men who served Catherine were Count Sievers, who helped with many of the domestic reforms; Betsky who was her helper in the field of education; and in military affairs, Marshal Rumyantsev, and above all, Suvorov, probably the greatest general in Russian history. Another of the Orlov brothers, Alexis, was a talented naval commander.

But Catherine was always her own chief minister, and she kept her favourites and her ministers in their places. She insisted on the maintenance of her despotic powers over a centralized bureaucracy. The new lands were Russified and local freedoms subordinated to the centre.

The Church was an essential part of the structure of the State and Catherine was punctilious in the performance of her public duties, but, after handing back the Church lands at the beginning of her reign to gain support, she secularized them again in 1763 and made the priests and monks public servants who were paid by the State.

The nobility had to be won over, for she could not afford to cross them and could not manage without them. Peter III had already freed them from their obligations to State service and she extended their privileges still further by her Charter to the Nobility in 1785. By this, they were exempted from personal taxation and corporal punishment; they could not lose their rank except by judgment of their peers; they were given the exclusive right to own serfs; they were granted the right to hold provincial assemblies where they could choose local officials from their own ranks; and in general, they were given power and influence without any responsibilities. What was not clearly faced was the fact that if the nobility who had enjoyed the privileges of serf ownership in return for their services to the State should be relieved of their duties, they could no longer justify their privileges. The abolition of serfdom was a necessary corollary of the emancipation of the nobility.

Domestic Reforms

The enlightened despots attempted to justify despotism by rationalizing the duties of kingship. They would care for the interests of the State as a good but firm father would, who knew what was best for his family. In 1767, Catherine, under the influence of her reading of Montesquieu's *De l'Esprit des lois*, of Beccaria's *Crime and Punishment*, and of the Encyclopaedists in general, drew up her Nakaz (Instructions) for the delegates to a great representative assembly that was to reform the law. The Nakaz was a wide-ranging document, even after it had been cut down by the nobility to whom Catherine showed it before publishing it in its final form. The principles and sentiments it expressed were admirable by the enlightened and humanitarian standards of the eighteenth century and when the assembly met it discussed very fully from 1767–1768 the problems of serfdom, the relations between the central and the local governments, trade, and all the mandates brought to the assembly by the delegates from the provinces.

Catherine had enjoyed composing the Nakaz (she had spent two years over it) and she listened to the discussions it provoked, but the net result in practical reforms was almost negligible, for the outbreak of the Turkish War and of Pugachev's rebellion made other matters more pressing.

There was some necessary reform of the Senate at the beginning of the reign and local government was reorganized in 1775. The Empire was divided into fifty guberniyas (provinces) of 300–400,000 inhabitants under governors-general, and each guberniya was subdivided into uyezds (districts) of 20–30,000 inhabitants, each with its own local organization. The Charter to the Nobility followed this reform of local government. Proposals to extend self-government to the towns by a charter in 1785 remained little more than reforms on paper.

The greatest problem was that of serfdom; yet although it was discussed by the Great Commission and Catherine was aware of the nature of the problem, the vested interests were too great, and serfdom was in fact intensified during Catherine's reign at the same time that the nobility extended their privileges. Serfdom was extended to the new lands gained by diplomacy and conquest and by the massive grants of Crown lands to favourites.

Pugachev's Rebellion, 1773–1775

The most serious internal crisis of the reign occurred while Catherine was preoccupied with the partition of Poland and the Turkish War. Peasant discontent had increased with the growth of the privileges of the nobility and the spread of serfdom to the new lands and to the industrial workers. There was also opposition to the establishment of central control over the formerly non-Russian lands, while the cossacks, the Old Believers and many of the orthodox clergy were opposed to Catherine's religious policy. There were also persistent rumours that Peter III had intended to emancipate the serfs and that his wishes were being flouted.

There had already been nearly fifty risings since 1762, and the discontent was especially serious in the south and the south-east. Here,

Emilian Pugachev (1726–1775), an illiterate Don Cossack who had served in the army and had many brushes with authority, appeared as the leader of the cossacks of the Urals in 1771. At first the revolt was not taken too seriously by Catherine, but by 1773 Pugachev was at the head of a large, if assorted army, and the whole of the southern and south-eastern parts of the empire were in revolt.

Pugachev claimed to be Peter III and set up a court; he promised to emancipate the serfs; to abolish military service; to restore the cossack privileges and to grant religious freedom to the Old Believers. It was class warfare; the poor against the rich, and fearful atrocities were committed against landowners and priests. Many soldiers deserted to the rebels and all who had a grievance against the State flocked to support them or fished in the troubled waters created by the revolt. Indeed, to a great extent, Pugachev was only a tool in the hands of Catherine's enemies, particularly the Poles.

Orenburg was besieged by the rebels from October 1773 to March 1774; Kazan was taken, and Moscow was threatened before the revolt was checked by General Bibikov and later by Suvorov. Pugachev was eventually betrayed, taken to Moscow in a cage in August 1774, and executed by quartering in January 1775.

The revolt had shown the internal stresses and weaknesses of the State beneath the dominating international position that Catherine's diplomacy had gained for Russia. The result for the peasants was an intensification of serfdom while the nobility won their Charter. After 1775 Catherine's internal position was secure: there were only twenty more outbreaks in the rest of her reign, although there were nearly 300 in the short reign of Paul.

National Finance

The national revenue increased from about £4½ million to £6 million in Catherine's reign, thanks to the conquest of new territories, to the increase in the poll tax, to new customs duties and the growth in trade and industry, and to the revenues from the lands formerly belonging to the Church. Yet, for the first time in Russian history, a national debt was created, and Catherine had to resort to loans and the issue of paper currency. The net result was inflation, and the rouble which had been worth from four to five shillings at the beginning of the reign, was worth only about two shillings at the end. There was always a budget deficit and the financial burdens on the peasantry increased as the State got deeper into debt. This was due partly to the corruption which was always a feature of tsarist officialdom, but more to Catherine's personal extravagance and the cost of her wars.

Catherine regarded the national exchequer as her own private purse and lavished gifts of cash, jewels, palaces and estates upon her favourites, or upon persons she wished to win over to her support, and her own patronage of the arts was on a magnificent scale. Her extravagance also reached beyond the court, for the nobility throughout the country tended to imitate the splendours of St Petersburg and Moscow, and indirectly the peasantry were obliged to pay the cost of the new fashions, the country houses and entertainments that were the mark of a cultured gentleman and his family.

Cultural and Scientific Developments

French cultural influences were dominant at court, and Catherine wrote and spoke in French except when it was expedient to speak Russian. Princess Dashkov says that Catherine spoke French to divert attention from her German origin, and it was the ideas of the French encyclopaedists that influenced her early ideas on government, but the liberalism and humanitarianism of her early years tended to disappear with the constant flattery that surrounded her, her diplomatic successes, the strain of government and the outbreak of the French Revolution. The Russian nobility were permitted to travel in Europe and romantic literature was widely read, but it was an alien culture that was being aped rather than absorbed or related to their own experience.

Catherine encouraged historical writing and founded the Free Economic Society to study agriculture. She took a special interest in roads and canals, established foundling hospitals in St Petersburg and Moscow, the Smolny Institute for the education of young ladies, a public library in St Petersburg and a college of medicine. Much was done in the field of geography and map making and the first Russian dictionaries were compiled. Catherine herself, was inoculated for smallpox when it was a revolutionary medical innovation to submit to such treatment. She even permitted some satirical writing to appear but her wrath fell upon Radishchev when he seemed to go too far in criticizing serfdom. Educational reforms remained largely on paper, and there was always a censorship to inhibit genuine intellectual freedom.

The Succession

Catherine's son, Paul, had been taken from her at birth by the Empress Elizabeth, and no love had developed between them. He was the rightful heir of Peter III, yet his mother was ruling in his place. He was consequently the focus of plots against Catherine and she devoted all her attention to her grandsons, Alexander and Constantine, whom she in turn took away from their parents. She planned to disown Paul and nominate Alexander as her successor, while it was her ambition, stated in her will, that Constantine should inherit 'The Great Eastern Empire'.

Foreign Policy

Catherine found more scope for her vanity, ambition and talents in the direction of foreign than in domestic affairs. Although she chose able men to carry out her work, she was her own foreign minister, directing policy by personal correspondence with the other crowned heads of Europe. No abstract philosophical principles were allowed to influence her relations with other states, for her conduct of foreign affairs was unscrupulous, realistic and opportunistic. The aims were to add to the territory of Russia and to the personal glory of Catherine. If at the same time attention was diverted from pressing domestic problems, so much the better—they were in any case more difficult to solve and brought less renown to the person attempting to deal with them.

Catherine added nothing new to the traditional policies of Russia, but she was more successful in pursuing them than anyone had been since Peter the Great; there was the expansion of the frontiers to bring in nearly all the Russian lands; the drive to gain access to the Baltic and the Black Seas; the expansion across Siberia; and the dream of reaching Constantinople. These aims were bound to lead to conflict with Sweden, who controlled the Baltic coast; with Poland, a Slav country, but with an alien faith that persecuted the orthodox minority; and with Turkey in control of the Black Sea coast as well as Constantinople, and infidel into the bargain. These countries in turn were allied with other European powers that felt their interests were involved, and no action could be taken against Russia's neighbours without alarming their allies; in particular, Austria, Prussia, France and Britain.

From 1726 until the accession of Peter III the basis of Russian policy, especially against the Turks, had been the alliance with Austria, and indirectly from 1756, with her ally, France. Panin's scheme in the first part of Catherine's reign was for a grand northern alliance, of Poland, Prussia, Sweden, Saxony and Britain, led by Russia, against the southern grouping of Spain, France and Austria. The pursuit of this dream meant giving up the proven alliance with Austria and France against Turkey, but it was not in fact a scheme that was likely to succeed, for the interests of the proposed allies were too diverse, and in any case they were unlikely to submit to Russian leadership. Nevertheless, it was flattering to Catherine to suppose that they might. In the second part of her reign her policy favoured the even more ambitious 'Greek scheme' whereby the Turkish Empire would be partitioned as

Poland had been, and a new Eastern Empire would be carved out of it, to be given to her grandson Constantine.

Poland

The reign began with a denunciation of Prussia and of Frederick II, for it was politic to do so, but in fact the Prussian alliance made by Peter III was useful, and it was renewed in 1762, as both Prussia and Russia were interested in keeping Poland weak. Catherine also began with a declaration of pacific intentions, and mediated with Prussia and Austria to end the Seven Years War. The state of Poland in the eighteenth century, however, offered opportunities for Russian intervention that could not be missed, and Catherine was at war, somewhere, for most of her reign.

Poland and Lithuania had been united since the fourteenth century and constituted the largest, most anarchic and defenceless state in Europe. Since the sixteenth century the monarchy had been elective, and the king (unless he was very strong) was no more than a pawn in the hands of the Polish nobility and of the great powers who surrounded him. In addition the Polish diet, in which only the nobles were represented, was reduced to impotence by the 'liberum veto', by which any single member could nullify legislation. The nobility were arrogant, selfish and divided by factions; the peasantry were poverty stricken and downtrodden, and there was no germ of national unity. The long history of Polish-Russian enmity had been intensified by the success of the Jesuits and other agents of the Counter-Reformation in converting the Poles, a Slav people, to Roman Catholicism. The orthodox minority were persecuted and this offered a standing excuse for Russian intervention in the affairs of Poland. Such interference was easy, for all Poland's neighbours had a vested interest in maintaining her weakness.

The Duchy of Courland was under Polish suzerainty, but the Empress Anna had forced her favourite, Biren, upon it as ruler, although he was later exiled to Siberia. The Polish king, Augustus III of Saxony, wished to gain the Duchy for his son Charles, but at the very beginning of her reign, Catherine, posing as the defender of Polish interests, forced the Poles to accept Biren again as Duke of Courland, although she had to use threats, bribes and direct military occupation to do so.

In 1763, Augustus III died and the majority of the electors wished to choose his son, Charles, as king, and force Biren out of Courland. Catherine, in alliance with Frederick II, by similar threats, bribes and military occupation, secured the election of her ex-lover, Stanislaus Poniatowski in September 1764.

Thus Catherine had succeeded in reducing Poland to the status of a Russian satellite, and for a time the country was to all intents governed by the Russian ambassador. But the Poles were stirred by the national disgrace, and began a movement for reform which gained ground in spite of Russian and Prussian attempts to discourage it. Eventually civil war broke out, in which the reformers and the anti-Russians were aided by the French, and Suvorov had to be sent to crush them. In order to help the Poles the French also urged the Turks to attack Russia and the Polish rising merged into the first Turkish War of 1768.

The Partitions of Poland

The division of Poland by her three neighbours at the end of the eighteenth century introduced a new element of cynicism and immorality into international power politics. The idea was suggested by Frederick II of Prussia in 1769, and he was joined by Russia and Austria in the first act of partition in August 1772, by which the Poles, threatened by Russian guns and purchased by Russian bribes, were obliged to accept the treaty which sanctioned the loss of 25,000 square miles (two-sevenths of their land) and five million out of their twelve million people. Russia took White Russia and Polish Livonia, while Austria and Prussia took corresponding areas adjacent to their own dominions in the south and the west.

This loss of territory stimulated a national revival among the Poles. The constitution imposed upon them by the partition treaty ensured their continued political weakness and Russian domination, but the outbreak of the French Revolution in 1789, the preoccupation of Austria and Russia with the Turkish War, and the friendly attitude of the new King of Prussia emboldened the Poles to renounce the constitution in 1789 and to introduce a new one of their own in 1791, which included major political reforms, such as the abolition of the liberum veto[1] and the establishment of hereditary monarchy. This was an affront to Catherine's pride and ambitions, and she determined to restore the old constitution and to stamp out 'Jacobinism'.

In 1792, Russian armies again marched into Poland and the second treaty of partition was made with Prussia; this time Catherine took what was left of White Russia, half of Lithuania and the whole of the Ukraine. Prussia took further territory in the west of Poland. In July 1793, the Polish king was obliged to agree to this second dismemberment of his country and to recognize Russian suzerainty.

The result was a Polish revolt led by Thaddeus Kosciuszko who

[1] The right of any Polish deputy to veto any measure introduced in the diet.

declared war on Russia in 1794 and set up a provisional government in Warsaw. For a time the rebels were successful, for Prussia, Austria and Russia were in disagreement, but the Polish resistance was doomed to failure when the three powers invaded the country from all quarters, and in 1794 Suvorov took Warsaw.

Prompted by Catherine the allies agreed on the third and final partition which removed Poland from the map of Europe in October 1795. Russia took Courland and what was left of Lithuania, while Prussia and Austria took what was left in the west and the south.

The partitions of Poland had brought Catherine great accessions of territory and population, and she had completed the gathering in of the Russian lands in the west. She had fed her craving for glory and acclaim, but what she had done was not really in the long-term interests of Russia. Polish enmity towards Russia had been intensified, and she now had a strengthened Prussia on her western frontier when it suited her better to have a large and weak Poland under Russian influence between them. The partitions demonstrated the 'moral bankruptcy' of eighteenth-century diplomacy.

Turkey

Catherine pursued the traditional Russian policy of hostility to the Turkish Empire with a new emphasis derived from the imagination of Potemkin. The Turks were Muslims ruling over numerous Slavs and orthodox Christians, and they possessed the whole of the Black Sea coastline and the region of the Caucasus which might be legitimately regarded as the natural frontiers of the Russian Empire in the south. There was no free access for Russian shipping to the Black Sea and the Mediterranean, and the Tartar subjects of the Porte in the Crimea were a nest of robbers and pirates who constantly attacked the southern provinces of the Empire. Above all, the Turks held the coveted prize of Constantinople.

To defeat the Turks; to win over their territories; to extend Russian protection to all Christians; to unite Russian national, religious and economic interests in a crusade for the good of Europe and the glory of the empress—this was the dream shared by Potemkin and Catherine. Unfortunately, the radical shifts in the balance of power in eastern Europe likely to result from the realization of such schemes alarmed not only the Turks, but also Austria and Poland, France, Prussia, Sweden and Britain, who were determined to gain what they could while resisting Russia and helping the Turks when it suited them to do so.

The First Turkish War, 1768–1774

Catherine's ambitions were no secret and the Turks were justifiably alarmed. She had for some time been attempting to stir up the subject peoples against the Porte, and the Turks in turn were prepared to help the Poles against Catherine in spite of the distribution of Russian bribes at Constantinople. Urged on by France, the Turks declared war on Russia after a body of Russian troops pursued some Poles into Turkish territory and burned the town of Balta.

Both sides were ill prepared for the war, and Frederick II referred to it as a fight between the blind and the one-eyed. The Tartars invaded from the Crimea, and the Russians occupied Moldavia and Wallachia. One of the most portentous events of the war was the sailing of a Russian fleet from Kronstadt to help the Greeks. After sailing round Europe and showing the Russian flag on the high seas for the first time, they defeated the Turks at Tchesme off Chios, in 1770.[1] In 1771 the Russians took the Crimea and their successes alarmed Austria who had her own ambitions in eastern Europe and saw them threatened: the result was an alliance between Austria and Turkey in 1771. It was the consequent danger of the development of a general European war that prompted Frederick II to propose the first partition of Poland. Catherine was to give up Moldavia and Wallachia, while Austria would not attack Russia, and they would all seek compensation in Poland. A puppet khan was set up by Catherine to rule the Crimean Tartars, and she now set her sights on Constantinople, but the partition of Poland and Pugachev's rebellion together with the length and cost of the war brought it to an end in 1774 by the Treaty of Kutchuk-Kainardji.

This was a great triumph for Catherine, for while she handed back Bessarabia, Moldavia, and Wallachia to the Turks, she retained Azov and Kerch, and the right of free navigation for Russian shipping in Turkish waters. The Crimean Tartars were declared 'independent' (meaning ripe for annexation by Russia) and religious liberty for the orthodox was promised within the Turkish Empire. The Treaty of Kutchuk-Kainardji marks the true beginning of the Eastern Question, which was to be a major problem in European affairs throughout the nineteenth century.

The Annexation of the Crimea, 1783

Catherine realized that co-operation with Austria was essential for the success of her Turkish ambitions, and partly due to Potemkin's dreams, the alliance with Prussia was abandoned in 1781 for alliance with

[1] The Russian fleet had British officers.

Austria, who agreed not to oppose Russian designs on Turkey. In 1778 the khan was obliged to recognize Russian suzerainty, and in 1783 the Crimea was annexed. By the Convention of Constantinople of 1784, the Turks accepted the Russian action. In 1783, also, Catherine imposed her suzerainty over Georgia.

New Russia

The task of consolidating the new lands acquired at Kutchuk-Kainardji was sought by Potemkin, who was made Governor-General and given plenary vice-regal powers in 'New Russia', as it was called. He founded Kherson on the Dnieper, encouraged immigration and the work of colonization, planned the annexation of the Crimea, founded Sevasto-pol in 1784, began the construction of a Black Sea fleet, and chose the site of Ekaterinoslav ('Catherine's Glory'—now Dnepropetrovsk), to be the future capital of the new province.

Potemkin also stage-managed the great tour of the new lands made by Catherine in 1787. This was a triumphal progress, designed to impress the whole of Europe with the magnificence of Catherine's achievements, and no expense was spared—even though the country was suffering from acute famine at the time. Almost the whole court, with invited guests and foreign ambassadors, left St Petersburg in February and travelled by enormous sledges to Kiev, where they waited for the ice to break, and then travelled by boat down the Dnieper. They were joined by the King of Poland and the Emperor of Austria, Joseph II, and travelled to inspect Kherson, Bakhchisaray and Sevasto-pol. The return was via Poltava, where Peter I's victory was re-enacted. Potemkin was created Prince of Taurida and showered with gifts for his services to the empress.

The Second Turkish War, 1787–1792

The great journey to the south had been deliberately provocative to the Turks, as well as impressing Prussia, Britain and France with Russia's successes to the extent that the Turks expected help from them against Russia when they declared war in 1787. Austria, who hoped to get Moldavia and Wallachia, declared war on the Turks in support of Russia, and at first, the joint forces were successful. Suvorov took Ochakov in 1788 and defeated the Turks at Fokshani in 1789; but Sweden saw a chance for revenge against Russia and attacked her in 1788, Austria withdrew after the revolt of her Netherlands, and Turkey was saved by the Triple Alliance of Britain, Holland and Prussia. Peace was made in 1792 at Jassy, where the Sultan accepted the loss of the Crimea and confirmed the Russian gains of 1774. In addition,

Catherine gained a further stretch of the Black Sea coastline where the port of Odessa later developed.

Thus Catherine had not achieved all her ambitions, but at great cost in men and money she had defeated the Turks, gained the Crimea, and established Russian control of the Black Sea coast—an adequate sequel to Peter I's work in reaching the Baltic.

Relations with the rest of Europe

From the death of Peter I in 1725 to the accession of Catherine, the conduct of Russian foreign policy tended to be manipulated by the intrigues of the other European powers at the Russian court. Catherine put an end to this, and attempted to make Russia the arbiter of Europe: to a great extent she succeeded. Her Turkish schemes, the partitions of Poland and her exploitation of the situation created by the French Revolution are very much a part of general European history in the late eighteenth century.

On at least two occasions she did in fact act as arbiter; the first was when she mediated between Austria and Prussia over the Bavarian succession to secure the Peace of Teschen in 1779; the second was when she formed the Armed Neutrality against Britain in 1780.

She showed great skill in playing off Prussia and Austria, the two powers who, if they acted together, could offer most resistance to her schemes in eastern Europe. From 1764 to 1780 she allied with Prussia, for that was necessary with respect to Poland; and from 1781 she allied with Austria, for that was necessary with respect to Turkey. The 1793 partition of Poland favoured Prussia, while the 1795 partition favoured Austria, and she urged them both to get involved with the French Revolution in order to divert their attention from eastern Europe.

Sweden she hoped to keep under control by using bribes and intrigues to build up a strong pro-Russian party in Stockholm, and the alliance between Sweden and Russia was confirmed in 1783, but while the Russian armies were occupied in the south during the second Turkish War, Gustavus III saw an opportunity to regain the Baltic Provinces, and, urged on by Britain and Prussia, he allied with the Turks and attacked Russia in 1788.

For a time St Petersburg was in danger, but Gustavus had his own difficulties at home, and made peace with Catherine at Verela in 1790. The treaty made no changes.

At the very end of her reign Catherine embarked upon a war with Persia in response to an appeal for help from Georgia over which she had assumed suzerainty in 1783. It was left to her successor to complete what she had begun by annexing Georgia in 1801.

France and the French Revolution

In spite of the dominance of French culture at the Russian court, France was one of Catherine's chief diplomatic opponents. In particular the French opposed her eastern schemes and gave help to Turkey and Poland. With the outbreak of the French Revolution Catherine, who had always insisted on maintaining her autocratic powers, put behind her all her early philandering with the ideas of the Philosophes, and presented a resolute opposition to the spread of revolutionary ideas. Russian travellers in France were recalled, and all French persons in Russia were obliged to swear loyalty to the king and opposition to the revolution. Voltaire and Rousseau became forbidden reading. She did not understand that the 'ancien régime' was on the way out, and saw the revolution as merely a problem of maintaining authority. Within Russia the régime became more repressive, and radicals like Radishchev were persecuted, as were suspect organizations such as the Freemasons.

Catherine's opposition to the ideas of the French Revolution did not prevent her from exploiting the situation it created for her own advantage, and she encouraged Prussia and Austria to get embroiled with France while she pursued her schemes in eastern Europe. Indirectly, she probably helped the revolutionaries, for had it not been for the partitions of Poland, Austria and Prussia might have brought more effective forces against them.

After the third partition of Poland Catherine was able to turn to France, and she was preparing to come to the aid of Austria against France when she died.

Catherine's Achievement

In her later years Catherine grew fat and lost her teeth, but she still retained her regal presence and continued to act the autocrat. There was undoubtedly some degeneration of her powers, for years of flattery had fed her vanity and ambition, and her megolomania grew on Potemkin's imagination to encompass dreams of European and world domination. Nevertheless, there were certain obvious gains in her reign: by conquest and annexation she had added about 560,000 square miles of territory, together with its natural resources and population to Russia—much of this was fertile and productive, and the great grain lands of the south could now be developed and the corn exported from the ports on the Black Sea. There had been some internal reforms, and by her skill in diplomacy and her patronage of the arts Catherine had gained international prestige for Russia and a reputation for splendour.

There was another side to this real achievement; the divisions between the nobility and the people had grown, while the condition of the peasantry had worsened, and Russian involvement in European affairs was to prove a mixed blessing, as much for the Russians themselves as for their apprehensive neighbours who now faced the complexities of the Eastern Question, and the existence of a powerful autocracy threatening, or appearing to threaten, the European balance of power.

QUESTIONS

1. To what extent does Catherine II deserve to be called 'The Great'?
2. Compare Catherine II's aims with her achievements in domestic affairs.
3. Give an account of the expansion of Russia under Catherine the Great.
4. Discuss Catherine II's policy towards either (a) Poland, or (b) Turkey.
5. Give an account of the partitions of Poland.
6. Give an account of the causes, course, and results of Pugachev's rebellion.
7. Discuss Catherine II's attitude towards the French Revolution.
8. Find out what you can and make notes on the following: The Orlov brothers; Princess Dashkov; N. Panin; Stanislaus Poniatowski; Potemkin; Suvorov; enlightened despotism; the Nakaz; the Charter to the the Nobility, 1785; A. Radishchev; T. Kosciuszko; the Hermitage; the great journey to the Crimea, 1787.

Further Reading

ALMEDINGEN, E. M. *Catherine the Great*: a portrait. Hutchinson, 1963.

ARETZ, G. *The Empress Catherine*, trans. H. C. Schnur. Godfrey and Stephens, 1947.

DESCARGUES, P. *The Hermitage*. Thames and Hudson, 1961.

GOOCH, G. P. *Catherine the Great and other studies*. Longmans, 1954.

GREY, I. *Catherine the Great*. Hodder and Stoughton, 1961.

FITZLYON, K., ed. *The Memoirs of Princess Dashkov*. Calder, 1956.

LANG, D. MARSHALL. *The First Russian Radical: A. Radishchev*. Allen and Unwin, 1959.

MAROGER, D., ed. *The Memoirs of Catherine the Great*. Hamish Hamilton, 1955.

MARSDEN, C. *Palmyra of the North*. Faber, 1942.

PUSHKIN, A. *The Captain's Daughter*. Dent, 1937. (A story of Pugachev's rebellion.) Trans. N. Duddington.

RADISHCHEV, A. N. *A Journey from St Petersburg to Moscow*, trans. Leo Wiener. Cambridge, Mass., 1958.

REDDAWAY, W. F., ed. *Documents of Catherine the Great*. Cambridge U.P., 1931.

The Memoirs of the Comte de Segur (1825). Ed. E. Cruickshanks. London, Folio Society, 1960.

SOLOVEYTCHIK, G. *Potemkin: A Picture of Catherine's Russia*. Butterworth, 1938.

THOMSON, G. SCOTT. *Catherine the Great and the Expansion of Russia*. 2nd edn. English Universities Press, 1947.

WALISZEWSKI, K. *The Romance of an Empress*. London, 1894.

CHAPTER VIII
PAUL: 1796-1801

Paul had spent his unfortunate early life brooding on his wrongs and making plans for the time when they should be put right. He was certain neither of his paternity nor of the extent of his mother's guilt in his father's death in 1762, but he considered himself the rightful heir to the throne from which Catherine excluded him until her own death thirty-four years later. Catherine treated him well, but allowed him no power or authority: he was, for example, appointed Grand Admiral of the Navy, but was never allowed to visit the main naval base at Kronstadt. In consequence Paul retired to his estate at Gatchina where he indulged his violent moods and fits of temper in drilling his soldiers mercilessly and terrifying the local inhabitants.

He was, as Catherine realized, unfit to rule, and his mental instability verged on madness. He was determined to be regarded as the tsar and to assert his authority, and like Peter III, he took Frederick II of Prussia as his model. Unfortunately his actions were capricious, and his lack of control and understanding went unchecked when he at last achieved the power he dreamed of. What was consistent was his determination to oppose and undo everything that his mother had stood for, and the reign began with some gruesome acts of revenge: Peter III's body was exhumed and placed beside Catherine's; Alexis Orlov was made to carry the crown in the funeral procession; the Princess Dashkov was persecuted and sent into exile, and Potemkin's bones were dug up and cast into a ditch.

The conspirators of 1762 having been punished and the chief royal favourite having been dishonoured, Paul set about reversing Catherine's policies: there were to be no more wars of conquest, no more coups d'état and no more royal favourites; order was to be re-established within the State, and all things French were to be rooted out. There was method in Paul's madness; unfortunately he lacked the capacity to rule according to his own vision of his role.

Domestic Policy

Paul had a well-founded fear of assassination and of Palace revolutions. In addition, his mother's philandering with the ideas of the Philosophes and the spread of Jacobinism alarmed him. He felt it necessary to strengthen the autocracy, but his ideas of his divine right and of his absolute powers were so exaggerated that his actions were often arbitrary, contradictory and incomprehensible.

He began well in 1797 by defining the law of succession to follow the rule of primogeniture. This put the monarchy and the administration on a much more stable basis than had been known since Peter 1's decree of 1722. Next he repealed parts of the Charter to the Nobility and attempted to reduce the privileges of the guards regiments that had so often conspired against the throne. The army and the navy were reformed, new uniforms on the Prussian model were introduced, and Paul gained some popularity with the rank and file, as he did with the peasantry, when in 1797, the barshchina was limited to three days per week with no work on holidays. There was an amnesty for political prisoners condemned by Catherine, including Radishchev; education and commerce were encouraged; the price of salt was reduced; reserves of grain for distribution in time of famine were set up; religious toleration was extended to the Old Believers; tariffs were revised; the Donets coalfield was discovered, and industry developed; but on the other hand, the Armed Neutrality led to loss of trade; little was really done for the serfs whom Paul continued to grant away by the thousand; and above all, he lost the support of the nobility whom he had antagonized by his reforms and his arbitrary actions. They were expected to perform their military duties and were replaced by bureaucrats in the work of government. They were also forbidden to travel abroad or to wear foreign (that is, French) fashions. There was a rigid censorship, and the importation of books, and even of music, was forbidden.

Foreign Policy

Catherine had allied with England, Austria and Prussia and had ordered Suvorov to plan a campaign against France. Paul revoked this, dismissed Suvorov, recalled the expedition to Persia, apologized for the partitions of Poland and declared that there would be no more wars. But his pacific intentions could not be sustained with the growth of French ambitions. His attempts at mediation to check French expansion in 1797-1798 came to nothing, and France went on to conquer the Low Countries, Italy, Switzerland and Egypt, at the same time establishing republics all over Europe. When French help was given to the Poles preparatory to the establishment of a republic there, when Napoleon expelled the Knights of Malta, of whom Paul regarded himself as the protector, and when he turned from Egypt to attack the Turkish Empire, Paul brought Russia into the Grand Alliance with Austria and England against France in 1798.

A fleet was sent into the Mediterranean, the Ionian Islands were captured and French shipping was attacked. Suvorov was recalled from the exile to which Paul had sent him to lead an army that would enable the Austrians to drive the French out of Italy. Another army was sent to help the English in the Low Countries. The success of these Russian forces alarmed Paul's allies and the Austrians foiled Suvorov's plans to invade France by diverting his army to Switzerland where it was checked, although not beaten, in the mountains. Suvorov returned to Russia to die with only a remnant of his army, while the Duke of York, the Commander-in-Chief in the Low Countries, had failed to achieve anything.

In disgust with his allies Paul withdrew from the alliance in 1800 and began to consider the advantages of working with Napoleon. He now saw his former enemy as the restorer of authority in Europe, and Napoleon exploited this remarkable change in his fortunes. Together they revived the Armed Neutrality of the North against England and they were planning a fantastic partition of the Turkish Empire and invasion of India when Paul was murdered.

The Assassination of Paul, 23 March 1801

Paul's tactless treatment of the officer class, his violent and capricious moods, the tales of his madness and unfitness to rule, all fostered the inevitable plots of the guards and the nobility to remove an emperor who inspired fear for their lives and dismay for their interests as well as genuine concern for the welfare of the country. A group of conspirators, with the connivance of the Grand Duke Alexander, whose liberal ideas were at odds with the absolutism of his father, entered Paul's fortress palace with the object of forcing him to abdicate, but they were the worse for drink, and Paul was struck down and strangled. The grand duke was shocked by this turn in events. Nevertheless the empress, who claimed the right to rule in place of her murdered husband, was obliged to give way to her son who became Alexander I.

Paul's short reign is significant for certain tendencies that became apparent at the end of the eighteenth century. Russian armies and navies were operating in central Europe and the Mediterranean and had begun to threaten India. Russian military prestige and the size of the armies alarmed the other European powers and the bogy of Russophobia was already apparent in western Europe by 1800. Russia began to recognize the importance of the problem of serfdom and the obligation of the State to do something about it. Indeed the whole conception of the State underwent change: it was no longer to be regarded as the personal possession of the sovereign, to be administered as a kind of private household, but as a trust, involving duties and responsibility. This in turn involved a diminution of the exclusive powers and privileges of the nobility and a greater reliance on a professional bureaucracy, while territorial gains were to be no longer for the greater glory of the ruler, but to serve the growing national will and interest. Finally, there was the emergence of anti-autocratic sentiments among the gentry and of criticism of the tsarist system.

QUESTIONS

1. What led to the assassination of Paul 1 in 1801?
2. What is the significance of the reign of the Emperor Paul 1 in Russian history?
3. Give an account of the part played by Russian armies and navies against France in the reign of Paul 1.
4. Discuss the relations between the Emperor Paul and Napoleon.
5. Comment on the reforms of Paul 1.
6. Write short notes on the following: Suvorov's campaigns; A. A. Arakcheyev; Count Pahlen; the campaign against India in the reign of Paul.

Further Reading

ALMEDINGEN, E. M. *So Dark a Stream*: a study of The Emperor Paul of Russia 1754-1801. Hutchinson, 1959.
BLEASE, W. L. *Suvorov*. Constable, 1921.
PARES, B. *History of Russia*. Rev. edn. Cape, 1955. (For the military campaigns.)
WALISZEWSKI, K. *Paul the First of Russia*. Heinemann, 1913.

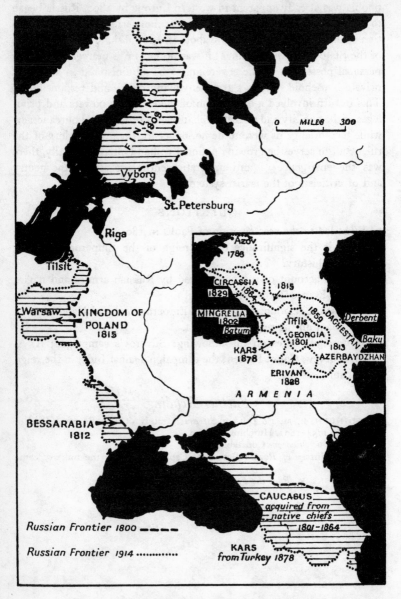

FINLAND 1809

Vyborg

St. Petersburg

Riga

Tilsit

Warsaw

KINGDOM OF POLAND 1815

BESSARABIA 1812

0 MILES 300

Azov 1786

CIRCASSIA 1829 1815 1864

MINGRELIA 1802 Batum

Tiflis

GEORGIA 1801

KARS 1878

ERIVAN 1828

1859 DACHESTAN

Derbent

Baku

1813 AZERBAYDZHAN

A R M E N I A

CAUCASUS acquired from native chiefs 1801-1864

KARS from Turkey 1878

Russian Frontier 1800 —— ——

Russian Frontier 1914 ....

THE EXPANSION OF RUSSIA IN THE NINETEENTH CENTURY

CHAPTER IX

RUSSIA IN THE NINETEENTH CENTURY

Alexander I: 1801–25
Nicholas I: 1825–55
Alexander II: 1855–81
Alexander III: 1881–94
Nicholas II: 1894–1917

At the beginning of the nineteenth century, a triumphant Russia expelled the French invaders and Russian armies marched across Europe to impose peace at Paris and Vienna: in the early twentieth century, the European powers used the opportunities of peacemaking at Versailles to build a wall of buffer states across eastern Europe to keep the Russians out. In the meantime, Russia had earned the reputation of 'the gendarme of Europe and the hangman of Asia', and Russophobia had intensified, particularly in Britain; European socialist ideas had been adapted to Russian social and political conditions; and the Romanov dynasty, together with the society that depended upon it, had disappeared in a revolution that marked the end of the old Russia and the beginning of a new world.

The tragedy of tsarist Russia was that it could only end in revolution, and the literature of the nineteenth century reflects the atmosphere of impending social disaster, together with resignation to the fate in store.[1] The structure of an autocratic society could admit no radical change unless imposed from above, yet to do so would involve limiting the autocracy. The need for reform was widely recognized, yet attempts to carry it out foundered because of the inherent stresses and contradictions in Russian society. The governments alternated between liberal proposals and reactionary policies; between stern military discipline and well-intentioned weakness or incompetence: the dreamy Alexander I was followed by Nicholas the disciplinarian; Nicholas by Alexander the Liberator; he by the determined reactionary Alexander III; and Alexander by the ineffectual Nicholas II.

[1] Especially the boredom and frustration of the nobility.

Social revolution was not prevented by the abolition of serfdom, which undermined the structure of Russian society without satisfying the peasants' need for land: indeed most of them were worse off economically as free men than they had been as serfs. Meanwhile economic developments were taking place that were transforming Russia from a feudal to a capitalist society, with a discontented urban working class that was to provide the means for the Bolshevik revolution.

At the same time Russia was extending her control over Siberia, and probing towards Afghanistan, India, Persia, the Middle East, the Balkans and the Mediterranean, building up her empire and helping to create the international tensions that were to lead to the First World War and the downfall of the tsarist régime. Indeed, a series of disastrous imperialist wars; the Crimean, the Russo-Turkish, and the Russo-Japanese wars all had revolutionary effects at home and brought the final revolution nearer.

The Government

The tsarist government was an autocracy; both theoretically and legally, the tsar exercised unlimited power, and by his own will he could issue orders, over-rule judgments, make and unmake the law. The only recognized influence upon him was the interpretation he cared to place upon his obligation to carry out what he thought was God's will. Yet in practice, the autocracy was limited by a number of factors, chief of which was that the tsar could only act through and with the support of the dvorianstvo whose members made up the court, the chief ministers, the officers in the army and the local administrators. Another important limitation on the power of the tsar was that although he had the power to make the laws he had very little to see that they were carried out; indeed Russian history is full of acts and well-meant reforms that remained dead letters because of the incompetence or the obstruction of the officials who were supposed to execute them. The vast distances and poor communications throughout the empire hindered the efficiency of the administration, and centuries of oppression had made the Russian peasant a past master in the art of evasion. Tradition and protocol also imposed some limits on what the tsar could, and could not do, although this applied rather to matters of lesser importance.

Clearly the efficiency of an autocracy depends upon the character of the autocrat: the Romanov dynasty produced some remarkable men and women, but few of them would deserve the title of statesman. In spite of their shortcomings they were, nevertheless, regarded with a superstitious veneration by the mass of the peasantry because they were regarded as God's anointed and the fathers of the people.

All the Government officials acted as the tsar's agents and were responsible to him. The Council of State, set up in 1801, discussed proposed laws but the tsar was free to accept or reject its findings and often acted without consulting it at all: the Senate, established by Peter I, was little more than a court of appeal: the Committee of Ministers set up in 1802 was not a corporate body like the English cabinet, for there was no chief minister, and each one was directly responsible to the tsar alone: the Procurator of the Holy Synod was a minister for Church affairs and the tsar was head of the Church: the Third Section was an independent organization charged with exercising police surveillance not only over the people but also over all the Government institutions.

The Administration of the Empire

The empire was divided into six regions for administrative purposes: Russia proper, Finland, the Baltic states, the Caucasus and Siberia.

Russia proper was divided into forty-six guberniyas (provinces), of roughly 300–400,000 inhabitants, with a gubernator (governor) appointed by the tsar. The Governor was assisted by the Assembly of the Nobility of the Province which elected certain provincial officials. Each province was divided into districts of approximately 30,000 inhabitants. Within the districts, the land was divided among the estates of the nobility, and on the estates the people were organized in the village communities of the mir. The landowner acted as the agent of the tsar and governed the villages of the estate in his name. He was responsible for maintaining order, collecting taxes and providing recruits for the army. All adult villagers took part in the village assembly and elected its starostas, or elders. The mir assumed corporate responsibility for the village: it allotted and redistributed the land and paid the taxes.

The Russian People

Figures for the population are very unreliable and little better than guesses, but it is probable that the population of Russia in 1725 was about thirteen million. At the end of the eighteenth century it may have been thirty-six million, including the people in the territories acquired by conquest, and about twenty-nine million in Russia proper. These acquisitions continued in the nineteenth century, so that the population became very diversified in race, language, religion and in general cultural standards. Russians were always in the majority and formed the largest national population in nineteenth-century Europe—a fact that tended to increase the growing Russophobia of their European neighbours.

Population

1796	36 million
1815	45 million
1835	60 million
1851	67 million
1858	74 million
1897	129 million (74 per cent in European Russia)

Of this population in the middle of the nineteenth century 95 per cent were rural dwellers and 88 per cent were serfs. About 3 per cent were free peasants; 2 per cent were merchants; 2 per cent were nobles, and 1 per cent were churchmen of various kinds. The urban population was only about eight-and-a-half million in 1861, but it had increased to sixteen-and-a-half million by the end of the century.

Although the great majority of the Russian people were peasants they owned only about 1 per cent of the land before 1861; about two-thirds of it belonged to the State, including the Church and the imperial family, and the rest to the nobility. Not all the landowners were wealthy: some were, for they owned hundreds of square miles of land and thousands of serfs, and they could live on an extravagant scale. About 100,000 nobles owned 30 per cent of the land, but three-quarters of them owned less than a hundred serfs; many of them lived beyond their means and were hopelessly in debt, with their estates and the serfs upon them mortgaged beyond redemption.

There were different degrees of serfdom, but broadly speaking, the common people (narod) consisted of State serfs, who paid obrok and poll tax, and the serfs in private ownership, two-thirds of whom paid barshchina, and the rest obrok. After emancipation, according to the Marxists, there tended to be two classes: the richer and more successful peasants (kulaks) and the impoverished and landless rural proletariat.

In 1859 there were about 10·7 million male serfs on the private estates and about 12·8 million on the lands belonging to the Crown and the State; these with their families constituted about forty million 'souls', as they were officially known. Generally speaking the lot of the Crown peasant was better than that of the serf on the private estates, for he was, at least to some extent, subject to the law of the land instead of the arbitrary will of the private owner, but for the Russian people as a whole, life was a grim blend of poverty and ignorance, plague and famine, brutality and servility, oppression and extortion. They lived on what they could produce and by bartering the surplus whenever there was one; they were at all times subject to the arbitrary whims of landowners and the corruption of Government officials; and drunkenness, rebellion or flight were the only means of escape or protest.

In effect the landowner had complete power over his serfs, for the laws were usually ignored or evaded. The estate and the serfs upon it, belonged to the landowner: they were invested in or bought and sold in the same way as the rest of the property. The peasants could not leave the estate without permission and a passport; they could be transferred to another estate or a factory at will; they could be sent to Siberia or drafted into the army at the wish of the owner; they could not marry without his consent, and they might indeed, be forced to marry against their own wishes someone chosen by him. Female serfs were especially subject to their master's wishes and the owner could and did inflict corporal punishment—indeed the beating in the stables was a normal feature of everyday life. If opposition to the owner's severity provoked open rebellion, as it frequently did, then he could call in the police or the military to crush it and inflict wholesale punishment upon the community. There were 148 peasant risings between 1826 and 1834; 216 between 1835 and 1844; and 348 between 1845 and 1854.

There was no redress for the serf: he could not sue his master in the courts even if he did know what the law allowed him; for example, the law of 1797 limited the barshchina to three days a week, but this was often extended to four or five and there was little the serf could do about it. Usually the serf worked the owner's land for part of the week and his own strips, for which he paid barshchina or obrok, for the rest, but this varied from place to place. In the less fertile north, the owners preferred to receive obrok, for labour was less in demand, while in the fertile areas of the south, where labour was needed, barshchina was insisted on.

With the growth of the population and the development of the great noble households in the eighteenth century an increasing number of domestic serfs were taken into service, usually from the children of the field serfs. These held no land, and were little more than domestic slaves, but they did occasionally get opportunities for education and advancement as musicians, teachers, scientists, and so on. There were probably about one-and-a-half million domestic serfs in the nineteenth century.

Intellectual Movements

In spite of the repressive governments there was lively intellectual activity in nineteenth-century Russia, even though many of the intellectuals were obliged to spend much of their time in exile. Siberia was the university of the political agitators and every city in western

Europe had its colony of Russian exiles all furiously debating their own particular points of view and, in spite of the censorship and the police, keeping contact with events in Russia without any great apparent difficulty.

Slavophils and Westernizers

The contact with western European ideas during and after the wars with Napoleon stimulated much questioning of the existing social and political conditions in Russia among the educated classes. Two distinct schools of thought emerged in the early nineteenth century: the Slavophils and the westernizers. They had much in common. Both groups drew their inspiration from European philosophers such as Hume, Voltaire, Kant, Schelling, Hegel, and from socialist thinkers such as Saint Simon, Proudhon, and later Marx. Both were influenced by the romantic writers such as Goethe, Schiller and Chateaubriand and tended to idealize the Russian peasant; both shared a love of Russia with criticism of the incompetence, corruption and repression of the governments; both were against serfdom, against the division of exploiters and exploited, and both appealed to what they thought was the true spirit of Russian history.

The Slavophils held that this spirit found its expression in the Orthodox Church and the traditional Russian social and political institutions. They believed that Russian civilization was inherently superior to that of western Europe, for it was based upon true Christianity and the communal organization of the mir. They maintained that the reforms of Peter the Great had introduced an alien element into the natural development of Russian society, and they wanted a spiritual reform of Russian society that would enable it to carry out the missionary work of spreading Russian civilization. They were opposed to individualism, and although they claimed to be non-political, they were, in fact, ultra-conservative. When it came to putting their ideas into practice they supported the autocracy against revolutionary movements and fostered Great Russian nationalism. They were not a united group and there were changes in their ideas as time went on, but the most prominent Slavophils were the following: N. Karamzin, 1766–1826, who was opposed to the introduction of any kind of constitution; I. Kireyevsky, 1806–1856, who was convinced that the orthodox faith was the basis of Russian society and that its historical evolution would only be perverted by the introduction of non-Russian ideas and customs; A. S. Khomyakov, 1804–1860, who extended the claims of the Slavophils to include all the Slav peoples; K. S. Aksakov, 1817–1886, who was opposed to the bad influence of western ideas on the purity of the Slavophil ideal and gave support to the repression at home and the Pan Slav movement abroad.

The westernizers on the other hand, believed in the unity of European civilization; they saw that Russia was backward before Peter the Great, and favoured the introduction of western European methods of social, economic and political organization. They were radical in politics and often atheistic in religion, and had no place in their schemes for a State Church. They believed in the rights of the individual, and held that the State existed for his material welfare, and that it was not the mystical and moral structure that the Slavophils made it.

The more prominent westernizers were: P. Chaadayev (1793–1856), who questioned the greatness of Russia's past, attacked orthodoxy and demonstrated Russia's isolation from the rest of Europe; V. Belinsky (1811–1848), the literary critic who upheld the superiority of reason and knowledge over the autocracy of the Church and the State; A. Herzen (1812–1870), who spent most of his life in exile and was one of the most noted of the liberal, and later socialist, publicists; and M. Bakunin (1814–1876), who carried the practical application of the westernizers' ideals to the extremes of anarchism.

The governments had no sympathy with either school and punished with exile those who managed to evade the censorship. The revolutionary ideas of the westernizers were clearly opposed to the autocracy, but the specifically Russian nature of the Slavophils was embarrassing to a government that had increasing numbers of non-Russian peoples under its control. Unfortunately, the educated classes were outside and against the Government, when under a different system, they might have been working with it for the reforms and improvements that were so necessary. The differences between the Slavophils and the westernizers illustrate the tensions within Russian society and the ambivalent attitude that history and geography have combined to produce throughout Russian history.

The Narodniks

The Russian 'intelligentsia' were not, as in the rest of Europe, essentially bourgeois: they came chiefly from the professional classes and the nobility. They were townsmen and products of the universities and had little in common with the peasantry. They were divided into groups and 'circles' where socialist and revolutionary political ideas were discussed in the abstract. In the 1860s certain members of the radical intelligentsia took up the ideas of Herzen and Chernyshevsky that socialism must be taken to the people in the belief that it could be established through the traditional communal organization of the mir without passing through the capitalist stage of economic development. To do this, and to gain practical experience, thousands of university students went out into the countryside in the 1870s to live with the peasants and to preach socialism. The 'to the people movement' (V. Narod) was a hopeless failure, for the peasants were unable to understand the message preached by these strange enthusiasts from the cities, but many of the disillusioned narodniks later joined the revolutionary socialist movements.

The Arts

Literature and music, in particular, flourised among the arts in Russia in the nineteenth century. The first Philharmonic Society was not formed until 1802, yet a succession of great composers gave universal appeal to the Russian spirit: Glinka (1804–1857); Balakirev (1836–1910); Tchaikovsky (1840–1893); Mussorgsky (1839–1881); Rimsky-Korsakov (1844–1908); Glazunov (1865–1936); Borodin (1833–1887); Rachmaninov (1873–1943). In literature, the contribution was equally great and universal: Pushkin (1799–1837); Lermontov (1814–1841); Gogol (1809–1852); Turgenev (1818–1883); Dostoyevsky (1821–1881); Tolstoy (1828–1910); Goncharov (1812–1891); Belinsky (1811–1848); Chekhov (1860–1904); Gorky (1868–1936). At the end of the century the Russian ballet achieved world renown under the direction of Diaghilev and Fokine, and Russian scientists, although sadly limited by the lack of official encouragement, were making their contribution to the advancement of knowledge with the work of men like Mendeleyev and Pavlov.

Economic Developments

By comparison with western Europe, the Russian economy remained backward and undeveloped until the rapid growth fostered by Bunge and Witte in the reign of Nicholas II. The population was largely rural; there was little capital available for investment; and the incompetence and corruption of the administration made it difficult to obtain credit. Even agriculture, the major economic activity, was unproductive, until the second half of the century, based as it was upon serfdom and hampered by the social system from introducing new methods.

Since private enterprise could not develop to any great extent, the stimulus to economic progress had to come from the State, which for military and political reasons found it desirable. Yet demand remained low because of the poverty of the people, and although there was some large-scale factory development in the first part of the century much of the total production still came from domestic workers. New industries tended to concentrate in a few centres such as Moscow, St Petersburg and Warsaw, and there were less than half a million industrial workers in 1850, many of them seasonal.

Communications were the key to Russian economic development, but they remained inadequate because of the vast distances and the lack of capital. Over 5,000 miles of road were built in the reign of Nicholas I, but plans to build railways were obstructed on the grounds that they were a danger to morals and that 'by encouraging frequent purposeless travels' they would 'foster the restless spirit of our age'. The first railway was built from St Petersburg to Tsarskoe Selo in 1837; the Moscow–Warsaw line was begun in 1839; and the Moscow–St Petersburg line in 1842, but at the death of Nicholas I there were only 650 miles of track in the whole of Russia. By 1904 there were 39,000 miles, but in relation to the area and the population this was hopelessly inadequate, more particularly so in the absence of useable roads.

Tariffs were high in the hope of encouraging domestic industry, but exports trebled and imports increased fourfold in the first part of the century. Most of this foreign trade was in the hands of alien merchants; in 1847 exports were worth 134 million roubles, but only 2 per cent of this trade was in Russian hands.

Industrialization increased rapidly in the 1890s, thanks to the work of Witte and large-scale foreign investment. There were spectacular increases in textiles, mining, metallurgical, coal and oil production, and joint stock companies and banking services grew in proportion. After Witte had based the finances on the gold standard in 1897, foreign loans poured in, so that foreign investment represented half the total capital, and sometimes as much as 90 per cent in particular industries such as mining and railways. In 1914 one-fifth of the total expenditure represented interest payments. Thus by 1917 Russia was a capitalist state and the factory system was well developed, often in very large scale enterprises. Nevertheless, compared with the United States and western Europe, Russian production, although increasing rapidly, was well behind, and industrialization was far from complete.

QUESTIONS

1. Distinguish between the aims and ideals of the Slavophils and the westernizers, and assess their significance in nineteenth-century Russian history.
2. Discuss the origins and importance of the Narodnik movement.
3. Give an account of the main developments in either: (a) Russian literature; or (b) music in the nineteenth century.

4. Outline the main features of Russian economic development before 1917.
5. Discuss the nature of the Russian autocracy in the nineteenth century. What prospects were there for peaceful reform?

Further Reading

BILLINGTON, J. H. *Mikhailovsky and Russian Populism.* Oxford U.P., 1958.
HARE, R. *Russian Literature from Pushkin to the Present Day.* Methuen, 1947.
LEONARD, R. A. *A History of Russian Music.* Jarrolds, 1957.
MIRSKY, D. S. *History of Russian Literature.* Routledge, 1949.
SLONIM, M. *An Outline of Russian Literature.* Oxford U.P., 1958. Home University Library.
VENTURI, F. *Roots of Revolution: A History of the Populist and Socialist Movements in Nineteenth-century Russia.* Weidenfeld, 1960.
See also books recommended for chapter XVI.

CHAPTER X

ALEXANDER I—'THE BLESSED' 1801–1825

For Russia, as for the rest of Europe, the developments of the first part of the nineteenth century were dominated by the French Revolution and the ambitions of Napoleon. Alexander played a leading part in the defeat of Napoleon, and Russia emerged as the greatest land power in Europe until the rise of Germany later in the century.

Personal Character and Education

Alexander had been taken away from his parents by his grandmother, Catherine II, who had attempted to have him brought up according to her own ideas. She drew up instructions for his education whereby he was to be trained 'in accordance with the laws of reason and the principles of virtue', and engaged as tutor for him a Swiss, Laharpe, a man with liberal and republican ideas who visualized a more democratic form of government and the end of serfdom.

In 1801, Alexander was a young man with liberal inclinations but, at the same time, with a realistic sense of the need to retain his despotic power; he was handsome, gifted, charming, sentimental, weak and lazy. The difficulty of keeping on terms with Catherine and with Paul at the same time had made him a master of dissimulation, of being all things to all men and of evading issues by using his charm, actor that he was, and hiding his true feelings. This gave him a reputation for elusiveness and complexity of character; Napoleon called him the 'Talma of the North'; Pushkin likened him to the sphinx; but Metternich said that he was incapable of pursuing a single line of thought. He was always troubled by the responsibility he shared for his father's death, and during the war of 1812 he underwent a religious conversion, aided by sessions with a female mystic of doubtful piety, which convinced him that he was the saviour of Europe and of the need to apply Christian principles to international diplomacy abroad, and to education at home.

Domestic Policy

In spite of all the talk of liberal reforms in his early years, Alexander in fact, achieved very little, chiefly because military and diplomatic affairs in the struggle against Napoleon and in the peacemaking afterwards left him with no time for domestic affairs, but also because his enthusiasm for reform waned, and there was a reversion to some of the worst aspects of Paul's reign after 1815. He began by promising to rule according to Catherine's model, and for the first two years surrounded himself with a group of young friends with ideas similar to his own.

The Young Friends

The privileges which had been lost by the nobility under Paul were restored; the secret police were closed down; there was an amnesty and exiles were permitted to return; students were permitted to travel abroad again; foreign books could be published in Russia and education in general for the nobility was encouraged by the founding of a Ministry of Instruction in 1802, and the establishment of universities, high schools and lyceums.

The central government was reorganized by the restoration of the Senate and the creation of eight new ministries and a permanent council.

For the peasantry there was the Law of Free Agriculturalists of 1803 which permitted landlords to free their serfs provided they also gave them some land to work. Not surprisingly, not many did so, but that was as far as the reforms of the Young Friends went. By the end of the reign only 47,000 out of seventeen million serfs had been freed in this way. Alexander found his friends too impractical and until 1812 he came to rely more and more upon the advice of Speransky.

Speransky, 1772–1839

Speransky was the son of a village priest and was a professor of mathematics and physics at an ecclesiastical seminary until he attracted the notice of Alexander who took him to Erfurt in 1806. Napoleon described him as 'the only clear head in Russia'. From 1809 to 1812 he was sole minister and all powerful. Alexander asked him to draw up a plan for the reorganization of the empire, to devise a new legal code and to advise generally.

Speransky's constitutional proposals were designed to separate the functions of the Government while preserving a strong central administration. There was to be a sovereign and a State council, with a duma to act as the legislature, a senate to act as the judiciary, and ministries to act as the executive. There were to be definite functions for each department, and the State council was to consist of delegates from the duma, which in turn would receive delegates from district councils, who would represent the townships consisting of representatives of the landowners. Alexander was enthusiastic but got no further than creating the State council with Speransky as Secretary. The new law code based upon the Code Napoléon was also drawn up by Speransky, submitted to the Council, and similarly pigeon holed.

Speransky next considered the need for financial reform, but the opposition to him was growing; he was regarded as too French and Alexander sacrificed him to preserve his own popularity. He was dismissed in 1812 and later, as Governor-General for Siberia, he devised a new scheme of government there.

The war of 1812 was a turning point. The dismissal of Speransky marked the end of attempts at liberal reforms, and Alexander, preoccupied with the task of remaking Europe, relied to a great extent in domestic matters upon Count Arakcheyev as Chief Minister, Prince Golitsyn as Minister of Ecclesiastical Affairs and Public Instruction, the Baroness Krüdener (his mystical mistress), and the Archimandrite Photius. Arakcheyev gained a notorious reputation for arbitrary rule, and the secret police and the censorship were restored, but the most unpopular feature of this period was the introduction of military colonies. Certain areas near the frontier were set aside, and here the peasants were obliged to cultivate the land, free of tax, but also to train as soldiers. Theoretically these colonies would have provided for the maintenance of a large regular army, cheaply and efficiently, but it did not work out that way.

Thus Alexander's domestic policy achieved very little: there had been some land reform and some useful changes in the administration but the high hopes of the early years came to nothing in the repression of the later part of the reign. There was, however, some economic progress that owed little to Government action: exports rose in value, factories increased in size and number, and serfdom was ended in the non-Russian Baltic lands. Nothing much could be done for the chronic financial problem of expenditure exceeding income except the traditional issue of more paper currency, which only tended to lower the value of the rouble.

Foreign Policy: the First War against Napoleon

Foreign affairs became Alexander's main interest and Russia became one of the arbiters of European affairs during his reign. In 1801 he hoped to remain neutral in the general conflict with France: he stopped the preparations for war against England begun by Paul and resumed friendly relations with Austria. But the extension of French power by Napoleon became so alarming that Russia was drawn into the third coalition against him and in 1805 a Russian army under Kutuzov went to aid the Austrians but was defeated at Austerlitz, and obliged to retreat. In 1806 Russia made an alliance with Prussia, but Napoleon defeated the Prussians at Jena, although the Russians checked the French at Eylau. Napoleon gained another victory at Friedland in 1807, Prussia was occupied by the French and the Russians had to retreat again.

The Treaty of Tilsit

In 1807 Napoleon and Alexander met at Tilsit to make peace and an alliance. Alexander was in financial difficulties and he had other wars on his hands against Turkey and Persia. By the agreement at Tilsit Napoleon was given a free hand in western Europe while Alexander was to be free to deal with eastern Europe, especially with Sweden and Turkey. Russia also agreed to assist Napoleon against Britain by enforcing the Continental System[1] in northern Europe. This agreement was forced upon Alexander by the circumstances and was ratified at Erfurt the next year, but Alexander realized that Europe was not big enough for both Napoleon and himself.

The Swedish War, 1808–1809

Alexander was now free to continue his other wars, but he turned first against Sweden who would not join the alliance against Britain. In 1808 Russian troops invaded Finland, drove the Swedes out, and crossed the ice to invade the Aland Islands and the Swedish mainland. Finland was incorporated with Russia before the peace was made at Frederikshamm in 1809. Alexander promised to respect the existing laws, religion and customs of the Finnish territory.

The Turkish War, 1806–1812

Spasmodic warfare had been conducted since 1806 with the Turks who had French support, but after Tilsit Russia had a free hand, and Kutuzov crossed the Danube and defeated them at Slobozia in 1811. Peace was made in 1812 by the Treaty of Bucharest when Russia gained Bessarabia.

The Persian War, 1805–1813

Catherine II had established a Russian protectorate over Georgia and Alexander annexed it in 1801. Persia's efforts to regain control over

[1] Napoleon's scheme to close the ports of Europe to British trade.

Georgia brought the war with Russia in 1805 which ended successfully for Russia in 1813 with the acquisition of Baku.

The Second War against Napoleon: the 1812 Campaign

The alliance with France in 1807 was not popular in Russia. The change in policy towards Austria, the presence of a French mission in St Petersburg, the economic loss to Russia which the enforcement of the Continental System entailed, the 'French' reforms of Speransky, the discourtesies arising out of a proposed marriage between Napoleon and a member of the tsar's family, and the double dealing of Napoleon, all contributed to a worsening of Franco-Russian relations, and both sides began to prepare for the coming war: There was also much opposition on religious grounds to the reorganization of Roman Catholic Poland which Alexander was obliged to accept.

In June 1812, Napoleon crossed the River Niemen and invaded Russia with an army of 600,000 men, marching towards Vilna and Smolensk (the direct route to Moscow). The Russian armies under Barclay de Tolly and Bagration were smaller and spread over a wide front, and Napoleon succeeded in dividing them. The Russians decided to retreat and join up again, which they did at Smolensk. Although this was a sensible plan it was unpopular because it seemed humiliating, so Alexander dismissed Barclay de Tolly, and ordered the troops to stand and fight the French. This they did and were obliged to retreat again. Kutuzov replaced Barclay de Tolly and a very bloody battle was fought at Borodino, when half the armies were lost. The decision was now taken to abandon Moscow which the French occupied. Napoleon was hoping for offers of peace, but they did not come. Moscow was burned and the French were short of supplies, while Russian armies to the south were a constant threat, so Napoleon decided to leave Moscow and winter in Smolensk. The Grand Army was harassed all the way by the Russian armies marching parallel to the line of retreat. Only a demoralized remnant of the once great French army succeeded in crossing the Russian border.

Alexander was determined to crush Napoleon, and the Russian armies followed the French back into Europe. They were joined by Prussia, Austria, Sweden and Britain and in 1813 was fought the battle of Leipzig, the 'Battle of the Nations', which resulted in the freeing of Germany from French control. In 1814 Prussian and Russian armies entered Paris and Napoleon abdicated. Alexander was granted the title, 'The Blessed', by the Senate.

The Congress of Vienna

The victorious allies met at Vienna to reward and to punish and to
re-make the map of Europe. Alexander was determined to bring all
Poland under Russian control, and his insistence almost provoked
another war between the allies. Eventually he got most of the Duchy of
Warsaw that had been created by Napoleon, reconstituted as the Kingdom of Poland, with himself as king.

Meanwhile Napoleon escaped from his exile in Elba and the allies
were obliged once more to go to war against France. But it was
Napoleon's last gamble, and he was defeated at Waterloo in 1815. A
Russian army took part in the occupation of France, and Alexander
on his second visit to Paris, proposed his scheme for a Holy Alliance.

The Holy Alliance

The 1812 war had been a great religious experience for Alexander and
he now proposed to the allied sovereigns that they should in future
conduct international affairs in accordance with 'the supreme truths
dictated by the eternal law of God the Saviour' and that they should be
guided by the commandments of 'love, truth and peace', and rule their
subjects 'as fathers of their families'. Most of the rulers of Europe paid
lip service to the ideal although they all probably shared with Castle-
reagh, the English Foreign Minister's view, that it was a 'piece of
sublime mysticism and nonsense'. Nevertheless Alexander was too
powerful to be openly opposed.

The Quadruple Alliance and the Congresses

Peace was effectively maintained after the defeat of Napoleon by the
Quadruple Alliance of Russia, Prussia, Britain and Austria, and by
periodic meetings of the great powers to discuss matters of common
interest. In these the dominating personality was that of the Austrian
Chancellor, Metternich, who converted the Holy Alliance into a kind
of trade union for kings, and the Congresses into a means of suppressing
liberal and nationalist movements wherever they might occur, but it
was Alexander who earned the reputation for Russia of being the
symbol of reaction in early nineteenth-century Europe.

Alexander's Achievement

Alexander was not so inconsistent as is sometimes supposed, and his
early interest in reform and constitutions was always to be seen in the
light of the need for authority, law and order, which so far as Russia
was concerned, could only proceed from the person of the tsar. He
was instrumental in the defeat of Napoleon and the remaking of Europe,

and was sincere in his aims; it was not entirely his fault that the Holy Alliance and the Congress system got a bad name in the eyes of nineteenth-century liberals. He insisted on generous terms for the defeated France and made the restored Bourbons accept a constitution. Poland and Finland were also granted constitutions, but Russia was not. The Kingdom of Poland, Finland, Bessarabia and Georgia were added to Russia, although not all of them were Russian lands. Alexander's personal prestige in Europe was high and Russia had established the myth of invincibility which haunted so many minds after the disaster of the 1812 campaign. Within Russia too, in spite of the repression of the later years of Alexander's reign there was the beginning of the great age of Russian literature with which Pushkin's name is associated.

The Decembrist Revolt, 1825

The wars against Napoleon had a great effect upon the intellectual and political life of the Russian nobility. Under Catherine II and Paul they had tended to avoid their military duties, but under Alexander they once more performed their traditional services in the army. Many of them spent several years in Germany and France in the armies of occupation and got used to the idea of travel about Europe. They became acquainted with the ideas of the German philosophers, the French socialists and the English parliamentary reformers, and everywhere they found social and political conditions that contrasted with the backwardness and conservatism of Russia. They returned to Russia imbued with the ideas of the Romantic movement in literature and liberalism in politics and began within the army to form groups that discussed the need for reform, for constitutional government, and for freeing the serfs.

In 1816 a group of young guards officers, led by Prince Trubetskoy, formed the Union of Salvation, to discuss literary developments and the need for reform. Their aims were to abolish the autocracy, to free the serfs, to end the military colonies and to achieve political reform through revolution. This became the Union of Welfare in 1818, which in turn split into a northern and a southern group, where the chief character was Paul Pestel, who went further than the rather vague and idealistic reformers in the north and advocated violent revolution and a republic rather than a constitutional monarchy.

Alexander knew of the plots of the reformers but did nothing about them and refused to let Arakcheyev suppress them although they had in fact gone underground.

In 1825 Alexander died at Taganrog[1] and since he had no legitimate

---

[1] Some believe that Alexander's 'death' was arranged, and that he continued to live as a holy man in Siberia until 1864. See Strakhovsky, *Alexander I*.

children, the succession by the law of 1797 should have gone to his eldest brother, Constantine, who was Commander-in-Chief in Warsaw at the time. But Constantine who had made a morganatic marriage had renounced his claim to the throne, and Alexander had secretly transferred the succession to his younger brother, Nicholas. Not knowing this, the court officials proclaimed Constantine as Emperor, and Nicholas took the oath of loyalty to him. Constantine refused to accept the crown and took the oath of loyalty to Nicholas. Thus for a period of three weeks there were two emperors, neither of whom wished to assume the role.

This farcical situation the members of the northern group decided to exploit when Constantine refused to go to St Petersburg, and Nicholas accepted the throne in December 1825. Some troops refused to take the oath of loyalty to Nicholas and were joined by a mob shouting for Constantine and the Constitution, although it seems some of them thought that the Constitution was Constantine's wife. Nicholas attempted to disperse the crowd peaceably, but after one of his spokesmen had been shot, the loyal troops were ordered to fire and the crowd soon dispersed. Another revolt in Kiev organized by the southern union was also suppressed.

An investigation and trial were held and forty of the leaders were sentenced to death although only five were executed, and many more exiled. Thus ended the last of the Palace revolutions, but it was the first of the political revolutions in that, vague and incompetently handled though it was, there was some kind of political programme in the minds of the leaders. It created martyrs for the revolutionary movement against the tsarist system, but the immediate effect was to harden Nicholas's determination to crush all liberal tendencies everywhere.

QUESTIONS

1. Describe the part played by Alexander I of Russia in the defeat of Napoleon.
2. Liberal abroad, reactionary at home. How far is this a fair assessment of Alexander I?
3. Give an account of the Decembrist revolt, 1825, and indicate its significance.
4. Find out what you can and make notes on the following: Laharpe; Speransky; the 1812 campaign; the Congress of Vienna; the Congress system; Paul Pestel; the Treaty of Tilsit; the Continental system; the Holy Alliance; Feodor Kuzmich.

Further Reading

MAZOUR, A. G. *The First Russian Revolution, 1825*. Cambridge for California U.P., 1937.

PALÉOLOGUE, G. M. *The Enigmatic Czar: The Life of Alexander I of Russia*, Eng. trans. Hamish Hamilton, 1938.

RAEFF, M. *Michael Speransky, Statesman of Imperial Russia, 1772–1839*. The Hague, 1957.

SEGUR, P. P. *Napoleon's Russian Campaign*, trans. J. Townsend. M. Joseph, 1959.

STRAKHOVSKY, L. *Alexander I of Russia*. Williams and Norgate, 1949.

TOLSTOY, L. *War and Peace*. Various editions.

YOUNG, I. 'Alexander I', in *History Today*. May, 1961.

CHAPTER XI

NICHOLAS I

'The Gendarme of Europe', 1825–1855

Nicholas was very different from Alexander: he had not expected to be emperor and was not trained for it. He was married to Alexandra, daughter of Frederick William III of Prussia and preferred drilling soldiers to the work of preparation for statecraft. His mental capacities were rather limited, but he was honest and hard working, with a keen sense of duty and a great respect for discipline. He was good looking, vain and tactless, determined to rule and to make Russia 'the cornerstone of despotism in the world'. During his reign all the apparatus of the police state and of thought control were strengthened, but in spite of this, the revolutionary undercurrents within Russian society continued to grow as did the Russophobia of the western European countries, particularly Britain and France.

It was unfortunate that the reign began with the Decembrist revolt. The consequences were that Nicholas's distrust of the nobility was strengthened and he relied upon professional bureaucrats who were dependent upon his favour for the administration, while the nobility withdrew from public life and thus created a gap between the Government and the upper ranks of society which fostered a resolute opposition to the reforms which Nicholas realized were necessary and which he attempted to introduce in a controlled way while retaining the absolute power of the autocracy.

Domestic Policy

Nicholas personally supervised the investigation and punishment of the Decembrist conspirators and this dealt a crushing blow at the nobility, but he then turned to the need for reform that the revolt had indicated.

Arakcheyev and Photius were dismissed and Speransky was recalled, but Nicholas was influenced most by the historian, N. M. Karamzin.

A special committee was set up to consider reform of the administration, both central and provincial, to devise ways of improving the condition of the State peasants, and to regulate the differences between the social classes. Most of the recommendations of the committee came to nothing, however, because the outbreak of revolutions throughout Europe in 1830 alarmed the reformers.

Most of the business of the State was conducted by 'His Majesty's own Chancery'. This was a private cabinet of the sovereign, the scope of which Nicholas extended, to give himself direct personal control over almost every aspect of the Government. Two of the chief ministers or directors responsible to him were Speransky and Benckendorff. Speransky was given the task of codifying the law, of putting into order some 40,000 acts. This was done by 1833 and was a major achievement. Benckendorff was responsible for the Third Department—the secret political police, an independent organization within the State with wide powers of censorship and espionage.

This was linked with the work for education for which Count Uvarov was minister from 1833–1849. Nicholas wanted this to be encouraged but controlled in order to produce enough trained officials for the State. There was to be only primary education for peasant children while secondary education was reserved for officials and nobles. Revolutionary ideas were to be prevented at all costs from attacking the ideal of a society where the citizens did as they were told and accepted the station in life to which it had pleased God to call them. After the outbreak of revolutions in Europe in 1848 this repression of all intellectual life went to extremes: the teaching of philosophy was abolished, the number of students at the universities was strictly limited, travel abroad was prohibited, the censorship was still further strengthened and military discipline and uniforms were introduced to the universities and secondary schools.

Attempts were made to deal with the chronic problem of financial chaos and here Nicholas relied upon his Finance Minister, E. F. Kankrin. The wars with France had been ruinous financially, but all the Government could do to balance chronic budget deficits was to issue more paper currency, which only had the effect of making inflation worse, and of creating two kinds of currency in circulation: paper and silver, with no stable exchange rate between them. Kankrin attempted to redeem the paper money by building up a gold and silver reserve and by establishing deposit banks and issuing Government stock. Agricultural and industrial output were encouraged by tariffs and for a time he was successful, in stabilizing the currency, but his work was undone by the cost of the wars in which Nicholas became involved.

The problem of serfdom was clearly recognized by the nineteenth century, and Nicholas meant the serfs to be free ultimately, but it must be done gradually, and within the already existing machinery of the State. A secret committee was set up to plan measures under Count Kiselev. Speransky advised that if the Government took the lead the private landlords would follow. A Ministry of State Properties was established in 1837 to organize the Crown peasants into self-governing communities and other measures were taken to provide instruction in better farming methods, extra land for the peasants, the supply of grain in time of shortage, etc. In 1842 a law was issued giving landlords the right to emancipate serfs if they wished to do so, but nothing was done to oblige the landowners to do anything.

The tragedy was that nothing could be done about serfdom within the existing framework of the Russian State. Almost everyone recognized that something must be done and the realization that plans were being considered stimulated peasant discontent still more. The population was growing rapidly, but productivity was not; there was a growing surplus of agricultural labour that could only find employment as domestic servants, and landowners were heavily mortgaged, often beyond hope of redemption. The conditions of labour on the land and in the factories produced constant strikes and riots—there were several hundred agricultural revolts in the reign of Nicholas.

The domestic policy of this reign was summarized in Uvarov's motto of 'Orthodoxy, Autocracy, Nationality', by which was meant that the Russian citizen must accept without question the authority of the tsar and the Church for the good of the country. The attempt to strengthen the central authority resulted in a great increase of the bureaucracy and of the graft and corruption that were a part of it.

Religious Policy

In religious matters the Orthodox Church was regarded as an instrument of State to keep the people in order. Strict orthodoxy was insisted on within the Church: discipline was strengthened, theological colleges were supervised and village priests were made part of the general system of thought control and espionage. A determined drive was made to win back to the orthodox faith the Old Believers and the various sects who were persecuted by imprisonment and banishment to Siberia. The members of the Uniate Church in the former Polish lands had particular pressure put upon them and in 1839 the Uniate Church came to an end when its bishops were persuaded to accept the orthodox faith. Attempts were also made to convert the Protestants, Roman Catholics and Muslims within the Empire, and the Jews in particular were subjected to pressure of various kinds to force them to become Russian in all things.

Yet in spite of the repression and the thought control there was a great growth of philosophic dispute between the Slavophils and the westernizers, and an increasing flow of middle class or 'raznochintzy'[1] to join the ranks of the noble intelligentsia, and it was the golden age of Russian literature. Much of this writing was used as a vehicle for social and political criticism.

Foreign Policy

Nicholas has been called 'The Gendarme of Europe' and this indicates his general attitude towards foreign affairs. Liberalism and Nationalism, the two great revolutionary forces of nineteenth-century Europe, were a threat to his vision of order and authority, and he gave his aid to their suppression wherever they might raise their heads, but it was the Eastern Question that dominated foreign affairs in his reign. The foreign minister was Count Nesselrode but the policy was Nicholas's.

The Persian War

The reign began with a war against Persia (1826–1828) which had never really accepted the incorporation of Georgia into the Russian Empire. The Russian armies under Paskevich entered Persia, took Tabriz, and moved towards Teheran. By the Treaty of Turkmanchay, 1828, Russia gained Erivan and the land on the left bank of the Arax, and put an end to Persian claims to the Caucasus. It was many years, however, before the various tribes were subjected and brought under Russian control.

Revolutions in Europe

The revolution in France in 1830 sparked off other revolutions; in Belgium and Poland in particular. Nicholas detested Louis Philippe who had replaced the reactionary rule of Charles x with a form of constitutional monarchy. When the Belgians revolted against the Dutch in violation of the Treaties of Vienna of 1815 Nicholas was prepared to send troops against both the French and Belgian revolutionaries but the outbreak of revolution in Poland at the same time occupied his attentions.

The Polish Revolt

Polish patriots wished to have their country restored to the frontiers it had known before the partitions of the eighteenth century, and were

[1] lit. people from various ranks.

particularly opposed to the Russian domination that had been imposed upon them by Alexander I. The rising began in Warsaw in 1830 and the Russians were at first driven out by the Poles who demanded the independence of Poland and the cession of Lithuania. When Nicholas refused, he was deposed as King of Poland. The next year Russian armies returned and the rising was crushed. The Polish constitution was abolished, the leaders of the rising fled into exile, and a deliberate policy of Russification was introduced into Poland. A similar policy was applied to Lithuania and west Russia which had been infected by the Polish rising. Russian became the official language, religious persecution of non-orthodox Christians began, property was confiscated from Polish landowners and given to Russians and the Russian educational policy was introduced. Poland as an independent state was crushed.

In 1833 Nicholas proposed an alliance between Russia, Prussia and Austria, by which all three were pledged to take common action against revolutionaries. They were successful until 1848 and even obliged Switzerland to refuse political asylum to refugees.

Revolts broke out again throughout Europe in 1848, but Nicholas was successful in preventing them from spreading to Russia and Poland while energetically helping to crush them elsewhere, especially in Hungary. With the flight of Metternich from Vienna in 1848 Nicholas was left as the sole champion of autocracy in Europe; he was not to know of the significance of the publication of the *Communist Manifesto* which also occurred in that year. When Austria appealed for help to crush the Hungarian revolt Nicholas sent an army which defeated the rebels at Vilagos and forced them to surrender in 1849. Nicholas also persuaded Frederick William of Prussia to refuse the throne of Germany offered to him by the German revolutionaries.

The Eastern Question

From the time of Alexander I to the outbreak of the First World War the problems arising out of the Eastern Question were a major factor in European diplomacy. It produced a series of international crises and wars, in all of which Russia was vitally concerned. The basic fact was that the Turkish Empire which consisted not only of modern Turkey, but also of all the Balkans south of the River Danube, the countries bordering the eastern Mediterranean, Egypt and much of North Africa, was in decline and the ambitions of the other powers in Europe were in conflict about the disposal of the 'sick man's' goods. Russia hoped to gain Turkish territory in the Caucasus, the western Black Sea area, and to extend her influence in the Balkans where there were many people of Slav origin—and of course there was always the glittering prize of Constantinople itself. But such an extension of Russian territory and influence would have upset the balance of power in Europe and have brought Russia into the Mediterranean. This prospect was strongly opposed by the foreign ministers of Austria, France and above all of Britain, and they were bound to oppose Russia by supporting the Turks, difficult though it was on occasion to do such a thing, for the Turkish Government was notoriously corrupt, inefficient and repressive, and was furthermore non-Christian.

Austria too was pursuing her ambitions in the Balkans, particularly after the unification of Germany under Bismarck, who drove Austria out of Germany, and urged her to pursue her 'drang nach Osten' in order to embroil her with Russia.

France had always regarded the Levant as her special sphere of interest and was generally hostile to Russia while Britain was concerned for her lines of communication through the Mediterranean to India and the Far East and was jealous of French ambitions. Out of these conflicting aims and interests the general series of incidents known as the Eastern Question arose. Essentially it was a diplomatic matter but the excuse was often a religious one, for periodically the Turks massacred a few thousand Christians somewhere in their empire and Russia claimed the right to protect all Greek Orthodox Christians while France claimed the right to protect the Roman Catholics. Such rights if granted by the Turks left the way open for other forms of intervention, thus it was said for example of the Crimean War that it was a war fought to give a few wretched monks the key of a grotto.

THE EASTERN QUESTION IN THE FIRST PART OF THE NINETEENTH CENTURY

Greek Independence and the Turkish War

The Greeks had revolted against the Turks in 1822, and Alexander had been torn between his desire to crush rebellion on the one hand, and on the other to exploit the situation at the expense of Turkey and for the benefit of Russia. The other countries of Europe were reluctant to aid revolutionaries, and were opposed to Russia acting on her own. On the other hand there was a widespread opposition to Turkish repression in the Balkans and a romantic sympathy for the Greeks in their struggle. The Sultan called in the aid of his vassal in Egypt, Mehemet Ali, who invaded Greece and defeated the rebels. Nicholas joined with Britain and France in 1827 in a protest to the Sultan against Turkish atrocities, and a joint fleet was sent to watch the Turkish-Egyptian fleet, which was later destroyed at the Battle of Navarino in 1827.

The Turks held Russia responsible for this disaster although it would be more correct to blame the British admiral, and demanded reparations from Russia. These Nicholas refused, and war broke out in 1828.

The Turkish War, 1828–1829

Russian armies crossed the Danube and seized Varna. From this base they moved through the Balkans, captured Adrianople and threatened Constantinople. Meanwhile to the east of the Black Sea another Russian army took Kars and Erzerum.

The Turks sued for peace which was made at Adrianople in 1829. Russia gained the eastern Black Sea coast from the mouth of the Kuban to Batum, the delta of the Danube, an indemnity, and commercial concessions in Turkey. Thus Russia had gained an important foothold in the Turkish Empire and the other powers of Europe were duly alarmed.

The First Mehemet Ali Affair, 1833

Mehemet Ali claimed that he had not been adequately rewarded for the help he had given the Sultan against the Greeks and decided to reward himself by invading Syria. The Sultan, Mahmud, in desperation accepted the Russian offer of help. The appearance of a Russian army at the Bosporus in 1833 alarmed Britain and France who acted jointly to forestall Russia by sending an expedition against Mehemet Ali, while a Franco-British fleet was sent to the Dardanelles. Russia concluded a treaty of alliance with Turkey at Unkiar Skelessi in 1833 which included a secret clause that seemed to indicate that Turkey would close the straits to all except Russian warships. It may be that Nicholas was only trying to establish a strong position in the event of a possible future collapse of the Turkish Empire but to Britain and France it looked as if Russia was out to get exclusive control of the straits, and they were determined to undo the terms of Unkiar Skelessi at the first opportunity. This came with the second Mehemet Ali affair.

The Second Mehemet Ali Affair, 1839–1841

This time Britain and France were the real opponents when Mehemet Ali again made a bid for more territory at the expense of the new Sultan who was only a boy. A Franco-British fleet was sent to the straits to warn Nicholas not to attempt to seize them as a protective measure against the Egyptians, but Nicholas joined Britain and France in collective action and the struggle became one between Britain, who supported the Sultan, and France who supported Mehemet Ali.

A general conference was held in London in 1840 to discuss the matter and by the Straits Convention of 1841, signed by Russia, Britain, France, Austria and Prussia, a joint protectorate over Turkey was set up and the straits were closed to the warships of all nationalities when Turkey was at peace.

In 1844 Nicholas paid a State visit to Britain during the course of which he tried unsuccessfully to come to some arrangement about the future of Turkey. Another crisis occurred in 1849 when Austria and Russia demanded that the Sultan should give up Kossuth and other Hungarian exiles and Britain and France once more sent fleets to Turkey as a warning to Russia.

The climax of the Eastern Question in the first half of the nineteenth century and of the reign of Nicholas came with the Crimean War.

The Crimean War

The Crimean war has been called one of the most unnecessary wars in history, and it was certainly one of the most incompetently conducted wars by all the countries concerned. The tensions created by the Eastern Question and the general fear and suspicion of Russian intentions in the nineteenth century brought in Britain and France against Russia in support of Turkey, while Piedmont joined in to gain French support and Austria and Prussia stood watchfully by.

On two occasions, in 1844 and 1853, Nicholas suggested to Britain a division of the Turkish Empire, which he referred to as 'the sick man' of Europe. Palmerston, the foreign minister, was alarmed at Russian ambitions and the extension of Russian influence towards the Mediterranean and India. Russian gains at the expense of Turkey would seem to threaten British interests and communications with the empire. There was general hostility in England to the reactionary nature of the tsarist régime and British trading interests were affected by the increase of Russian trade in the Turkish market.

In France, Napoleon III had a personal grudge against Nicholas, who treated him as a usurper, and he needed a successful war to bolster up his dreams of military glory. It would be better still if it could be a war that would gain the support of the Roman Catholic Church, and France had a traditional interest in the Levant.

Austria was apprehensive about Russian ambitions in the Balkans and in the Danube valley and the Emperor Francis Joseph had already had Russian troops in his territories at the time of the Hungarian rising in 1848.

Yet in spite of the general anti-Russian feeling throughout Europe in the nineteenth century Nicholas fancied that he could depend upon

Britain not to intervene in a dispute with Turkey and he also felt that since Francis Joseph owed his throne to Russian help in 1848 Austria too would not oppose his activities in the Turkish Empire.

The immediate cause of the war was a squabble between Greek Orthodox and Roman Catholic monks over the guardianship of the Holy Places at Bethlehem, particularly the possession of the key to the main door of the Church of the Nativity. The right to protect Christians in the Holy Land had been traditionally claimed by France, but the right lapsed during the Napoleonic wars and Russia assumed it. Napoleon III revived the French claim and the Sultan conceded it, with the result that Russia protested.

Nicholas not only claimed this right, but now extended it to cover all orthodox Christians, throughout the Turkish Empire, although in fact, Russia only had the right to protect Christians in Galata, a part of Constantinople. The other powers feared that if the Sultan agreed to the Russian demand Russia would use it to extend her political and military influence in the Turkish Empire, and Britain in particular urged the Sultan to stand firm against Russia. The British Ambassador in Constantinople also had a personal grudge against Nicholas and needed no encouragement in this.

The War

In 1853, Nicholas invoked the terms of the Treaty of Kutchuk Kainardji and invaded the principalities of Wallachia and Moldavia to bully the Sultan into giving way. Turkey, assured of British support, demanded their evacuation; it was refused and war began between Russia and Turkey.

Britain and France sent their fleets to the Dardanelles as a warning to Nicholas to go no further, but Nicholas, fearing that they might join up with the Turkish fleet, ordered the Russian fleet to attack, and at Sinope, the Turkish fleet was destroyed.

This naval defeat for Turkey was regarded as a massacre in France and Britain even though Russia and Turkey were at war. War feeling was high and Britain and France demanded that Russia evacuate Wallachia and Moldavia and recall her fleet to Sevastopol. Russia refused and Britain and France declared war in March 1854.

Thus began the war that Thiers said was fought to a give a few wretched monks the key of a grotto, but which was to prove a watershed in Russian history.

Nicholas was dismayed to find that neither Prussia nor Austria supported him, and indeed, Austria demanded the withdrawal of Russian troops from the Danube provinces. When they left in July 1854,

Austrian troops marched in and remained in occupation throughout the war.

The war could have ended at that point, but the French and British were determined to use the opportunity to limit Russian power and ambitions and it was decided to destroy the Russian naval base in the Crimea. Anglo-French naval attacks were made on the Russian Baltic and White Sea coasts and on Kamchatka in the Pacific, but the main attack was against Sevastopol, which withstood a siege lasting 349 days. The allied incompetence was only equalled by the Russian, and except for the courage of the private Russian soldier and the genius of Todleben the engineer who fortified Sevastopol, the Russian story of the Crimean war is one of unrelieved disaster. There was incompetent leadership, bad organization, great loss of life and waste of material, widespread corruption in the supply services, complete loss of military prestige and financial ruin for the State. In particular, the lack of adequate roads and railways and the need to keep troops on the Austrian and Prussian frontiers limited the Russian defence, but it was the general technical, economic and administrative backwardness and the faulty leadership that was the cause of the Russian defeat. It was certainly not the military superiority of the allies.

Nicholas died, or as some thought, committed suicide, in the winter of 1855, and it fell to his successor, Alexander II, to save what he could by making peace on the best possible terms and to deal with the internal crisis in Russia brought about by the war.

Alexander began peace negotiations immediately, but could not accept the terms offered, and still refused to agree after the fall of Sevastopol in September 1855. In December, Austria threatened to join in, and in January 1856, Alexander agreed to a peace conference which was held at Paris.

The Treaty of Paris, 1856

The Russian demand for a general protectorate was dismissed and the Black Sea was neutralized; neither Turkey nor Russia was to have warships there, and the Russian and Turkish naval bases were to be demilitarized, and the fortifications destroyed. The straits were closed to foreign warships, and Kars which had been taken from Turkey by Russia at the end of the war was handed back. Wallachia and Moldavia were declared independent, under Turkish suzerainty and they later formed the kingdom of Rumania. The Danube was internationalized and the Sultan promised to treat his Christian subjects better in future.

QUESTIONS

1. To what extent did Nicholas I deserve the title, 'the Gendarme of Europe'?
2. What was the Eastern Question? Describe Russia's interest in it.
3. Discuss the causes of the Crimean War and its consequences for Russia.
4. Find out what you can and make notes on the following: the Third Department; Uvarov; the Polish Revolt 1830; the Hungarian Revolt 1848; the Holy Places; Todleben.

Further Reading

AKSAKOV, S. *A Russian Gentleman*, trans. J. D. Duff. Arnold, 1917.

CUSTINE, MARQUIS DE. *Journey for Our Time*, Russia in 1839. ed. and trans. P. P. Kohler. Barker, 1953.

GOGOL, N. *The Government Inspector*, trans. D. J. Campbell. Heinemann. Drama Library and Everyman.

—— *Dead Souls*, trans. G. Reavey. Oxford U.P. 1957. World's Classics and Everyman.

GONCHAROV, I. *Oblomov*, trans. N. Duddington. Everyman, 1953.

GRUNWALD, C. DE. *Tsar Nicholas I*, trans. B. Patmore. Saunders, 1954.

HERZEN, A. *My Past and Thoughts, the Memoirs of Alexander Herzen*, trans. C. Garnett. 6 vols. Chatto and Windus, 1924–27.

LERMONTOV, M. *A Hero of Our Times*, trans. E. and C. Paul. Oxford. World's Classics.

SUMNER, B. H. *Russia and the Balkans*. Oxford U.P., 1937.

TURGENEV, I. S. *A Sportsman's Sketches*. Dent, 1932.

CHAPTER XII

ALEXANDER II
'The Tsar Liberator', 1855–1881

The stern rule of Nicholas was followed by the well-intentioned reign of Alexander II, who while equally determined to maintain the autocracy, attempted to introduce a series of reforms, the most important of which was the abolition of serfdom. Yet the reign ended in assassination, after many attempts on his life, and the revolutionary movement continued to gather strength.

Nicholas had said: 'By taking upon myself all that was hard and difficult I intended to leave to you a peaceful, well-organized, prosperous country . . . but providence has decreed otherwise'. Instead Alexander inherited the disaster of the Crimean War and the appalling shortcomings in the Government and in the state of Russian society that it revealed. Alexander realized, with respect to serfdom, that 'It is better to begin to abolish bondage from above than to wait for the time when it will begin to abolish itself spontaneously from below'. Unfortunately the verdict on his efforts must probably be 'too little too late'.

Personal character of Alexander II

Alexander was thirty-seven when he succeeded his father, and he had been better trained and educated than most tsars, though with a strong German and military influence. His father sent him on journeys through Russia, Siberia and Europe, and introduced him to the work of government by making him a member of the State Council, appointing him to a commission on serfdom and giving him military appointments during the Crimean War.

Alexander could be stubborn at times, but he was not really a strong enough character for the role he had to play. Usually mild and indolent, he had fits of temper and while he was consistent in his determination to force through the emancipation of the serfs, at other times he tended to hesitate, to accept what had been done in his name, or to take the line of least resistance. There was a romantic streak in him that went ill with his conservative, disciplined upbringing and the realities of government in a revolutionary situation. His early 'liberalism' was unsatisfactory to his critics and left him bitter and disillusioned at the end of his life, while as an autocrat he was ineffective. He was really a conservative who was obliged to introduce reforms by the pressure of events.

His first marriage was a love match against parental wishes, but he later took as his mistress Catherine Dolgoruky, whom he married soon after his first wife's death. This affair lost him any popularity he might have had, and the lessening of his personal authority over his family and at court was reflected in the general decline in the effectiveness of authority throughout the State.

There were many attempts on Alexander's life: shots were fired at him on several occasions; the royal train and the royal palace were blown up; tunnels were dug under the streets to blow up the royal carriage as it passed; and finally a bomb was thrown directly at the tsar—it missed, but a second mutilated him horribly and he died soon after. Yet when it happened, no one seemed to care.

Domestic Policy

It is sometimes said that Alexander's reign began with a period of liberal reform and ended with a period of reaction, but in fact, he was considering further constitutional reforms just before his death, while he had no intention of lessening the power of the autocracy. Apart from the conservatism of his upbringing, it was, paradoxically, only the power of the tsar that could force through liberal reforms against the vested interests of the landowners and the nobility, and it was, of course, essential to take repressive action against the revolutionaries and those who were plotting his death.

The Abolition of Serfdom, 19 February 1861

The need to reform or abolish serfdom had been under discussion since the reign of Catherine II, but all suggestions for action had come to nothing in face of the social and political problems which it raised and the vested interests concerned. The tsar could only act through the great nobles, who were, of course, the beneficiaries of serfdom; and the army, the taxation system and the very structure of the State rested on the basis of serfdom. Consequently, when serfdom was abolished, it was more than a liberal reform; it amounted to a revolution that prepared the way for the later revolutions of 1905 and 1917.

Even when the desire and the determination to do something were present, as with Alexander II, there remained the problem of deciding the method of emancipation. Were the serfs simply to be given their social and political freedom, or were they to be emancipated and given economic freedom through the possession of land? If they were to be freed and given land, how were they to pay for it, and how were the landowners to be compensated? Furthermore, there was no uniformity in the serf and landowning system, which varied throughout Russia with the fertility of the soil and the density of the population. Indeed in the Black Earth region there was serious overpopulation and there would not be enough land for redistribution whatever happened.

Many suggestions had been made before Alexander's reign but it was the realization of the economic, social and military backwardness underlying the defeats during the Crimean War, as well as the growth of liberalism, and a sense that serfdom was, in any case, an uneconomic method of production, that made action necessary in the early years of Alexander's reign.

In 1856 a secret committee was formed which proposed emancipation by degrees, but Alexander insisted on a quick and final solution. After a tour in 1858, Provincial Committees were set up to make suggestions, and a Main Committee was created with the tsar as president. After prolonged discussion, Alexander steered its report through the Main Committee by overruling the opposition of the landowners, and submitted it to the State Council. The manifesto was signed in 1861.

The Terms of the Act of Liberation

The complicated acts of 1861 (there were sixteen altogether) applied only to the twenty-two million serfs in private ownership: similar legislation was applied to State-owned serfs in 1866.[1]

After a period of 'temporary bondage' (two years), the serfs were to be liberated without compensation to their owners for the loss of their labour, and the right to hold men in servitude was abolished for ever. But the land, except that part of it formerly worked by the serfs as their own plots, remained the property of the landowners.

The peasants who needed extra land could pay the owners rent, in cash or labour, or they could purchase it by redemption payments to the State over a period of forty-nine years. The landowners on the other hand were compensated immediately in Government bonds for the loss of their land, and a special fund was set up for the purpose, but details of price were left to be decided by mutual agreement between the owners and the peasants and official arbitrators were appointed.

The question of how much land the serf should have varied from

[1] Slavery was abolished in the United States in 1863.

place to place with the fertility of the soil, but, of course, the landowners desired to sell off the least favourable lands and keep the best for themselves, and there were many disputes about access to water, forests and meadows. Landowners could, if they chose, allot only one quarter of the maximum allowance, without payment and without compensation. This happened in the more fertile areas where the owners retained the bulk of the good land and the peasants were reduced to starvation on their 'beggars' quarters'.

Two important points must be made here: first, that only the field serfs—those who normally worked in agriculture—got land; the domestic serfs, if they no longer served in the noble households, could only drift to the towns to join the urban workers; secondly, the peasants did not become freeholders, for the title to the lands was transferred to the village commune which now became responsible for many of the functions formerly exercised by the landowners.

The process of land settlement following the emancipation required a series of acts during the next thirty years before it could be regarded as complete.

Results of the Emancipation of the Serfs

About forty million peasants were eventually set free: half of them Crown or State owned and half of them private. They were no longer dependent on the will of the landowner, and were free to marry, to own property, to engage in trade, and to sue and be sued in the courts; but they were still a class apart and the lowest in the social hierarchy. They could not choose their occupations, they were still liable to corporal punishment and they still needed internal passports. They were subject now to the authority of the village commune and its elders who were responsible for the division of lands, the redemption payments, the poll tax, the drafting to army service, the maintenance of law and order, the billetting of troops, the repair of the roads and other administrative matters.

The peasantry had claimed that all the land rightfully belonged to them and the nobility had as firmly claimed it for themselves. Alexander could therefore only impose a compromise, and the complicated procedure of the act attempted to do this, but disappointment was inevitable; for the peasants, for the landowners, and for the liberals and intellectuals who supported the emancipation on social and moral grounds.

The peasants gained their freedom and the landowners lost about a third of their land, but the former were disappointed because their allotments were too small and over-valued, and the latter lost their social and economic power and their raison d'être. The power of the nobility rested on their land and the servile labour that worked it. Since the nobility were responsible for the civil and military administration, the power of the tsar rested on that of the nobility: thus the emancipation undermined the very structure of tsarist society. Few of the nobility were interested in agriculture and they were already deeply in debt. Emancipation hastened their decline as a class, although some prospered through the application of capital and enterprise in the Black Earth regions.

The peasantry as a whole were no better off economically, for the redemption payments were onerous and long drawn out, and many of them defaulted. They often received less land than they had worked as serfs and they lost their common rights in the forests and meadows. The consequences were that they often became a discontented rural proletariat seeking to supplement their incomes by working on the landowners' estates or in near-by towns.

The discontent manifested itself in hundreds of riots and disturbances, and from this time the revolutionary movement developed rapidly in Russia, so that there is a direct link between the emancipation and the events of 1917. The emancipation was a turning point in Russian history and further reforms were necessary, for the State was obliged to provide the services formerly the responsibility of the landowner and a new system of local government and of the administration of law and order had to be devised to replace the machinery that had been based on the old social order.

Local Government Reform

The Act of Emancipation obliged the freed serfs to combine in village communities and the communities were grouped in volosts (townships), with prospects of future self-government. The law on zemstvos (locally elected councils) of 1864, provided for the election of an assemby in each uyezd (district). There were to be three separate groups of voters: the nobility, the wealthy townspeople, and the peasants, with power weighted very heavily in favour of the nobility. Yet it must be remembered that the nobility were the only people with any experience in local administration and their services had to be retained. In a sense, the power they gained in the zemstvos was compensation for what they had lost by the emancipation.

The zemstvos were to be responsible for all local administration, such as the collection of State and local taxes, the provision of health and education services, and communications, but not the control of the police which remained with the central government.

In 1870 the towns were granted elected dumas (councils), with similar functions to the zemstvos in the rural areas. All who paid taxes could vote, but there were still three separate classes of voters.

The powers and functions of the zemstvos and dumas were limited, but they were the nearest tsarist Russia ever came to democratic self-government, and they did provide a useful training ground and experience for future political leaders, and much useful work was done by them, particularly for education in rural areas.

Education

Much was done to liberalize the educational system against the opposition of the Church, and particularly while Golovnin was Minister of Education, 1861–1866. In 1863, in response to student unrest, considerable autonomy was granted to the universities, and in 1864 it was decreed that anyone who could pass the examinations should have a secondary education, while higher education was made available to women. The zemstvos and dumas did much for primary education, establishing village schools at the rate of about a thousand a year. In 1856 there were 8,000 elementary schools in the empire: in 1880 there were 23,000. These schools and their teachers became the real agents of progress in the villages.

Legal Reform

This was made necessary by the emancipation and by the manifold abuses in the old legal system. A commission was appointed in 1861 to study other European legal systems and to suggest reforms. These were promulgated in 1864 with a radical revision of the law and its methods: procedure was simplified, the penal system was modified, trial by jury was introduced and the administration of justice was made more prompt and fair, although not always for the peasants.[1]

Military Reforms

These were made very necessary by the disasters of the Crimean War and owed much to the enlightened policy of D. A. Milyutin, Minister of War, 1861–1881. He was interested in social and educational problems and placed stress on the education of the men and the training of the officers. Military service was reduced from twenty-five to sixteen years and the army was no longer used for penal reform. Corporal punishment was limited and the military colonies were abolished. The general efficiency of the administration, the commissariat, transport and engineering branches was improved, strategic railways were built,

[1] Peasants remained subjects to their own 'volost', or communal courts.

and new arms and equipment were introduced. Most important of all was the introduction of conscription in 1874 after prolonged resistance from those sections of society which had formerly been able to obtain exemption from military service. It was an important step towards the achievement of social equality.

Financial Reform and Economic Development

Reutern, the Minister of Finance, 1862–1878, did much to promote economic development as well as the reform of Government finance. The accounts were centralized instead of being administered independently by the various departments, methods of auditing were improved and the budget was made public for the first time in 1862. In 1866 a State Bank was created and considerable railway development took place: the mileage increased from 600 to 14,000 in Alexander's reign, and railways were the key to Russia's economic development. One result was a great increase in grain exports; from an annual average of 76 million poods[1] at the beginning of the reign, to 257 million poods in 1880. Commercial and industrial development increased apace with the rapid growth of banks and joint stock companies and the imposition of protective tariffs in 1877.

Alexander's Liberalism

Alexander was not truly liberal: he could not be, for his own inclination as well as his position as tsar meant that he had to insist on the preservation of his personal authority and order within the State, but he had had liberal-minded tutors and his reign began with an apparent burst of enthusiasm for necessary reform. Reforming ministers were appointed in numbers at the beginning of the reign and there was always his brother, the Grand Duke Constantine, an ardent reformer, at his side to urge him on; indeed, probably much of Alexander's 'liberalism' was the result of his giving way to the promptings of others rather than of his own convictions. There was, however, genuine relaxation of the severities of the reign of Nicholas: the coronation manifesto in 1856 made considerable concessions and hinted at more to come; there was an amnesty for political prisoners, religious persecution was modified, the universities regained much of their freedom and the censorship was relaxed. There followed the liberation of the serfs and the other reforms, but already by 1862 the dangers of relaxing control were apparent in criticism, discontent and disorder, and a return to repression was the obvious corollary. Restrictions were reimposed on the

---

[1] One pood = 36 lb.

universities and the zemstvos in the 1870s and the censorship was restored, while the activities of the secret police were intensified. Constant demands for constitutional reform fell on deaf ears. Thirteen noblemen who addressed a demand for a national assembly to the tsar in 1861 were sent to a lunatic asylum.

The Importance of Alexander's Reforms

The Crimean War and the reign of Alexander II can be seen to be a watershed in Russian history: in that period the social and economic transformation took place that divides medieval from modern Russia. The nobility gave way to the bureaucracy as the agents of power and authority, the intellectual ferment stimulated by the reforms hastened the revolutionary movement, and the industrial revolution made rapid progress. In spite of the weakness of Alexander's character his achievement bears comparison with that of Peter the Great, or indeed of any other Russian ruler. He was not successful, but he did much. The reforms tended to be piecemeal, many of them being the consequence of the emancipation rather than of a carefully thought out plan, and there was all too often a wide gap between the letter of the law and the time and manner of its operation, so that the old and the new order continued to exist side by side. The transformation was incomplete, but there was no going back: the fall of the tsarist system had begun.

The Growth of Discontent and Revolutionary Activity

Alexander's reforms satisfied no one: the conservatives were opposed to all that had happened, the peasants felt that they were worse off and that they had been deprived of their rights, the liberals were disappointed at the extent of the reforms and the return to repression, and the revolutionaries were actively plotting the destruction of tsarist society. Agriculture was still backward and unproductive, for the peasants were ignorant and lacked capital, so that famines were recurrent, while the development of manufacturing industry created new social and economic problems in the towns. Added to this, the great reforms were slow to show any immediate practical benefits to the bulk of the population.

The most vocal critics of the Government were the intelligentsia, a tiny minority of the population, mostly members of the nobility and town-bred middle classes with a university education, who had liberal or socialist ideas and a strong social consciousness, but little, if any, direct contact with the Russian people, and no practical political experience. The Populists, or Narodniks, took their name from the 'V narod' (to the people) movement which reached its height in the

1870s. Under the influence of Alexander Herzen and N. G. Cherny-shevsky, students and professional people went out to preach revolutionary socialism to the peasants in the countryside. The peasants were quite unresponsive: they wanted land not ideas, but the Narodniks provided many of the leaders of the later revolutionary movements. Secret revolutionary societies such as the 'Zemlya i Volya' (Land and Freedom), 1876, and the 'Narodnaya Volya' (Peoples' Will), 1879, were formed. Their victims included the Chief of the Secret Police in 1878, the Governor-General of Kharkov in 1879, and after several attempts, Alexander II in 1881.

The Polish Revolt, 1863

Polish national feeling had been growing throughout the nineteenth century: there was a widespread desire for national independence and a return to the frontiers that existed before the partitions at the end of the eighteenth century. The general discontent was heightened by economic distress, and the desire for liberal reforms was expressed by the Polish landowners and the Roman Catholic clergy.

Alexander's policy at first, was one of concessions and reform, together with firmness in maintaining order and in resisting the nationalist demands, for the retention of the western lands was regarded as essential to the security of the empire.

The reign began with an amnesty for political prisoners and exiles and a relaxation from the repressive rule of Nicholas I. There was a concordat with the Roman Catholic Church; elections for local and district assemblies were to be permitted; education was to be allowed to develop on Polish lines; and political activity was tolerated through the so-called Agricultural Societies. But concessions were not enough for the Polish patriots: nationalist demonstrations increased in size and number between 1860 and 1863, and clashes with the police eventually led to the imposition of martial law.

Alexander persisted in his policy of proposing reform while resisting nationalist demands, until an attempt to crush the revolutionary societies by drafting their leaders to the army led to risings throughout Poland in January 1863, and guerilla warfare continued until 1865.

The Polish revolt was doomed to failure for the nationalists were disunited and poorly led. The peasantry took little part, and the 10,000 or so students and members of the middle classes who formed the bulk of the rebels were faced with 80,000 Russian troops, who enjoyed the enthusiastic support of Prussia, and the less willing help of Austria, while Britain and France gave little but verbal help to the Poles.

The Polish revolt changed Alexander's policy. It seemed that conciliation was a failure, henceforth nationalism must be crushed, the Polish gentry and the Roman Catholic clergy must be punished, and the peasantry must be won over by land reform. Poland must be Russified.

In 1863 the Polish kingdom disappeared and was incorporated within the empire as the Vistula region under the control of a governor-general. The rebels and their leaders were executed or deported to Siberia, heavy fines were imposed, estates confiscated and Roman Catholic monasteries were closed. Russian became the official language.

By the land reform of 1864 the Polish serfs were given their freedom, with more generous allotments of land, and at lower prices, than were offered to their fellow serfs in Russia: thus the Polish peasantry were rewarded by punishing the landowners who had offended against Alexander.

The Polish revolt together with the attempts on his life helped to turn Alexander from his early liberalism to the repression of the later part of his reign.

Finland

In Finland, as in Poland, the nationalists desired to separate from the Russian Empire, and the liberals wanted reforms and some kind of representative government. Alexander insisted on the necessary benefits of Russian rule but wished to introduce moderate reform and to encourage economic development. On the whole he was more successful than in Poland. Railways and steamship services were introduced, and these, in turn, helped the development of the agricultural and forestry industries, but the Finns were demanding more independence as well as economic advances.

The Finnish Diet had not met since 1809, and Alexander was reluctant to grant self-government for fear that he might have to do so in the rest of the empire, but in 1864, elections for the Diet were permitted and the Finns were allowed to govern themselves according to their constitution.

Foreign Policy

Alexander's first task in foreign affairs was to bring the Crimean War to an end (see chapter XI). After that he wanted peace and an end to the diplomatic isolation of Russia. It needed a period of peace to put Russia's internal affairs in order, and in any case, wars had a tendency to encourage the growth of revolutionary ideas, and this was to be prevented. But in spite of Alexander's desire for peace he was at war with Turkey again before the end of his reign, and the imperialist ambitions of some of his army officers and governors, together with the economic motives of the merchants, led to a rapid expansion throughout central Asia and the Far East, which brought him into conflict with the other imperialist powers, particularly Britain.

Much of this expansion was unplanned, for Alexander was too weak to exert his authority over his agents, and he eventually began the war with Turkey in spite of his early determination to avoid it. Nesselrode was replaced as Foreign Minister by Gorchakov at the beginning of the reign; the Austrian alliance was dropped, and it was sought to strengthen the friendship with Prussia, while a rapprochement developed with France, but Britain, alarmed at Russian expansion, became more hostile, especially while Disraeli was in control of foreign affairs.

The Far East

Defeat in the Crimean War meant that expansion westwards was checked for the time being, but control over Poland was ensured after the revolt of 1863, and railway and economic development led to almost unchecked expansion eastwards in the late nineteenth century.

The weakness of China had been demonstrated by Britain during the Opium Wars of the 1840s. Nicholas had appointed N. Muravyev as Governor-General of eastern Siberia in 1847, and a commission was set up to investigate the possibility of expanding trade with China. Muravyev disregarded the terms of the Treaty of Nerchinsk, 1689, which had given the Amur region to China. He founded Nikolaevsk, occupied Sakhalin and part of Korea, and encouraged settlement there. During the Crimean War he annexed the whole of the Amur region, in spite of Chinese protests, in order to forestall any possible Anglo-French activity in the Far East. By the Convention of Aigun, 1858, the Chinese were obliged to recognize Russian possession of the left bank of the Amur and to grant favourable commercial privileges. These were confirmed and extended by the Treaty of Pekin, 1860, and the Russian Maritime Provinces were established and the port of Vladivostok (Lord of the East) was founded. Russia now had both sides of the Amur, a port on the Pacific coast, and economic concessions in China. At the same time the Russo-Chinese border in Turkestan was revised.

The Sale of Alaska, 1867

The Treaty of Nerchinsk, 1689, checked Russian expansion towards China, but traders and adventurers, keeping well to the north, moved into Kamchatka and the Kurile Islands. Attempts to open up trade with Japan had little success until the Treaty of Shimoda, 1855, which gave the Russians certain trading rights and possession of the northern Kuriles. Meanwhile the penetration of Alaska had begun. Peter the Great had commissioned Vitus Bering to explore the area which bears his name, and following his discoveries, Russian fur traders moved into the Aleutians and Alaska. The Emperor Paul granted a charter to the Russian-American Company which established trading posts down the west coast of the North American continent as far as California. Alexander I claimed the Pacific coast as far as the fifty-first parallel and Russian activities in the north Pacific alarmed Spain and Britain as well as the United States. President Monroe's message to Congress in 1823 was directed against all European powers, and Alexander revised his claim to the line of 54 degrees, 40 minutes north, in 1824.

The Company did not prosper, however, and during the Crimean War it became evident that Russia could not hold Alaska. In 1867 it was agreed to sell it to the United States for 7,200,000 dollars, which was considered a bargain then, but it is interesting to consider the position of the United States today if Alaska were not the forty-ninth state and the Russians were still there.

Central Asia

In central Asia the subjection of the three Muslim khanates of Kokand, Bukhara and Khiva was regarded as a civilizing mission. The tribes were disorderly and there was growing demand for the raw material which the area could provide: hemp, tobacco, silk, cattle and horses, gold and cotton. Tashkent was taken in 1865 by Chernyaev; Bukhara was occupied, and the governor-generalship of Turkestan was created in 1866, with Kaufmann in control, 1867–1883. He completed the subjection of central Asia by taking Bukhara and Samarkand in 1868, and Khiva in 1873. Turkmenia was added after the capture of Geok-Tepe in 1881, and in 1884 the submission of Merv opened the road to Herat. This rapid and successful expansion alleviated some of the humiliation felt by defeat in the Crimea but the extension of Russian influence towards Afghanistan aroused Britain's fears for India.

The Caucasus and Persia

The conquest of the Caucasus was a long-standing imperial ambition and under Prince Baryatinsky, as Viceroy at Tiflis, it was completed in 1864. This accomplished, Russian forces began to move south of the Caspian towards Persia. Krasnovodsk was established as a base in 1869 and a Trans-Caspian military district was set up in 1874. The Trans-Caspian railway was begun in 1879 and expansion continued towards Persia and Afghanistan. Russia gained economic concessions in Persia

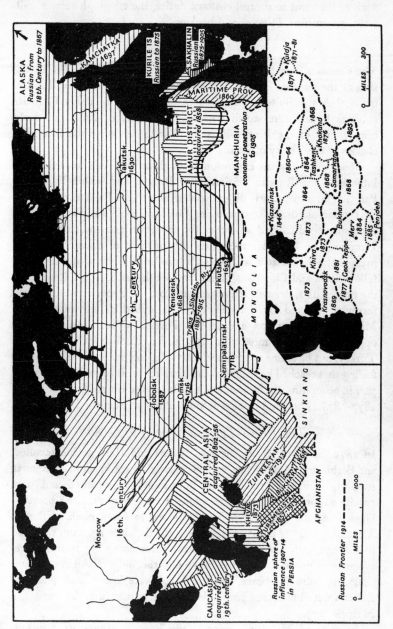

RUSSIAN EXPANSION IN CENTRAL ASIA AND SIBERIA

ALASKA
Russian from
18th Century to 1867

KAMCHATKA
1697

KURILE IS
Russian to 1875

SAKHALIN
(Russian
1875-1905)

MARITIME PROV
1860

AMUR DISTRICT
acquired 1858

MANCHURIA
economic penetration
to 1905

Yakutsk
1630

17th. Century

Yeniseisk
1618

Irkutsk
1652

Trans-Siberian Rly
1891-1915

Semipalatinsk
1718

Tobolsk
1587

Omsk
1716

MONGOLIA

SINKIANG

16th. Century

Moscow

CENTRAL ASIA
acquired 1802-56

TURKESTAN
1857-1913

KHIVA
1873

BUKHARA 1868

TURKMENISTAN
1857-1913

AFGHANISTAN

CAUCASUS
acquired in
19th century

Russian sphere of
influence 1907-14
in PERSIA

Russian Frontier 1914 ------

0   1000
MILES

Kuldja
1871 1871-81

Kazalinsk
1846

1860-64

Tashkent
1864
1868

Khokand
1876

Samarkand
1868

1895

1864

1873

Khiva
1873

Bukhara
1868

Merv
1884

1873

Krasnovodsk
1869

1877

Geok Teppe
1881

1885

Penjdeh

0   300
MILES

such as the right to control customs duties, the telegraph service, railways, steamships, fisheries and banking.

The Eastern Question

The Crimean War did not solve the Eastern Question. Russian expansion at the expense of the Turkish Empire was checked for the time being, but the Sultan's promises that he would treat his Christian subjects better were worth nothing, and in 1870, Russia used the opportunity of the Franco-Prussian War to denounce the Black Sea clauses of the Treaty of Paris.

Meanwhile Russian expansion through central Asia towards India intensified anti-Russian sentiments in Britain, and within Russia the Pan Slav movement was directing attention to the Balkans once more. To the age-old dream of controlling Constantinople was now added the economic need to find an outlet for the grain and industries of the Ukraine. The Pan Slav movement, an offshoot of Slavophilism, expressed the idea that it was Russia's mission to liberate and unite her fellow Slavs and Christians in east and south-east Europe. It began in the universities, drew its main support from the upper classes, and was fervently fostered by the empress. It also had its adherents in the Ministry of Education and in the Foreign Office. Alexander was opposed to it, for it must ultimately lead to conflict with Austria and Turkey, but he seems to have been carried along by the wave of national feeling that reached its height in the early 1870s. It played an important part in generating the atmosphere that led to the Russo-Turkish War of 1877–1878, although it had spent much of its force before the war began.

The Russo-Turkish War, 1877–1878

In 1875 the Turkish provinces of Bosnia and Herzegovina revolted, and Serbia and Montenegro, believing that they could count on Russian support, joined in (1876). The Bulgarians also revolted and were cruelly suppressed by the Turks: these Bulgarian atrocities horrified Gladstone, and raised Pan Slav passions to fever pitch. Although Alexander and his ministers tried to keep the situation calm they had to contend with a wave of patriotism; volunteers were recruited and money was raised to help the Serbs and the Bulgars. Alexander continued to work for peace, but the Serbs were losing, and when the Sultan refused to accept proposals that were put to him, the war began in April 1877.

In spite of Milyutin's reforms the Russian armies were incompetently led and badly supplied, and the advance was held up for months by the stubborn Turkish defence of Plevna. By the time they reached Adrianople, they found that Disraeli had sent the British fleet to Constantinople as a blunt warning to go no further. Austria, too, was preparing for war, so a hasty truce was made at San Stephano, 1878, by the terms of which Russia would have gained Bessarabia, and a 'big' Bulgaria would have been created—independent, but it was hoped, under Russian influence.

This, the other powers, led by Britain, could not agree to, and they threatened war if the terms of San Stephano were not revised.[1] Alexander gave way, and at Berlin, in 1878, with Bismarck claiming to play the part of an honest broker, Russia retained her conquests from Turkey in Asia Minor and Bessarabia, and the independence of Serbia, Montenegro and Rumania was recognized, but the big Bulgaria was drastically reduced. Britain took Cyprus from Turkey, and Austria occupied Bosnia and Herzegovina. From here a sequence of events led to the outbreak of war in 1914.

The settlement at Berlin in 1878 was regarded as yet another humiliation for Russia at the hands of the other powers in Europe, but the gains, nevertheless, were quite considerable; Batum and Kars, to the east of the Black Sea and Bessarabia, to the west, had been added to the empire, and there had been a lesson on the hypocrisy and unreliability of Austria and Prussia in spite of the Dreikaiserbund of 1873. But the most important immediate consequence was a renewed outbreak of revolutionary activity within Russia.

The Importance of the Reign of Alexander II

Alexander's reign is significant for a number of reasons: it saw the beginnings of the break-up of the old Russia; free labour replaced serfdom, and the influence of the nobility declined. There was considerable economic development: capitalist enterprise and foreign investment were accompanied by the speculation and corruption that was common in other European countries with the progress of the industrial revolution, with the difference that capitalism in Russia was from the first aided by the State to a greater degree than elsewhere. Imperial expansion beyond the bounds of the Russian lands took place, with the acquisition of what were, in effect, colonies in central Asia, and the strains and stresses which this economic development produced combined with the impetus of the reforms and the results of the Turkish war to stimulate the revolutionary movement. For in spite of the reforms the essential structure of tsarist society remained and the assassination of Alexander II delayed further constitutional development for a quarter of a century.

[1] Disraeli, for example, drafted Indian troops to Malta.

QUESTIONS

1. Give an account of the abolition of serfdom in Russia indicating the problems involved and the results that followed.
2. Give an account of Russian expansion in central Asia and the Far East in the reigns of Alexander II and Alexander III.
3. Describe Alexander II's reforms and explain why they failed to satisfy Russia.
4. The Russo-Turkish War of 1877-1878 was a continuation of the Crimean War. Discuss.
5. Find out what you can and make notes on the following: the Russians in Alaska: the Narodniks; A. Herzen; N. G. Chernishevsky; Vladivostok; The Pan Slav movement; San Stephano; the Bulgarian Atrocities; the Siege of Plevna; the Dreikaiserbund; Loris-Melikov; General C. Kaufmann; Trans-Caspian Railway; N. Muravyev.
6. Discuss the place of the reign of Alexander II in Russian history.
7. Give an account of Alexander II's policy towards: (a) Poland; (b) Finland; (c) Turkey.
8. Trace and explain the growth of unrest in Russia after the Crimean War.

Further Reading

ALMEDINGEN, E. M. *The Emperor Alexander II.* Bodley Head, 1962.
FURNEAUX, R. *The Siege of Plevna.* Blond, 1958.
GRAHAM, S. *Tsar of Freedom: the Life and Reign of Alexander II.* Nicholson and Watson, 1935.
MOSSE, W. E. *Alexander II and the Modernization of Russia.* English U.P., 1959.
PALÉOLOGUE, M. *The Tragic Romance of Alexander II of Russia.* Hutchinson, 1926.
ROBINSON, G. T. *Rural Russia under the Old Régime.* Macmillan, New York, 1949.
SETON-WATSON, H. *The Decline of Imperial Russia.* Methuen, 1956.
SUMNER, B. H. *Russia and the Balkans, 1870-1880.* Oxford U.P. 1937.
TOLSTOY, L. *Anna Karenina*, trans. A. Maude. Oxford. World's Classics.
TURGENEV, I. *Fathers and Children*, trans. A. Pyman. Everyman, 1962.

CHAPTER XIII

ALEXANDER III
'The Peacemaker', 'The Peasant Tsar', 1881–1894

Alexander II's eldest son, Nicholas, died as a result of a fall from a horse—a form of exercise ordered by his father because he thought the boy was too soft and needed strengthening. The second son became Alexander III. He was simple and dull, happily married, a devout churchman, very tall and strong physically (he could bend horseshoes with his bare hands), liked the theatre and music, and played the trombone.

He had opposed his father's reforms and the lesson of assassination seemed to be that reform did not pay. Alexander III proclaimed his belief in the necessary powers of the autocracy, which his tutor, Constantine Pobedonostsev, Chief Procurator of the Holy Synod, 1880–1904, who remained a constant influence throughout the reign, had exalted as fervently as he distrusted western liberalism. The theme of Alexander III's reign became a return to the 'Autocracy, Orthodoxy and Nationalism' of Nicholas I, and he had the strength of body and will to carry it out, but not the understanding of the problems involved.

At the beginning of the reign there were hopes that Alexander might continue the constitutional reforms that his father had been considering before his assassination, but these hopes were soon dashed, and the reforming ministers that Alexander had inherited from the previous reign resigned.

Domestic Policy

The policies of Alexander III can be seen as a reaction to the 'liberalism' of Alexander II, but it was really an emphasis on the traditional procedure of tsarist governments. His aims were to strengthen the autocracy by crushing the revolutionary movements and by revising his father's reforms. He hoped to win the peasantry over, and to restore the power of the nobility. Meanwhile the economic development continued, and so too, did the discontent and the revolutionary activity, although much of it had to be organized from abroad.

Repression

Revolutionary agitators, as distinct from the general unorganized body of discontent, were never large in numbers, and the Government activity in the later years of the reign of Alexander II had been almost successful in eliminating them. The killers of Alexander were caught and executed, and the 'People's Will' was crushed. The Chief of Police, Vyacheslav Plehve, suppressed the revolutionaries by execution and exile, and there was a general extension of police powers throughout the reign. In 1881, an emergency decree permitted the suspension of the normal operation of the law whenever and wherever it was considered necessary and its substitution by one of three grades of martial law. One of the victims of the police at this time was Lenin's brother—an incident that intensified Lenin's hatred of the tsarist system.

Dimitry Tolstoy, the Minister of the Interior, 1882–1889, carried out the policy of limiting Alexander II's reforms. The censorship was extended, the universities lost their autonomy, and Government control was extended over the whole field of education and the Church while it was sought to limit secondary and higher education to the upper classes. Technical education was encouraged, but student disorders were frequent. In 1890, the powers of the zemstvos were reduced, as were those of the town dumas in 1892. In the countryside, the establishment of Land Captains in 1889 deprived the zemstvos and village communities of much of their jurisdiction by transferring these powers back to the local gentry.

Nationalism and the Persecution of Minorities

Slavophil sentiments were strengthened by the humiliations suffered at the hands of the European powers in the Crimean and Turkish wars. In the late nineteenth century reaction to European hostility combined with the fear of revolutionary activity in a profound sense of Russian nationalism which the need for unity in support of the autocracy turned into an official policy of intolerance and persecution of the non-Russian peoples of the empire.

Of the total population, in 1897, of 129 million, over forty million were non-Russian, including nine million Poles, six million Finns, eleven million Turco-Tartars, and five million Jews (about half the world total). A deliberate policy of Russification was forced upon these peoples by rigorous political, social and religious persecution. In Poland, no Pole or Roman Catholic could hold official positions, and use of

Polish in the schools was forbidden; in Finland the semi-autonomous powers were removed and the country was progressively incorporated in the Russian State: in the Baltic provinces a campaign was waged against the Lutheran faith and the German language of the ruling classes; the use of the Ukrainian language was forbidden, and similar policies were applied to Armenia and central Asia.

Russification also meant imposing the orthodox faith on religious minorities within the empire; this included the Old Believers, Uniates, Roman Catholics, Moslems and Jews. Two of the sects were particularly severely persecuted; the Stundists, a Baptist group, and the Dukhobors. The worst persecution was of the Jews: here the aim was not to force them to become Russians but to eliminate them. Anti-semitism was not, of course, a new thing, but Alexander II had made certain concessions to the Jews. After his death they were suspected of being at the bottom of all revolutionary activity, and in Alexander III's reign, the pogroms[1] began. Thousands of Jews were murdered in south-west Russia, and their limited rights were still further reduced. Many who could emigrated, and they were encouraged to do so. Pobedonostsev thought the Jewish problem would be solved when one-third had emigrated, one-third had been converted to Russian Orthodoxy, and one third had disappeared.

Economic Development

Much of the economic development owed little to Government policy, but the work of two men was important; N. K. Bunge, as Minister of Finance, 1881–1887, and Sergius Witte, Minister of Communications and Minister of Finance from 1892.

Some concessions were made to the peasantry: in 1882, the redemption payments were reduced and made obligatory; the poll tax was abolished and replaced by an inheritance tax; and in 1884, a Peasants' Bank was created to enable them to buy more land. But the peasant population had increased to seventy-nine from fifty millions in 1860, and while some prospered, the average size of peasant holdings grew less. There was serious famine in 1891–1892, and the poverty of the peasantry as a whole worsened. Emigration to Siberia or to the towns was the only relief.

A Land Bank was also set up for the nobility in 1885 to enable them to retain their estates and this was far more generously financed than the Peasants' Bank.

Private capital was not available for investment, so much of the

[1] Officially sponsored anti-semitic riots.

industrial development was due to State investment and foreign loans. By 1901, 37,209 miles of railway had been built, including much of the Trans-Siberian and the Trans-Caspian railways, and of this, 75 per cent was State owned. Between 1880 and 1890, coal production increased from $3\frac{1}{2}$ to 5 million tons, oil from half a million to $4\frac{1}{4}$ million tons, and iron from 1 to 2 million tons. High tariffs and subsidies were imposed, and concessions granted, to encourage native industry, but it is significant that it tended to concentrate in one or two urban centres, in what was still essentially a backward rural country. The discontented urban proletariat in these centres was relatively easily controlled by the later revolutionary movements.

The laissez-faire industrial development was accompanied by the corruption and speculation, the exploitation, the long hours, low wages, bad working and living conditions that were familiar elsewhere in Europe, but there was an attempt at labour legislation, and a kind of paternal State socialism, while Bunge was in office. It was, however, undone after his dismissal in 1887. Child labour in factories was prohibited under the age of twelve in 1882; hours were reduced for women and children, and night work for women was regulated. Inspectors were appointed to supervise the administration of the acts, and regulations for the payment of workers and the extraction of fines from them by the employers were introduced.

Alexander gave support to Bunge and Witte in their efforts to bring order and economy to the State finances. A system of tax inspection was introduced and Witte was able to put Russia on the gold standard and build up enough reserves to encourage foreign investment. A Government monopoly of vodka failed to stop drunkenness, but did bring in welcome revenue to the treasury as well as ending the corruption that had accompanied the former system of farming the excise.

The Development of Political Opposition

Alexander's policy of repression almost stifled the revolutionary movements inside Russia until the later years of his reign. There were attempts on his life, but the badly organized, romantic and utopian revolutionary societies were incapable of achieving their aims through terrorism, and it was realized that to be effective, political opposition must be more highly organized and have a definite programme. There were no organized political parties in Alexander III's reign—only tendencies of thought among the intelligentsia, and discussion circles among workers. These groups were very small in numbers, and although they did not form a definite party, the largest politically conscious group in Russia were the liberals who were gaining their practical experience in the zemstvos. The Marxists formed the Social Democratic Labour Party in 1898; the Socialist Revolutionary Party was formed in 1902; and the Liberals formed the Constitutional Democrats in 1905.

Foreign Policy

Alexander announced on his accession that he intended to follow a peaceful foreign policy, and that he would concentrate on the material and moral development of Russia, but he could not avoid the pressure of outside events, and the policy of expansion in Asia was continued, partly to divert attention from the demand for reform at home; indeed the emphasis fluctuated between the defence of Slav interests in the Balkans and imperialism in Asia.

The European Balance of Power

European politics in the second half of the nineteenth century were dominated by the schemes of Bismarck. He sought first to eliminate Austrian influence from Germany and then to assert Prussian dominance over France. To achieve this he wanted to be sure that Russia would not intervene on his eastern frontier, and the Russo-Prussian alliance that he maintained, worked to their mutual benefit. He refused to help the Poles in 1863 and allowed Alexander II to denounce the Black Sea clauses in 1870. But after the trickery that surrounded the dealings at Berlin in 1878, the friendship began to wear thin, and Russia began to find that republican France could offer a more genuine blend of mutual interest in the common opposition to Germany.

Driven from Germany, Austria began to concentrate on her ambitions in the Danube valley and the Balkan states. This brought her into conflict with Russian interests, in spite of Germany's attempts to divert Russian attention from Europe towards Siberia and the Far East. France needed an ally after her defeat by Prussia in 1871, and although Bismarck attempted to keep up the Russian alliance to prevent this, he was bound to support Austria if conflict broke out in the Balkans. In 1879 he made the Dual Alliance with Austria which became the Triple Alliance with Italy in 1882—thus creating one of the power blocs that led to the First World War.

At the same time he made a separate treaty with Russia, and in 1881 the Dreikaiserbund was revived whereby Austria, Russia and Germany agreed to remain neutral if one of the others became involved in war. They also promised to maintain the status quo in Turkey, and recognized Russian interest in Bulgaria and Austrian interest in Serbia, Bosnia and Herzogovina. Germany also promised to support Russia against Britain in the Middle East, but by now there were ample reasons for Russia to distrust German assurances.

Bismarck was correct in fearing that Russia and France would move closer together, and with his removal from office in 1890, the Reinsurance Treaty which he had made with Alexander III in 1887 was allowed to lapse. Franco-Russian military conversations took place in 1890 which developed into a definite alliance in 1893. The military and political alliance was accompanied by a commercial treaty, and large-scale French loans to Russia—500 million francs in 1887, and several other large loans between 1889 and 1891.

The Eastern Question

Bulgaria had gained her independence thanks to Russian efforts, but she was frustrated in her ambitions by the Russian attempts to treat her as a vassal state. A series of plots, assassinations and coups d'état failed to establish Russian influence and strengthened the general suspicion of Russian intentions in the Balkans. Russia's conflict here with Austria, who enjoyed German support, brought the Dreikaiser-bund to an end and drew Russia and France closer together.

Ethiopia

One of the more extravagant manifestations of the Slavophil tendencies in the nineteenth century was a belief in the identity of the Orthodox and the Ethiopian churches. With the ostensible aim of bringing about the union of the churches a series of semi-official Russian expeditions were sent to Ethiopia, beginning with that led by Ashinov in 1888, and culminating in the establishment of a regular military and diplomatic mission in 1897. The real aim seems to have been to establish a foothold in Africa to counter British influence, and to create private commercial empires for individual Russian adventurers. The Government tried to hush up the Ashinov affair, but considerable traffic in arms and money took place, and Russians seemed to gain a good deal of influence at the court of Menelik II, although in truth he was probably only using them to counter Italian influence in East Africa. Indeed, the chief consequence of the Ethiopian adventures was a worsening of relations between Russia and Italy, who regarded that part of Africa as her special sphere of influence.

Central Asia and the Far East

The expansion which had been so rapid under Alexander II continued and brought nearer the danger of conflict with Britain who feared for the safety of India, and with Japan who had ambitions in Korea and

China. The colonization of Siberia became a positive alternative to granting reforms and settlement was greatly aided by the construction of the Trans-Siberian railway.

In 1884 Merv was taken into the empire and Persia ceded Serakhs. The proximity of these areas to the north-west frontier of India, and Russo-British intrigues in Afghanistan, produced the Penjdeh crisis of 18__ between Russia and Britain was averted by a compromise ___ Russia to keep Penjdeh but not the important Zufilkar ___ she also wanted.

___ ar East Japan had since 1858 been developing rapidly along ___ lines and was contending with China for influence in Korea. ___ a series of crises between Japan and China over Korea in ___4 and 1894 which led to war in 1894-1895. Before this, ___ he Russians had been attempting to extend their influence ___ d a Russo-Korean treaty of friendship was made in 1884. ___ as set for the conflict between Russia and Japan that was to ___ astrously for Russia in the next reign.

QUESTIONS

___ e economic policies of the Government under Alexander

___ e emergence of political parties in Russia at the close of the ___ nth century.

___ n account of the reign of Alexander III under the headings: ___ estic affairs; (b) foreign affairs.

___ st of the autocrats. Discuss this view of Alexander III.

___ ut what you can and make notes on the following: C. Pobe- ___ stsev; Sergius Witte; the Trans-Siberian Railway; the Pogroms; ___ e Dukhubors; the Penjdeh incident; the Sino-Japanese War; the ___ and Captains; the Franco-Russian Alliance.

Further Reading

JESMAN, C. *The Russians in Ethiopia.* Chatto and Windus, 1958.

LOWE, C. *Alexander III of Russia.* Heinemann, 1895.

SETON-WATSON, H. *The Decline of Imperial Russia, 1855-1914.* New edn. Methuen, 1952.

TISDALE, E. E. P. *The Dowager Empress.* Stanley Paul, 1957.

CHAPTER XIV

NICHOLAS II, 1894–1917
The last of the Tsars

Alexander III was the last of the autocrats: his son, Nich
neither his father's physique nor his clarity of mind and
will. Indeed, Alexander thought his son childish and unde
made no serious attempt to educate him in his imperial du
for sending him on a tour of the Far East, via Greece, E
and Japan and returning through Siberia in 1890–1891.
upbringing was strict and disciplined, and he became fluent
English and French, but apart from his interest in milit
was not a keen student, and appears to have had a very ord

Nicholas had the Romanov charm and a great faculty of
his feelings, which all too often meant that he could not be reli
ministers would leave him one day, confident that all was we
learn the next day that they had been dismissed or their
altered. His mystical belief in autocracy was complete: his a
carry on as his father had done and then to hand on his powe
tsarevich unchallenged. Yet Nicholas was no autocrat: his
characteristics were his weakness of will, although he could be stub
at times, and his extraordinary fatalism. He refused to listen to adv
but he was easily influenced by those near to him, and in consequen
the court was the centre of constant intrigues. The truth was probably
that Nicholas avoided difficult decisions by appearing to agree with
everyone and acted according to the influence of the last person to see
him.

The Empress

In 1894, Nicholas married Princess Alix, daughter of the Grand Duke
of Hesse, and a granddaughter of Queen Victoria. She had found
consolation from an unhappy early life in Lutheranism, and it was only
after much heart-searching that she was re-christened, as Alexandra
Feodorovna, into the Russian Orthodox faith. She was shy, awkward,

not very intelligent, often ill and hysterical, and never popular, but she was devoted to Nicholas and became a fanatical convert to the cause of her new religion and her new country.

After four daughters had been born, the joy at the birth of a son was saddened by the discovery that he suffered from haemophilia. Alexandra's life came to be dominated by two aims: (1) that the Tsarevich Alexis should live to inherit the throne, and (2) that he should inherit the powers of the autocracy undiminished. 'The Emperor', she is reported to have said, 'unfortunately, is weak, but I am not, and I intend to be firm.' After 1905 she came increasingly to exert her will over him in the matter of appointments and policy, and her meddling contributed no small part to the downfall of the Russian monarchy.

The imperial family were all clumsily murdered by the Bolsheviks in 1918. After a period of imprisonment, they were shot and bayoneted, and the bodies were cut in pieces, burned in acid, and thrown down a disused mine. But the brutal murder of a whole family, one of whom, the tsarevich, was so ill that he had to be carried, was only part of the greater tragedy of the civil war that accompanied the birth of the U.S.S.R.

Domestic Policy

It is difficult to extend the sympathy that one feels at the manner of the deaths of the imperial family to the lives of the tsar and the empress. They were completely out of touch with the Russian people, and an ominous sequence of events leads up to the revolution of 1917.

The reign began tragically when the crowd which assembled for the traditional distribution of gifts at the coronation ceremony in 1896, stampeded, crushing 1,300 people to death, and injuring many more: and yet, the same evening, the tsar and empress attended a ball. This apparent lack of personal sensitivity to what was appropriate for the occasion was repeated when the liberals in the zemstvos, who hoped that the new reign might give an opportunity for some relaxation from the repression of Alexander's reign, were rebuked for daring to hope for some kind of constitutional reform. Replying to their address, Nicholas said:

> It has come to my knowledge that lately, in some meetings of the zemstva, voices have made themselves heard from people who have allowed themselves to be carried away by foolish fancies about the participation of representatives of the zemstva in the general administration of the internal affairs of the state.
> Let every man know that I will devote all of my strength to the good of my people, but that I will uphold the principle of the autocracy as firmly and as unflinchingly as did my ever-lamented father.

Nicholas retained most of his father's ministers and officials, particularly Pobedonostsev, Witte and Plehve and they carried out his, or rather their, policies. Until 1905, Pobedonostsev was the chief influence on Nicholas, while Witte and Plehve were rivals for power and influence. The court went on its way with its intrigues and its corruption while successive ministers were arbitrarily appointed and dismissed; the bureaucracy lumbered inefficiently and corruptly on; the liberals became ever more frustrated in their hopes of constitutional reform; the peasantry and the urban workers were expressing their discontent in a flood of strikes, riots and outbreaks of disorder, and the underground revolutionary activity of the Social Democrats and the Socialist Revolutionary Party increased in intensity.

The policy of Russification continued throughout the empire, but particularly harshly in Finland; so too did the persecution of non-orthodox religious sects and the pogroms against the Jews. The constant demands of the liberals for political freedom and equal civil rights fell on deaf ears, while the police continued to repress all political agitation. There were variations, however: for example in the 1890s certain writers with Marxist views were permitted to express their ideas and were known as 'Legal Marxists'; the Government's aim was not, of course, to encourage socialist ideas, but to promote the divisions between the socialists—nevertheless Marxist ideas were enabled to spread, even if there were different kinds of Marxists. Another experiment between 1900 and 1905 was the idea of Zubatov, head of the Moscow police, who organized the first legal trade unions, which it was hoped, would attract support away from the revolutionaries and enable the police to keep an eye on the leaders. Similar police unions were created in other cities, but they were too successful in attracting support, and the Social Democrats were able to utilize them for their own revolutionary purposes. Zubatov had to resign in 1903.

In spite of ubiquitous police activities, the repression and police socialism, revolutionary activity continued and there was a renewed outbreak of terrorism: Plehve the Minister of the Interior had suggested that what was wanted to divert attention from the discontent at home was 'a successful little war'. The disastrous Russo-Japanese war of 1904–1905 only intensified the opposition to the tsarist government and Plehve himself was assassinated by the S.R.s in July 1904: so too in February 1905, was the Grand Duke Sergius, late Governor-General of Moscow and husband to a sister of the empress.

The 1905 Revolution

The assassinations of Plehve and the Grand Duke Sergius seen against the events of the Japanese war were a warning to the Government of impending trouble. A slightly more liberal Minister of the Interior, Sviatopolk-Mirsky, succeeded Plehve, and he hesitantly permitted the zemstvos to hold a conference in November 1904. They demanded more political and religious freedom, equality before the law, an extension of the powers of self-government, and a reform of the constitution to permit representative government. The most they got from Nicholas was a vague promise of reform and their demands were unheeded. The result was that the opposition became more radical and strikes and disorders increased.

In January 1905, a strike at the Putilov works in St Petersburg spread, and a peaceful procession of about 200,000 workers and their families, led by Father Gapon, a police agent in one of the legal unions, planned to march to the Winter Palace to present a petition to the tsar based on the demands put forward at the zemstvos conference. The marchers were fired upon and hundreds were killed and injured. This 'Bloody Sunday', as it was called, destroyed all hope that the tsar, as distinct from his ministers, would listen to the grievances of the people. There was renewed political agitation and an outbreak of strikes, including a mutiny on the battleship *Potemkin* in June.

Nicholas, supported by the empress, was determined not to surrender the prerogatives of the autocracy to any kind of representative or parliamentary assembly, but in March 1905 he reluctantly promised some kind of duma, or consultative assembly, and in August was obliged to go further and agree to promise that it would be representative, but he meant it to have a very limited electorate, weighted in favour of landowners and it would have no share in legislation. Sviatopolk-Mirsky was replaced as Minister of the Interior by Bulygin.

Meanwhile the liberals were forming unions of professional persons, and these in turn formed the 'Union of Unions', with Paul Milyukov as president. Many labour unions also joined the Union of Unions and it acted as the voice of left-wing liberal opinion. In July the All-Russian Peasants Union was formed and this too joined the Union of Unions.

The August proposals of the tsar, known as the Bulygin Law on the Duma fell far short of the liberals' hopes and they were divided on whether to accept the proposals in the hope of improving on them or to reject them completely. In the event the right-wing liberals decided to accept the proposed Duma and to try to convert it into something more like a representative parliament, while the left-wing liberals and the socialists decided to boycott the elections.

The year 1905 saw a series of riots and strikes in the industrial areas, peasant disorders in the country, mutinies in the army and navy, and national risings in the non-Russian parts of the empire. In October, a general strike developed almost spontaneously. This was what the revolutionaries had been waiting for, and the socialists were soon prominent among the strike leaders. In St Petersburg, Moscow and elsewhere, soviets, councils of strike committees, were created, and for fifty days the St Petersburg Soviet exercised control almost as a rival government.

This was the climax of the revolutionary movement in 1905, and in despair Nicholas turned to Witte, just back from negotiating the Treaty of Portsmouth in America. Witte's advice was that Nicholas must either establish a military dictatorship over Russia, or grant some constitutional reform. Against his own feelings, and the empress's wishes, Nicholas issued a manifesto on 17 October 1905, which promised civil liberties to the people; inviolability of the person; freedom of speech, conscience and assembly; an extension of the franchise for the elections to the promised Duma; and that no laws should be enforced without the consent of the Duma. There was no promise that the Duma should actually be permitted to initiate legislation; it was intended to be no more than a consultative body. To demonstrate the sincerity of its promises, the Government granted a limited amnesty, abolished the censorship, and ended redemption payments for the peasants.

The liberals rejoiced at what they thought was to be the beginnings of constitutional government, but certain sections of the nobility and the Church, with the backing of the police, formed right-wing groups and intensely patriotic monarchist societies to uphold the traditional ideas of autocracy, orthodoxy and nationalism. These groups carried on bitter propaganda against the liberals, and the notorious 'Black Hundreds'—gangs of thugs—carried out political assassinations and pogroms against the Jews in support of their aims.

The October Manifesto succeeded in splitting the opposition, for those liberals who were satisfied with its proposals organized themselves as the Octobrist Party; others who hoped to go further and transform the Duma into a parliament on the English model formed the Constitutional Democratic Party—the Cadets. The socialists on the other hand wished to keep up the revolutionary struggle, and for a time strikes, riots, peasant risings and mutinies continued. In November the St Petersburg Soviet attempted to overthrow the Government by calling another general strike as a prelude to armed revolution, but the response was poor and, in December, the Government arrested the entire Soviet of 270 persons. The Moscow Soviet attempted to stage an insurrection, but this too was crushed by the Government. Riots and revolts continued until 1907, but by the end of 1905 Witte had succeeded in crushing the danger of a successful armed rising against the Government. The Soviets had made themselves exclusively working class and lost the support of the intellectuals, while the employers' lockouts and the activities of the Black Hundreds helped in crushing the revolts.

Witte, now a count as a reward for his services, was also Chairman of the Council of Ministers, a function formerly performed by the tsar himself, and he was in effect Prime Minister. Through 1906 he was concerned with the restoration of order by punitive expeditions and the task of introducing enough constitutional reform to win over those who wanted representative government without at the same time seriously diminishing the powers of the autocracy. As a first step to limiting the powers of the proposed Duma he negotiated, in April 1906, a loan from France of 2,000 million francs which would make the Government independent of the Duma on financial matters, and he next set about revising the fundamental laws of the empire to allow for the creation of an elected legislative assembly.

The Dumas

From 1906 Russia had the appearance of a monarchy working through an elected assembly, but in spite of the hopes of the liberals it was never anything like a constitutional monarchy as in Britain.

The Dumas were never meant to have anything but limited powers, and these were in fact successively limited still more. The State Council became an Upper House with half of its members appointed by the tsar, and the rest by the Church, the nobility, the zemstvos, the universities, the chambers of commerce and the trade associations. The Lower House, the Duma, was to be indirectly elected for five years on universal manhood suffrage, but the traditional three classes of voters were retained, and were weighted in favour of the nobility.

The Duma could initiate legislation, but it could not change the fundamental laws and the consent of both houses was necessary. The Upper House, which was bound to be conservative, could outvote the Lower, and the tsar had the right of veto. Article 87 of the fundamental laws enabled the Council of Ministers (the Cabinet) to issue legislation by emergency decree when the Duma was not in session, although both Houses had to approve it later. Ministers were appointed by the tsar and responsible to him, not to the Duma, and foreign affairs and important sections of the budget such as the army, navy and court estimates were not to be the concern of the Duma. The tsar could call, adjourn and dismiss the Duma, although he must provide for the next session; he remained in command of the army and navy with the right to declare war and sign treaties. In fact the tsar was still almost absolute, but for the first time, his powers had been defined, and Russia had come the nearest she was to know to parliamentary government.

The First Duma, May 1906

The first national elections in Russian history (March and April 1906) were preceded by a reassertion of the divine right of the autocracy from Nicholas. Most of the socialists boycotted the elections, so the field was clear for the liberals who were returned, after a vigorous campaign as the largest single group in the Duma. The strength of the opposition to the Government demonstrated during the election alarmed Nicholas, and Witte, who was held responsible, resigned. The first Duma achieved little, for its demands for reforms, and the assertion of the principle that ministers should be responsible to it, were directly contrary to the intentions of the Government. Stolypin was promoted from Minister of the Interior to Prime Minister, and Nicholas dissolved the Duma. The bulk of the liberals, in indignation, crossed the border to Viborg, in Finland, and from there, appealed to the people to refuse to pay taxes or to report for military service until another Duma was called. The appeals met with little response, the liberals had put themselves in the wrong, and they were automatically disqualified from taking their seats again.

The Second Duma, March–June 1907

The activities of the members of the first Duma confirmed all the worst fears of those who opposed constitutional reform, and pressure was put on Nicholas by the right-wing groups to limit the Duma's powers. Meanwhile, Stolypin was carrying out his work of trying to win over the peasants and crushing the opposition to the Government. There was a good deal of Government manipulation of the elections to the second Duma, but in spite of this, and because the majority of the liberals were excluded, the membership was more left wing in opinion than the first, and the demand for reform and criticism of the Government continued. The second Duma was dissolved in June.

The Third and Fourth Dumas, 1907–1912 and 1912–1917

Before the elections to the third Duma, Stolypin, using the powers of Article 87 of the fundamental laws, revised the electoral law to cut the representation of the workers, peasants and non-Russian peoples from whom most of the criticism came, in favour of the landowners and the Russian elements in the population. This abuse of its constitutional powers by the Government succeeded in the return of a Duma that was more docile and the third and fourth Dumas lasted their full five year periods. Even so, criticism of the Government continued, particularly, for example, of the influence of Rasputin at the court.

The fourth Duma was sitting when the 1917 Revolution began and its members formed the first provisional government.

The Work of the Dumas

The Dumas achieved little practical legislation, for only 34 of the 2,197 bills enacted by the Government in this period were initiated by the Lower House, but much was done for education and agriculture. Indirectly, in spite of its legal limitations the Duma was able to influence army and navy reforms through the budget, and it was the only legal organ that could criticize the Government. Its members gained legislative experience and a beginning, however reluctantly on the Government's part, had been made on constitutional reform.

P. A. Stolypin

Peter Stolypin (1862-1911) was a wealthy landowner who had given good service to the State as a provincial governor with a reputation for fairness and firmness when he was made Minister of the Interior and then Chairman of the Council of Ministers in 1906. He was conservative, and a supporter of tsarism, but he saw the need for necessary reforms, and followed a dual policy of suppressing the revolutionary activity after 1905 and winning over the peasantry by land reform. He took a firm line in dissolving the second Duma and in revising the electoral law, and his period of office was efficient and successful. By introducing reform he intended the Government to keep its power by taking the initiative from the Duma.

Revolutionaries and suspects were swiftly dealt with by field courts martial, which executed hundreds of persons between 1905 and 1908 and exiled thousands to Siberia, and the non-Russian population of the empire, particularly Poles, Jews and Finns, suffered from Great Russian persecution. Finland, which had regained some of her autonomy in 1905, had it restricted again in 1910.

In the hope of influencing the elections to the second Duma, Stolypin used Article 87 to introduce his first land law, which permitted peasants to claim their land in one piece from the mir and to work it as individual land-holders. The law was extended by the third Duma to overcome the opposition of the mirs and between 1906 and 1914 half the peasant families in Russia had claimed their land from the mir. The Government gave further help by providing loans and arranging surveys so that the division and consolidation of the communal lands could proceed. This was a necessary first step to making peasant agriculture more efficient and by creating a class of peasant landowners the Government was successful in winning some support. At the same time, about three million independent farmers were aided by the Government in establishing themselves in Siberia.

By 1914 one in every four peasant households had converted their communal holdings into personal property and one in ten had consolidated them. The outbreak of war checked the development of Stolypin's land reform: if it had been allowed to continue it is doubtful whether the Bolshevik revolution could have developed along the lines it did. Stolypin himself, of course, made many enemies; from the empress and the extreme right to the radicals and the revolutionaries who saw his success with the peasants depriving them of their own support. He was assassinated by a member of the S.R., who was also a police agent, in 1911.

Rasputin

Gregory Efimovich Novykh, nicknamed 'Rasputin', meaning dissolute, was the son of a Siberian horse dealer. After a youth spent in drunkenness and lechery he obtained a reputation as a wandering holy man with powers of healing and clairvoyancy. In 1905 he was introduced to the court and rapidly made important contacts which brought him to the notice of the empress. He was uneducated, filthy and disgusting in his personal habits, and spent his nights drinking and whoring, yet the society which he set out to humiliate flocked to him. His pose as a holy man recommended him to the empress, but the secret of his success was the power that he seemed to exercise over the tsarevich. What the doctors could not do, Gregory, or 'our friend', as he became to the empress, seemed to do, either by drugs or hypnotism, or by the sheer luck of coincidence. The empress's faith in him was unshakeable, and from about 1911 his influence at court grew until he was making and unmaking ministers and exercising control over the direction of the war. For the imperial family, cut off as it was from the realities of ordinary life, Rasputin represented their only contact with the peasantry and he, knowing that his power depended upon it, emphasized the need for maintaining the autocracy.

The manner of his death was as bizarre as his life. After the tsar had gone to the front in 1915, the direction of affairs at home was left to the empress, and Rasputin reigned supreme. The loathing for him personally, and the disasters that he and the empress were bringing on the State, led to his murder in 1916. The assassins were not socialists or revolutionaries, but members of the aristocracy who felt it necessary to save the monarchy from further scandal. Led by Prince Yusupov, a group of conspirators lured Rasputin to a cellar where he was given poisoned food and drink. To their horror he seemed to be unaffected, and Yusupov shot him. Even so, Rasputin rose before he was shot again and was kicked and beaten. The body was then wrapped in a bag made from a curtain and thrown in the River Neva; yet when it was recovered it was found that he had apparently gone on struggling after being thrown in the water. The empress was, of course, heartbroken, and Rasputin was buried at the royal palace at Tsarskoe Selo, but the body was exhumed and burned during the Revolution.

Domestic Policy: Summary

It has been said that revolutions occur, not when things are at their worst but when they begin to improve. This seems to be so for tsarist Russia. Thanks to the work of Witte and Stolypin, economic development made rapid progress; order had been restored after the 1905 revolution, the opposition to the Government had been divided, and a beginning, however grudgingly, had been made on constitutional reform. Russia now had a legislative assembly, which though grossly unrepresentative, could and did voice criticism and influence policy. Civil liberties had been granted in principle, even if they were frequently denied in practice. The peasants, or rather the 'sober and strong' among them, according to Stolypin's phrase, were on their way to becoming independent farmers with their own land.

The population had doubled in the second half of the nineteenth century: the peasants accounted for 85 per cent, and the majority of them were illiterate, backward, and living in poverty that amounted to starvation in the famine years of the 1890s. Two-thirds of them were unable to support themselves entirely from the land, and in their hunger for more land, it was the landowner's property that they regarded as theirs by right, and which they began to take in the years of revolution. The Government, by encouraging emigration to Siberia, and by Stolypin's reforms, sought with some success to allay this, and the zemstvos and dumas did much to provide elementary education, health services and agricultural improvements.

There was a remarkable increase in industrial production, and the development of the railways opened up new industrial areas such as the Donets Basin, the Krivoy Rog ironfield, oilfields in the Caucasus, cotton growing in Turkestan, and sugar beet and wheat in southern Russia.

Foreign investment, particularly French, Belgian and British, stimulated this progress, although it also often brought undesirable political affiliations. For the industrial workers, conditions were often grim, but they achieved a limited right to organize, and there was some amelioration of working conditions, hours, pay and insurance. In 1912 strikers in the Lena goldfields were shot down, and industrial strife was on the increase again by 1914, but the aims were more economic than political.

In fact the revolutionary movement seemed to be losing its strength when the outbreak of war and the economic breakdown which followed exposed the shortcomings of the tsarist system and gave the revolutionaries their opportunity.

Foreign Policy

The First World War of 1914–1918 marks the climax of nineteenth-century European history; for Russia it meant the end of a dynasty and the end of a system. Wars, it is said, breed revolutions, and in Nicholas's reign there were two of each. In the Far East, the weakness of the Chinese Empire provided opportunities for the imperialist ambitions of the European powers and the new power of Japan; for Russia it led to the disaster of the Russo-Japanese war and the 1905 revolution. In Europe, the weakness of the Turkish Empire led to conflicts in the Balkans among the great powers and to the schemes of the new power of Germany; for Russia it led to the war with Germany and Austria and the 1917 revolution.

Since the formation of the Triple Alliance between Germany, Austria and Italy in 1882, Europe had been divided between two armed camps, and this with the imperial rivalries throughout the world led to a series of international crises which culminated in war in 1914. Before that happened, important diplomatic changes took place: Germany, under Bismarck, the ally and chief trading partner of Russia was replaced by France in 1891; and Britain, Russia's major opponent in the nineteenth century, became her ally in 1907. Thus the powers of the Triple Entente faced those of the Triple Alliance.

In spite of military reforms after the Japanese War Russia was not ready for another war in 1914 and it was not Nicholas's fault that it came when it did—indeed at the beginning of his reign he had been instrumental in calling the Hague Peace Conferences; the first in 1899, and the second in 1907. Against the opposition of Germany they did nothing to stop the armaments race, but a permanent international court of arbitration was established at The Hague and certain conventions for the more humane conduct of war were adopted.

Russia's part in bringing on the war lay in the influence of the Pan

Slav movement, the anti-Austrian feeling that strengthened the support given to Serbia, and Nicholas's hesitancy in the face of advice on the necessity for mobilization given to him by his military advisers.

The Far East

Nicholas's interest in the Far East was, perhaps, stimulated by his tour as tsarevich in 1890; but he was surrounded by speculators and adventurers at court who hoped for railway, mining and timber concessions; by ministers like Witte, who had dreams of securing a monopoly of the China trade; and by nationalists who were convinced of Russia's civilizing mission in Siberia and the East. The latter were encouraged by the diplomacy of Germany, who wished to divert Russian interest away from the Balkans and eastern Europe.

The Treaty of Shimonoseki, which ended the Sino-Japanese War in 1895, gave Japan the Liao Tung Peninsula, Port Arthur, Formosa, the Pescadores, Wei Hei Wei, and an indemnity. The treaty also made Korea an independent kingdom, and in 1895 Russia and Japan agreed to respect it. Japan's success both alarmed Russia and encouraged her eastern ambitions. In 1896, on the initiative of Russia, Germany and France joined in forcing Japan to return the Liao Tung Peninsula to the Chinese, and Witte secured a loan from France to enable the Chinese to pay the indemnity. He also succeeded in bribing the Chinese trade minister to grant Russia, by a secret treaty of alliance against Japan, the right to build a railway through Manchuria with a branch line to Port Arthur. This it was intended would give Russia economic control over Manchuria.

Other European powers forced economic concessions from China, and in 1898 Russia demanded Port Arthur and the southern tip of the Liao Tung Peninsula 'as compensation'. Manchuria rapidly came under Russian domination, and the Japanese were understandably incensed and alarmed at the Russian actions, for similar ambitions became apparent in Korea which they regarded as 'a dagger pointing at the heart of Japan'. Attempts were made by the Japanese to get Russia to recognize their interests in Korea in return for a recognition of Russian interests in Manchuria, but Nicholas's courtiers were determined to have Korea as well.

In 1900 occurred the Boxer Rising, when intense anti-foreign feeling in China broke out in attacks on foreign legations in Pekin. The European powers affected sent troops to crush the rebellion and when it was over, the Russian troops remained in occupation of Manchuria, in spite of Japanese protests. Britain, in need of allies after her isolation during the Boer War, and alarmed for her China trade, made an alliance with

Japan in 1902, and strengthened by this, the Japanese felt able to seek revenge and challenge Russian ambitions in the Far East.

Witte was against war and resigned, but Nicholas, encouraged by men like Plehve and princely speculators with concessions on the Yalu River, was following his own foreign policy, independent of the foreign office. He appointed Admiral Alexeyev as Viceroy in the Far East and the infiltration of Russians into Korea began. In 1903 the Japanese asked the Russians to remove their troops from Manchuria and to recognize the Japanese interest in Korea. Russia would not agree and the war began with a Japanese attack on Port Arthur which immobilized the Russian Far East fleet.

THE FAR EAST AND THE RUSSO-JAPANESE WAR

The Russo-Japanese War, 1904–1905

At first the Russians were confident of victory and despised the Japanese but once again the war was a tragic story of incompetence, corruption and disaster. The troops in the Far East were inadequate in numbers, the Trans-Siberian Railway, single-tracked and incomplete, could not maintain supplies, and there was a general lack of interest at home in the war that had been begun so far away and without the consent of the people.

The Japanese had not the resources for a long war and had to gain control of the sea to ensure the safe transport of troops to Manchuria. Korea was occupied, Port Arthur was taken in January 1905, and in February, the Russians were beaten at the bloody Battle of Mukden. The Russians were forced to adopt delaying tactics by retreating until reinforcements could arrive, and eventually perhaps, they would have succeeded, but the revolution at home obliged Nicholas to accept the American offer of mediation which the Japanese, faced with a longer war than they had bargained for, also accepted. This was not before the crowning disaster and disgrace of the war, for it had been decided in October 1904 to send the Baltic fleet halfway round the world to Port Arthur. After an epic voyage, during which British fishing vessels on the Dogger Bank were fired on as suspected Japanese torpedo-boats, the Baltic fleet reached the Far East in April 1905, only to be sent to the bottom by Admiral Togo and the Japanese fleet in the Straits of Tsushima: twenty-three Russian ships were sunk, and only four reached Port Arthur; 4,830 Russians were killed, and only 110 Japanese. The results of the war were a setback to Russian ambitions in the Far East, a complete loss of prestige, and a stimulus to revolution at home.

The Treaty of Portsmouth (U.S.A.), September, 1905

Witte was sent to America with orders to cede no territory and to agree to no indemnities: for the representative of the defeated party he did remarkably well in the terms he achieved. Russia renounced all interest in Korea, and gave up her rights in the Liao Tung Peninsula, Port Arthur, and in the South Manchurian Railway. She had to evacuate Manchuria, and the Japanese obtained the southern half of Sakhalin Island and fishing rights north of Vladivostok.

In 1907 and 1912 there were further agreements by which Russia and Japan agreed on the division of Manchuria into spheres of interest and Russia gained a free hand in Outer Mongolia. Japan annexed Korea in 1910.

Mongolia

The Chinese revolution in 1911 was an opportunity for advance in Mongolia. The Mongols, with Russian aid, revolted against their Chinese masters and Outer Mongolia declared its independence. A Russian-Mongolian treaty was signed in 1912 that confirmed Russian privileges, and although a treaty was made between Russia and China in 1913 that recognized Outer Mongolia as independent, it remained in effect a vassal state of Russia.

Relations with France

Nicholas inherited the entente with France made by his father in 1891. It provided for mutual consultation on international affairs and for mutual support in time of war and was followed by military conventions and agreements. Thereafter, French loans poured into Russia, which gained economically, but politically it often meant that Russia was obliged to give support to France against her own interests, for example, in pursuing an anti-German policy and a tariff war when Germany was Russia's best trading partner.

The link with France was the main theme in Russian foreign affairs from 1890 to 1917: it was used by Witte to obtain loans by giving France diplomatic support, notably at the Algeciras Conference, and it could be used against the central powers Austria and Germany, but on balance, Russia was made to serve French interests against her own.

Rapprochement with Britain

Throughout the nineteenth century Britain had been opposed to Russia, partly through dislike of the Russian system of government, and partly through fear that Russian expansion towards Constantinople and in Asia would threaten Britain's own imperial interests, especially in India. In Russia, official dislike of Britain had been constant, even while the liberals had hoped to gain a parliamentary system on the British model. In the early twentieth century, Germany represented a bigger threat to British as well as Russian interests, and the apparent liberalization of the Russian Government after 1906 helped to soften British feeling. British control of the Suez Canal also made the strategic position of Constantinople of less significance to the control of her imperial communications, and there was considerable British investment in Russian industry.

In 1907, Britain and Russia came to an understanding about disputed spheres of interest in Persia, Afghanistan, and Tibet. Both countries agreed to keep out of Tibet; Russia recognized British interests in Afghanistan; and Persia was divided into a northern zone for Russia, a southern zone for Britain, and a no-man's-land in between. Thus the alliance between Russia and France of 1891 and the entente between Britain and France of 1904 now became the Triple Entente of Russia, France and Britain.

Relations with Germany

The alliance between Russia and Germany was traditional, and dissolved only when it was realized that Germany could not continue to support both Russia and Austria when their interests conflicted in the Balkans. In spite of Bismarck's efforts, it was evident at the Congress of Berlin in 1878 that Russia could not depend on German support against Austria. The Dreikaiserbund was renewed in 1881 but could not succeed, and expired in 1887. Bismarck's last attempt to keep Russian friendship was the secret Reinsurance Treaty of 1887, but this, too, expired when Bismarck was dismissed in 1890.

Even though distrust of Germany and the need for loans forced Russia and France together, attempts were made to limit the dependency on France, and it was of course a major aim of German policy to break the alliance. Gestures towards maintaining good relations with Germany continued, and Kaiser William II gave support to Russian schemes in the Far East. There was a steady exchange of correspondence, and in 1905 the two emperors met at Björkö, where William persuaded Nicholas to accept a Russian-French-German alliance against Britain, but it was repudiated by both their foreign ministers, and William's attempts to keep France and Russia apart were abortive.

German ambitions in the Turkish Empire alarmed Russia which had a particular interest there, but in 1910 at Potsdam, Russia agreed to the German scheme for a railway from Constantinople to Baghdad in return for German recognition of Russian interests in Persia. This accord was broken when in 1913 the Sultan appointed a German military mission under General Liman von Sanders to reorganize the Turkish army. Russia, France and Britain protested to the Sultan, and Liman von Sander's official post was changed from 'Commander of the First Army Corps at Constantinople', to 'Inspector-General of the Turkish Army'. This was a device to ensure the continuance of German influence while removing the appearance of having a German garrison at Constantinople.

The Eastern Question

It was events in the Balkans that provided the immediate causes of the First World War. The weakness of the Turkish Empire, the championship of the orthodox faith and of the Pan Slav movement were a constant stimulus to the age-old Russian dream of seizing Constantinople. Austria, driven from Germany by Prussia in 1866, and encouraged to look elsewhere was pursuing her 'drang nach Osten' down the Danube valley and into the Balkans. Germany had dreams of building a railway from Berlin to Baghdad that would give her economic domination in the Turkish Empire and would rival British control of the sea communications with the East. The Balkan states themselves were afire with nationalist aspirations and every local crisis was magnified into an international event by the groupings of the great powers in the Triple Alliance and the Triple Entente.

At the beginning of his reign Nicholas was talked into approving a mad scheme to seize the Bosporus, put forward by his ambassador at Constantinople, but fortunately for the peace of Europe he was talked out of it again. For the time being Austria and Russia had an understanding to maintain the status quo in the Balkans and Nicholas's attentions were occupied by events at home and in the Far East.

After 1905 Austro-Russian rivalry in the Balkans began a new phase. Both countries had foreign ministers (Aehrenthal in Austria and Izvolsky in Russia) who were determined to push their respective interests. In 1903 the pro-Austrian rulers in Serbia had been replaced by the pro-Russian Karageorgeovitch family and Austria feared the extension of Serbian influence backed by Russia, among the millions of Slavs living in the Austrian Empire.

When the Young Turks revolted in 1908 the disturbances were an opportunity for the ambitions of the great powers. It was agreed at Buchlau that Austria should annex Bosnia and Herzegovina, which she had occupied since 1878, and that Russia should seek to revise the Straits Convention. Austria annexed the provinces immediately, but Russia could not get the general agreement to the freeing of the straits to Russian shipping. This produced the Bosnian crisis of 1908, for Serbia regarded the provinces as legitimately hers, and would have made war on Austria if she had been more sure of Russian support. Germany supported Austria, and Russia, angry at Austrian trickery, but unready for war, had to give way. It was not, however, the end of the matter.

Izvolsky was replaced by Sazonov who planned to strengthen the Balkan states and weaken the Austrian and Turkish Empires. Under his guidance was formed the Balkan League of Serbia, Bulgaria, Greece, and Montenegro. In 1912, to the amazement of Europe, the League waged successful war on the Turks and drove them almost out of the Balkans. But when it came to dividing the spoils Austria refused to permit Serbia to gain access to the coast and by way of compensation she attempted to recompense herself at the expense of Bulgaria. In a second war, Bulgaria fought her former allies and the Turks stepped in and recovered much of what they had lost. The result of the Balkan Wars for Russia was that Bulgaria looked to Austria and Germany for support, Serbia and Rumania looked to Russia, and Austria and Turkey were more anti-Russian than ever.

The final crisis came over Serbia which Russia felt as bound to support as Austria was determined to humble. On 28 June 1914, the heir to the Austrian throne was assassinated by a Serbian nationalist at Sarajevo. An Austrian ultimatum to Serbia was followed by a declaration of war. Russia mobilized hesitantly and Germany mobilized in return. On 1 August, Germany declared war on Russia, and Austria did so three days later. France assured Russia of support; Germany declared war on France on 3 August; and next day Britain declared war on Germany.

The 1914 War

The outbreak of war stimulated an outburst of patriotic fervour in defence of Mother Russia and for the support of Slavs elsewhere. In the Duma, a sacred union of all parties except the S.D.s was formed. Only the Bolsheviks[1] opposed the war and for their own reasons. But Russia was not ready: there was no provision for putting the economy on a wartime basis, there was no financial stability, and communications were inadequate. There had been some improvements in the army since 1905, but it was inferior in arms, supplies and equipment; there were, for example, only sixty artillery batteries to Germany's 381. There was a standing army of one-and-a-half million men, with three million on the reserve, and eventually something like fifteen million men were mobilized during the war, but they were in general, pitifully equipped, often without arms or medical services.

The plans were sound, but not well co-ordinated: (1) to relieve pressure on France by attacking Germany through East Prussia, and (2) to attack Austria via Galicia. At the same time, it was necessary to defend Russia against the Turks and to ensure that Japan did not join in in the Far East. The Grand Duke Nicholas was a competent Commander-in-Chief who earned the respect of the Germans.

Both sides attempted to enlist Polish sympathies: the Austrians by allowing Pilsudski to form a legion to fight the Russians and promising self-government after the war; the Russians by promising local self-government and religious freedom under Russian rule. Naturally the Poles hoped to gain complete political independence for a restored Poland after the war. The Slavs in south-east Europe in general looked to Russia for liberation from Austria as a prelude to their own national independence, but Bulgaria joined the central powers. Turkey, after some negotiation with Russia, also threw in her lot with Germany.

At first the Russian armies were successful: in the north their advance alarmed the Germans who sent Hindenburg to the eastern front. The

[1] See chapter XVI.

Battle of Tannenberg in August drove the Russians from East Prussia with the loss of 170,000 men, but the Germans were obliged to withdraw forces from the western front and France was saved at the Battle of the Marne. In the south, the Austrians drove into Russian Poland from Galicia, but they were defeated in a Russian counter-attack, and by September all Galicia was in Russian hands. The German attack on Warsaw was held, but the Russians failed to follow up their advantage when the Germans retreated and the winter checked activities for the time being. In the south, a Turkish attack in Trans-Caucasia was held, but Turkish and German control was established over the Black Sea.

The winter campaign against Austria continued with a steady advance, and in March 1915 the Russians crossed the Carpathians, entered Hungary, and took the key Galician fortress of Przemsyl and 120,000 men. In May, however, an Austro-German offensive under Mackensen destroyed the Russian forces and drove them out of Galicia. In the summer of 1915, a second Austro-German offensive, with the Germans attacking south from East Prussia, and the Austrians north from Galicia, forced the Russians out of Poland, Courland and Lithuania. The Grand Duke Nicholas made a good retreat to the line of Riga, Vilna, Pinsk, Tarnopol, but the Germans were content with control of Poland, for they regarded the western front as more important and did not want too many troops on the eastern front. Thus although the homeland was not invaded, the year 1915 was one of defeat for Russia. The allied attempt to force the Dardanelles in March 1915 was a fiasco, the Serbs were defeated in September, and the Balkans, as well as eastern Europe, were in the hands of the central powers. Russian losses were tremendous: their own estimates were 3,800,000 men in the first ten months of the war. The Grand Duke Nicholas, frustrated by personal intrigues, incompetent officers, inadequate supplies and general confusion, was replaced by the emperor himself, who assumed the supreme command in September. This was a disastrous decision, since it left the conduct of home affairs to the empress and Rasputin, while the emperor could now be personally identified with the conduct of the war.

In 1916 the allies planned a summer offensive in the west and Russia, at Chantilly in December 1915, agreed to mount an offensive in the east at the same time. The eastern front had remained fairly stable since 1915 for the Germans were concentrating on the west and the Austrians had to deal with Italy who had changed sides in May 1915. Meanwhile, Britain, France, the United States and Japan sent supplies to meet the desperate shortage of ammunition in Russia. Some regiments had no rifles, and the artillery was rationed to four shells a day.

In May, the Italians appealed for help, and Brusilov began his offensive along a 300-mile front. The Austrians were defeated, and once more the Germans had to come to their aid, but not before Brusilov had taken 450,000 prisoners, many of them deserters from the Austrian army. In spite of the great cost in men and material no further gains were made. The Rumanians entered the war at this stage, but were defeated, and the Germans were soon in Bucharest. This exposed the front in the south-west and was an extra drain on Russian resources. 1916 thus ended in stalemate on the eastern front, but once more the Russian action had brought much needed relief to the west.

In 1917 Brusilov made another offensive to aid the allies in the west: he was successful against the Austrians but was routed by the Germans. By this time, however, the armies were dissolving and the country was on the verge of revolution.

Wartime Diplomacy

Russia's aims were: to maintain the alliance with Britain and France and to enlist further allies where possible, to safeguard the Far East, and to provide for a division of the spoils when the war ended. Unfortunately, it lasted longer than anticipated and as new allies came in, the division of the spoils became more complicated, while the Bolshevik triumph in the 1917 revolution upset all previous calculation.

The conduct of the war illustrates how Russian interests were constantly sacrificed to the French alliance; the drives to the west brought relief to France but at great cost and no gain to Russia. In London in September 1914, Britain, France and Russia agreed not to make a separate peace. Had it not been for loyalty to the alliance, Russia could probably have made peace on favourable terms on more than one occasion during the war. The Bolsheviks were not bound by tsarist promises and made peace immediately. In 1916 a secret treaty was made with Japan confirming the status quo in the Far East, Russia played her part in persuading Italy to change sides, and in deference to France, in bringing Rumania into the war, although it was realized that she was more useful as a neutral than as an ally. In March 1915 it was agreed to partition the Turkish Empire: Britain was to let Russia have Constantinople and the straits in return for the neutral zone in Persia. At last the great prize of Russian foreign policy was within reach—but the war had to be won first.

The Home Front

The surge of national unity at the outbreak of the war did not survive the defeats and the disorganization that followed. It was replaced by a drop in morale, apathy, and then revolt. Troops deserted and joined the strikers at home. The blockade brought foreign trade to a standstill, although this did mean that more goods should have been available at home. The internal economy collapsed through lack of organization and faulty distribution more than lack of production, although this too was severely disrupted by an unselective call up, and the fact that peasants who could not obtain manufactured goods withheld food supplies. The transport system was inadequate and incompetently run, while strategic railways in the south-west and west were lost. Food and fuel shortages became acute in the cities, prices rose, and discontent manifested itself in mounting strikes, riots and rebellions in the non-Russian parts of the Empire.

Government planning, unprepared for a long war, was uncoordinated. The western provinces were placed under military rule and compulsory evacuation of the civilian population and refugees brought chaos, disease, and discontent to the provinces further east. The zemstvos and dumas that were organizing voluntary medical aid and supplies were forbidden at first from doing so, for fear that the powers of the central government would be weakened. The Duma was called only for a one-day session in August 1914, and for three days in February 1915, the Government preferring to legislate by Article 87. The discontent and criticism became so strong in 1915 that Nicholas reorganized the Government to deal with the munitions shortage and called a Duma for August. Although its members were conservative, they demanded more popular representation in the administration and the opposition formed itself into the Progressive Bloc. The Duma was adjourned in September sine die.

Nicholas and the empress seemed impervious to all warnings. He was probably happy amid his military advisers at the front, but at home, plots and intrigues continued at the court, where Rasputin and the empress were appointing and dismissing ministers and altering policies with bewildering rapidity.

QUESTIONS

1. To what extent were Nicholas II and the empress personally responsible for the revolution in 1917?
2. Compare Nicholas II of Russia with either (a) Charles I of England; or (b) Louis XVI of France.
3. Discuss the services rendered to Nicholas II by (a) Witte and (b) Stolypin.
4. Give an account of the 1905 Revolution under the headings: (a) Causes; (b) Course; (c) Results.

5. To what extent did the Dumas give Russia a constitutional monarchy?

6. Trace the development of political parties in Russia.

7. Give an account of the Russo-Japanese War, 1904–1905 under the headings: (*a*) Causes; (*b*) Course; (*c*) Results.

8. Discuss the consequences for Russia of the French alliance.

9. How did Russia become involved in the First World War?

10. Discuss either (*a*) how domestic events limited the successful prosecution of the war, or (*b*) how the conduct of the war influenced the 1917 Revolution.

11. Find out what you can and make notes on the following: the murder of the tsar and his family; Pobedonostsev; Plehve; Father Gapon; the mutiny on the *Potemkin*; P. Milyukov; the St Petersburg Soviet 1905; the Black Hundreds; the French loans to Russia; Stolypin's land reforms; Rasputin; the Chinese Eastern Railway; the Battle of Mukden; the Battle of Tsushima; the Björkö meeting, 1905; the Pan Slav movement; the Bosnian crisis, 1908; the Balkan Wars, 1912–1913; the Grand Duke Nicholas; Pilsudski; the Battle of Tannenberg; the Dardanelles campaign; Brusilov.

Further Reading

ALMEDINGEN, E. M. *The Empress Alexandra: 1872–1918.* Hutchinson, 1961.

CHARQUES, R. D. *The Twilight of Imperial Russia: The Reign of Tsar Nicholas II.* Phoenix House, 1958.

FLORINSKY, M. T. *The End of the Russian Empire.* Oxford U.P., 1931.

FRANKLAND, N. *Crown of Tragedy: Nicholas II.* Kimber, 1960.

HOUGH, R. *The Fleet that had to Die.* Hamish Hamilton, 1958 and Four Square Books, 1961.

HOUGH, R. *The Potemkin Mutiny.* Hamish Hamilton, 1960.

MAYNARD, J. *Russia in Flux.* Gollancz, 1941.

PARES, SIR B. *The Fall of the Russian Monarchy.* Cape, 1939.

SETON-WATSON, H. *The Decline of Imperial Russia, 1855–1914.* New edn., Methuen, 1952.

TROYAT, H. *Daily life in Russia under the last Tsar,* trans. M. Barnes. Allen and Unwin, 1961.

Part Two

INTRODUCTION

The year 1917 may be seen by future historians as one of the great turning points in history, not only for the Russian people, but for the world.

A handful of determined men, absolutely convinced of the rightness of their ideas, with great audacity and much good luck, exploited the revolutionary situation which existed, and which they had helped to create, to seize political power and to develop something new in the conception of social and political organization.

It was not to be just a change of government, but a radical new approach to the very nature of government and the exercise of power within the State. Marxism provided a new scientific and philosophic ideology for the ends and means of human society. The Bolsheviks, on this basis, set out to create a Utopia here on earth and to remould the very nature of the beings who were to dwell in it. Consequently, it is not possible to appreciate the significance of events within the U.S.S.R. without some understanding of socialist and Marxist ideas, and above all, of the role of the Communist Party as the vanguard of the revolution.

This must be borne constantly in mind when reading the narrative of domestic and foreign affairs. For a few years after 1917 the Bolsheviks lived in anticipation of a general world revolution when the people would rise against their oppressors and begin building socialism from below. The expected revolution did not come about, and with the failure of the German revolution and the rise to power of Stalin, there came the decision to build socialism in one country. The party would have to take the lead in imposing socialism from above. This is the significance of Stalin's second revolution—the forced collectivization of agriculture and the five year plans.

Nor must it be thought that politics in the U.S.S.R. are conducted on the same basis, or by the same standards, as in the so-called western democracies. In external affairs, Moscow is the centre of a world-wide political movement with a mission to spread its creed by any and every means, and certain of its ultimate triumph. In internal affairs, the Communist Party is concerned to extend its control over every aspect of national life; from the Government, the learned associations, the trade unions, down to the smallest sports and social club. Private expressions of opinion in the arts or in literature are no more permissible than are individual political opinions. Everything in public life must have an 'official' character as laid down by the party line.

The disillusion in the minds of many who welcomed the early idealism of the Russian revolution has been bitterly expressed in George Orwell's *Animal Farm*.

The stultifying effect of the stranglehold exerted by the party on national life was such that some kind of reaction was inevitable after Stalin's death. It has been Khrushchev's task to reconstruct Stalin's authoritarian edifice, giving it a new look more in line with the realities of the postwar world, while retaining the essential foundations of Marxism and the structure of the party leadership.

Lastly, in spite of the certainty of Marxist dogma and the authority exerted by the party, allowance must be made for what H. A. L. Fisher called 'the play of the contingent and the unforeseen'. The party found itself faced with problems that could not have been predicted in 1917 and it might be held by a non-Marxist that chance events and personalities can play as important a part in history as the operation of economic forces.

Lookin' for action?
call JANICE: 897-6563
(OR YOUR MONEY back)

CHAPTER XV

THE DEVELOPMENT OF EUROPEAN SOCIALISM

The term socialism suggests a complicated body of political and economic beliefs and principles together with emotional and moral attitudes that have led to great differences and indeed violent antagonisms between different kinds of socialists. Just as there are many Christian sects and churches with one claiming to be the true universal church so there are many distinct socialist groups: the British Labour Party, Social Democrats, Christian Socialists, Communists, Anarchists, Syndicalists, etc., with the Marxists claiming the certainty of the universal validity of their views.

While they vary considerably in their aims and the means they would adopt to achieve them, what they have in common is opposition to the great inequalities in wealth and the opportunities for the rich and privileged to exploit the labour of their less privileged fellow men which they believe the competitive economic system of private enterprise leads to. They would limit, or abolish, the right to hold private property, substituting public ownership of all the means of production, distribution and exchange; State control and planning of the economic system would replace competition, and equal opportunities for all men would lead to a happier state for the majority of mankind.

In this sense socialist ideas can be traced back to ancient times. Plato prescribed a form of communal society for his guardians in the *Republic* and there is much in the teaching of the Christian Church relating to man's relations with his fellows that is socialism without the political implications. Indeed the only truly communal societies that have been successfully established are the monasteries. Yet socialism, more strictly, means a body of ideas that men attempt to put into practice through political action. If they wish to change the social and economic order they must first gain political power directly or indirectly to do so.

In this sense socialism is a product of the late eighteenth and the nineteenth centuries. Two great historical events provided the conditions for the evolution of European socialism; the Industrial Revolution and the French Revolution. It was the great social and economic changes brought about by the Industrial Revolution which led to the growth of factories and towns, with their industrial working classes living and working in conditions of squalor and hardship, and yet at the same time creating vast new wealth which all too clearly was most unevenly distributed. At the same time the concentration of large numbers of discontented persons in the towns and factories made it possible to organize them in effective groups to make their demands known.

The French Revolution drew attention to the ideas of Liberty, Equality, Fraternity and the Rights of Man that were in turn the product of eighteenth-century Enlightenment and of the Romantic Movement. The French Revolution also provided a practical demonstration of revolt against the established order and gave valuable lessons for future revolutionary movements.

The early socialists were mostly French and English. Later in the nineteenth century Germany was the centre of European socialism while developments in Russia since 1917 have made Moscow the third Rome in more senses than one. Marx referred to the French and English socialists as Utopians in contrast with the scientific socialists who based their ideas on historical materialism. Until the development of large-scale national and international socialist organizations in the later nineteenth century the history of socialism is largely the story of the lives and ideas of individual socialists and their followers; of their rivalries and their experiments.

FRANCOIS NOËL BABEUF nicknamed 'Gracchus' (1760–1797), was one of the first to propose socialism as a practical policy. He formed the Société des Egaux in 1797, declaring that 'Nature has given to every man the right to the enjoyment of an equal share in all property.' He believed in the socialization of land and industry in order to abolish riches and poverty. Everyone had a right to education and a duty to work.

CLAUDE HENRI, COMTE DE ST SIMON (1760–1825), was one of the first to claim that history was a story of class struggles and to stress the importance of the economic factor. He believed that everything should be done to improve the lot of the poorest section of society and that to do this State planning was necessary. All the means of production should belong to a social fund and the State should appoint business experts to run the economy and avoid the present wasteful system.

Property as such would not be abolished, but the laws of inheritance would be put in order to prevent unfair and undeserved accumulations of wealth.

ROBERT OWEN (1771–1858), was the first Englishman who could be called a socialist although the way had been prepared by the ideas of the philosopher William Godwin, and Thomas Spence who had advocated nationalization of the land. Owen was a wealthy cotton manufacturer who was convinced that it paid to look after his workers by providing schools and improved living and working conditions for them. He was obsessed with the belief that character is the product of environment and education, and that what was necessary for human happiness was a change in the environment. He also experimented unsuccessfully with model communities, trade unions and cooperatives. After the failure of Owen's schemes the English working classes gave their attention to the Chartist Movement.

FRANCOIS MARIE CHARLES FOURIER (1772–1837), believed that it was possible for human beings to develop a 'Harmony of Passions' if they could be free of the restraints imposed by society, and that society must be reconstructed to permit this. It was not necessary to abolish private property but all land and natural resources should be held in common and society should be organized (voluntarily, not by State action) in cooperative communities known as 'phalanges' consisting of 1,600 persons. Much of this was Utopian nonsense, but Fourier did draw attention to the evils and inadequacies of the laissez-faire economic system.

LOUIS AUGUSTE BLANQUI (1805–1881), spent forty years of his life in prison as a result of his revolutionary activities. He saw that a successful revolution was only to be accomplished by a body of professionals and was the first to advocate a dictatorship of the proletariat.

PIERRE JOSEPH PROUDHON (1809–1865), was the founder of anarchism, an extreme form of socialism based on opposition to all forms of external authority on individual action. He was not opposed to property so much as to the State and to collectivism. He believed in Justice, Liberty and Equality and advocated what was termed 'mutuellisme'. It was he who drew attention to the power that the possession of property and capital gave to those who had it to exploit the labour of those who had not, and coined the phrase the 'exploitation of man by man'. In 1840 he published his work *Qu'est-ce que la Propriété?* and provided his own answer, 'La Propriété, c'est le vol'.

LOUIS BLANC (1811–1882), attributed the evils of society to competition and advocated State control of industry. He saw that reform could only come through the State, therefore the reformers must gain political power. He wanted public ownership with the workers in control, and a democratic parliamentary system. In 1848 he set up a short-lived system in Paris very like the soviets that were later set up in Russia. He was the originator of the phrase, 'à chacun selon ses besoins, de chacun selon ses facultés'.

MIKHAIL BAKUNIN (1818–1876), was among the first Russians to take an active part in European socialism. He was one of the most remarkable personalities of the period: he clashed with Marx, who had him expelled from the International, and succeeded Proudhon as the leading anarchist. The State-centralized socialism advocated by Marx seemed to be worse than the tyranny of the existing system. He wished to destroy the State as an organ of oppression by revolutionary action.

FERDINAND LASSALLE (1825–1864), was responsible for forming the first effective socialist party in Germany: the Allgemeine Deutsche Arbeitverein, in 1863.

KARL HEINRICH MARX, 1818–1883

Without question Karl Marx ranks as one of those men whose ideas have transformed and entered into every aspect of social and political life.

Marx was born at Trier, where his father, a Christian Jew, was a lawyer of enlightened and patriotic views. Karl was educated at Trier and then went to Bonn in 1835, and to Berlin in 1836 to study law. All the German universities at that time were under the influence of Hegel's philosophic ideas and Marx was so affected by them that he gave up law and took up philosophy with the intention of following an academic career. The death of his father and the ending of his financial support meant that Marx had to change his mind and he accepted an invitation to write for the *Rheinische Zeitung*, a radical newspaper of which he soon became editor. The Prussian Government was very repressive and anti-liberal, and Marx, at this time a liberal idealist, pursued a violently anti-Government policy. The paper was suppressed in 1843, and Marx, with his newly-wed wife, went to Paris where he met most of the French socialists as well as his life-long collaborator, Friedrich Engels (1820–1895), and Mikhail Bakunin (1818–1876).

In his controversies with the Prussian Government Marx had realized his ignorance of economics and economic history and he set himself the task of mastering these subjects. He read omnivorously and by 1848 he had worked out his system. He also set out to study why the French Revolution had failed and how another failure might be prevented next time. In addition to the influence of the French socialists he also at this time was much affected by the writings of Ludwig

Feuerbach (1804–1872), a German philosopher who claimed that ideas and religious beliefs are a product of environment; that 'Man is what he eats', and that 'It is not thought that determines Being, but Being Thought'.

Marx became editor of the *Deutsch-Französicher Jahrbücher*, but in 1845, owing to pressure from the Prussian Government he was expelled from Paris and went to Brussels where he continued his work of reading, writing, organizing and preparing for the coming revolution. In 1847 an international Communist League was set up and Marx and Engels produced a programme for it. This was the *Communist Manifesto* published in 1848.

The Communist Manifesto

This is one of the most important revolutionary pamphlets ever written and contains the kernel of Marx's ideas. The manifesto declares that the spectre of Communism is haunting Europe and that it is time that the party published its views and aims. It begins with the statement that 'the history of all hitherto existing society is the history of class struggles', and goes on to develop the fundamental Marxist propositions:

that in every historical epoch, the prevailing mode of economic production and exchange, and the social organization necessarily following from it, form the basis upon which is built up, and from which alone can be explained, the political and intellectual history of that epoch; that consequently the whole history of mankind (since the dissolution of primitive tribal society, holding land in common ownership) has been a history of class struggles, contests between exploiting and exploited, ruling and oppressed classes; that the history of these class struggles form a series of evolutions in which, nowadays, a stage has been reached where the exploited and oppressed class—the proletariat—cannot attain its emancipation from the sway of the exploiting and ruling class—the bourgeoisie—without, at the same time, and once and for all emancipating society at large from all exploitation, oppression, class distinctions and class struggles.

The suggested programme was as follows:

1. Abolition of property in land and application of all rents to public purposes.
2. A heavy progressive or graduated income tax.
3. Abolition of all right of inheritance.
4. Confiscation of the property of all emigrants and rebels.
5. Centralization of credit in the hands of the State, by means of a national bank with State capital and an exclusive monopoly.

6. Centralization of the means of communication and transport in the hands of the State.

7. Extension of factories and instruments of production owned by the State: the bringing into cultivation of waste lands, and the improvement of the soil generally in accordance with a common plan.

8. Equal obligation of all to work. Establishment of industrial armies, especially for agriculture.

9. Combination of agriculture with manufacturing industries; gradual abolition of the distinction between town and country, by a more equable distribution of the population over the country.

10. Free education for all children in public schools. Abolition of children's factory labour in its present form. Combination of education with industrial production, etc.

The *Manifesto* ends by defiantly declaring that:

The Communists disdain to conceal their views and aims. They openly declare that their ends can be attained only by the forcible overthrow of all existing social conditions. Let the ruling classes tremble at a Communist revolution. The proletarians have nothing to lose but their chains. They have a world to win. Working men of all countries, unite.

In 1848 Louis Philippe's government was overthrown in France; Marx was expelled from Brussels and went to Paris at the invitation of the socialists. From there he went to Cologne, restarted the *Rheinische Zeitung* and continued his political agitation. The paper was suppressed and Marx was arrested and tried for sedition but was acquitted. Nevertheless he was expelled from the Rhineland and returned to Paris. The Government did not welcome him there so he went to England in 1849 where he remained until his death in 1883.

The 1848 revolutions were a failure and Marx spent the rest of his life, much of it in great poverty and hardship, studying, writing, disputing especially with Lassalle and Bakunin, organizing and directing the forces that were intended to lead to the destruction of that very society that was giving him shelter and providing him with his material.

In 1864 the first International Working Mens' Association was formed and Marx took charge until it collapsed through its own divisions in 1876. Marx's major work, *Das Kapital*, volume I, was published in 1867. The later volumes were published after Marx's death by Engels (in 1885 and 1894).

Personal Character

Marx was a student and a prophet; his life was spent in reading, writing and preaching with an intensity and a single-mindedness that can rarely have been equalled. In his family and small circle of friends he inspired love and affection; to his opponents he was a bitter and jealous enemy, determined to dominate at all costs.

He once played the game of confessions with his children and his answers have the ring of truth:

Favourite virtue: simplicity.
Favourite virtue in Man: strength.
Chief characteristic: singleness of purpose.
Idea of happiness: to fight.
Idea of misery: submission.
Favourite occupation: bookworming.
Heroes: Kepler and Spartacus. (Spartacus led a slave revolt and Kepler conceived a new view of the universe as Marx did of history.)

MARXISM

Marx continued and brilliantly rounded off the three main currents of nineteenth century thought, the currents that flowed in the three most advanced countries in the world: classical German philosophy; classical British political economy; and French socialism.

Lenin

Marxism is the term given to the ideas of Karl Marx and Friedrich Engels and as developed by their followers. These are contained in their writings, especially in the *Communist Manifesto* and in *Das Kapital* but they are sometimes so open to interpretations which Marx did not define adequately that late in his life he declared that he was not a 'Marxist' himself.

It is possible to separate Marxism into three sections:

1. A philosophy of History known as Historical Materialism;
2. A system of economic thought;
3. A theory of the State and revolution.

1. The Philosophy of History

Hegel saw history as a continuous process which should be studied so that we can understand our present condition. Marx took the dialectical process which Hegel used and claimed to be able to predict the way that history would develop. Hegel's interpretation of the dialectical process was that for every given situation, or thesis, there is its opposite, or antithesis, and out of the conflict of these opposites, taking the best features of each will emerge a new situation or synthesis which in turn will be confronted as a new thesis with its own antithesis. Thus the process of history continues, always improving, until the absolute will be reached free of all contradictions. This dialectical process is governed by its own laws.

Marx claimed to have turned Hegel upside down, or rather right way up. He rejected Hegel's theory of ideas but took his dialectical method and added to it his views on scientific materialism.

For Hegel it was ideas that ruled the world, but Marx claimed that it was not ideas that brought about social change, but the prevailing methods of production of which ideas and morality are the result. Man must eat before he has time and leisure to think. His first concern is the production and exchange of goods, but since some men get control of the means of production, and classes are created when those who own the means of production control the labour of those who do not, all history becomes the history of class struggles, while the prevailing ideas at any time are the ideas only of the ruling class.

It must be remembered that Marx was a revolutionary: he was determined to upset the existing order of society. He lived at a time when the evil effects of the Industrial Revolution were most evident and before the development of powerful forces like modern nationalism and the idea of the welfare state. For him the dialectical process, based on apparently scientific principles, gave certainty to his views, which saw history as an inevitable process leading from the feudal thesis to the capitalist antithesis, and on to the socialist synthesis when the contradictions in society would be eliminated, there would be only one class, the proletariat, and eventually the State would wither away when true Communism was established.

Criticism

To anyone not already a convinced Marxist this interpretation of history is subject to considerable doubt. All too clearly it seems that once the theory has been affirmed the 'proof' is arrived at by a careful selection of convenient facts to support it. Although the economic factor is clearly very important in history and Marx's chief contribution to historical writing is the stress which he laid upon it, it is by no means true that the economic factor is the overriding motive in human actions. Nor does Marx seem to have been aware of other equally potent forces, such as nationalism, or the operation of chance in history. His own life, and that of Lenin for example, seem to illustrate the effect which one man's ideas and actions can have upon the course of history—another factor that he denied was important. In reducing the historical process to the operation of scientific laws, and in particular the war between the classes he is guilty of oversimplifying what is in fact an immeasurably complicated interaction of human desires and activities.

2. Marxist Economics

Marx's economic theories really amount to two main ideas:

(a) *the labour theory of value* which holds that the value of a commodity consists solely of a measure of the labour that has gone into producing it and by implication that the labourer alone is entitled to the reward due it;

(b) *the theory of surplus value* which holds that the worker is paid the minimum necessary to keep him alive and that the difference between the value of the wages paid to him and the price paid for the commodity is the surplus value which goes as profit to the employer. It is a measure of the degree of exploitation of the workers by the employers.

Marx went on to formulate certain laws from these theories which showed that capital would accumulate, but the number of capitalists would decline, and as they struggled to survive, the lot of the working classes would become more and more wretched until eventually they would rise and overthrow their oppressors.

Developments in the past hundred years have disproved Marx's assertions. The growth of joint stock companies has dispersed the ownership of capital, the middle classes have increased in numbers, the standard of living of the working classes has improved, the idea of the welfare state and public control have replaced laissez-faire economics and Marx's economic theories have been shown to be incomplete. Yet *Das Kapital* remains one of the world's most important books and Marx's central theme—that the propertied classes live on the labour of the non-property-owning classes, has a potent political attraction. There remain two important criticisms of Marxist economics: one is that if the labour theory of value is unsound, then all Marx's theories based upon it are no longer valid; the other is that Marx's main object was to expose and indict capitalism—after 1917, capitalism was overthrown in Russia, and then Marxist economists had to put theory into practice and find doctrinally correct, but effective substitutes for the working of the price system in relation to supply and demand, the profit motive as a spur to productivity and efficiency, etc. These problems have not yet been satisfactorily solved, particularly, e.g. with relation to agricultural economics.

3. The Theory of the State and Revolution

Marx held that the State was an instrument of oppression and coercion exploited for the benefit of the ruling class. With the abolition of classes the State would lose its raison d'être and wither away; only its administrative functions would remain.

The first task of the revolution then was to destroy the State. This would be achieved in two stages: first the bourgeoisie would overcome the remnants of feudalism by establishing some kind of democracy. The proletariat would assist in this, even though they were enemies, because it was a necessary first stage. Secondly, the proletariat would overcome the bourgeoisie and there would be a transitional stage, known as the dictatorship of the proletariat, retaining some of the machinery of the State, before the final stage of a Communist society was reached and the State would wither away.

Marx was very vague about the machinery of the Communist society that would ultimately be established: indeed he was as Utopian as any of the French socialists about this. For him the proletariat was essentially the industrial working class. He expected the revolution to come in the highly industrialized western European countries and did not contemplate an agricultural country like Russia or China achieving the revolution by skipping a stage in the dialectical process. Nor did he believe that a socialist State might develop through the already existing constitutional machinery.

Ends and Means

The materialist conception is that human nature and man's ideas and morality are a product of his environment and class. 'It is not the consciousness of human beings that determines their existence, but conversely, it is their social existence that determines their consciousness,' wrote Marx. Since the ideas at any stage in history are those of its ruling class and since history is a process of change from one stage to another it follows that there can be no absolute standards of morality or of right and wrong. What has happened is right and that which assists the revolution is right. Bourgeois morality will be destroyed with its class and only when the classless society has been achieved will it be possible to evolve a universal morality; until that time any means that will lead to the desired end are justified.

QUESTIONS

1. Trace the development of socialist ideas in Europe in the nineteenth century.
2. Attempt to distinguish between Socialism, Communism and Anarchism.
3. What do you understand by Dialectical Materialism?
4. Summarize the main argument of the *Communist Manifesto* and discuss the reasons for its success as a revolutionary pamphlet.

Further Reading

BERLIN, SIR I. *Karl Marx, his life and environment.* 3rd edn. Oxford U.P., 1963. Home University Library.

BOTTOMORE, T. B. and RUBEL, M. 'Karl Marx': Selected writings in *Sociology and Social Philosophy*. Watts, 1956 and Penguin, 1963.

BURNS, E. *Introduction to Marxism.* Laurence and Wishart.

BURNS, E. *A Handbook of Marxism.* Gollancz, 1935.

CARR, E. H. *Michael Bakunin.* Macmillan, 1937.

—— *Karl Marx, a study in Fanaticism.* Dent, 1934.

COLE, G. D. H. *A History of Socialist Thought.* 4 vols. Macmillan, 1953–6.

FREEDMAN, R. ed. *Marx on Economics.* Penguin, 1962.

GALLACHER, W. *The Case for Communism.* Penguin, 1949.

HUNT, R. N. CAREW *The Theory and Practice of Communism.* 5th edn. Bles, 1956 and Penguin, 1963.

JACKSON, J. HAMPDEN *Marx, Proudhon, and European Socialism.* English Universities Press, 1958.

KETTLE, A. *Karl Marx.* Weidenfeld and Nicholson, 1963.

MARX, K. *Das Kapital,* 1867–94. Various translations available.

—— *The Communist Manifesto.* Foreign Languages Publishing House, Moscow.

PLAMENATZ, J. *What is Communism?* London, National News-Letter, 1947.

RYAZONOFF, D., ed. *Karl Marx: Man, Thinker, Revolutionist. A Symposium.* M. Lawrence, 1937.

SABINE, G. H. *A History of Political Theory.* Harrap, 1937.

SPRIGGE, C. J. S. *Karl Marx.* Duckworth, 1938. Great Lives.

STALIN, J. *Dialectical and Historical Materialism.* In *Collected Works,* 3 vols Lawrence and Wishart, 1953–5.

STRACHEY, J. *The Theory and Practice of Socialism.* Gollancz, 1936.

WILSON, E. *To the Finland Station.* Secker, 1941 and Collins, Fontana Library, 1960.

WOODCOCK, G. 'Bakunin'. *History Today,* July 1961.

—— *Anarchism.* Penguin, 1963.

CHAPTER XVI

THE DEVELOPMENT OF THE REVOLU-TIONARY MOVEMENT IN RUSSIA

Revolutionary activity was endemic in Russia throughout the nineteenth and early twentieth centuries. Opposition to the tsarist government and the system it represented came from a great variety of uncoordinated sources: from the intelligentsia, from the students, from the peasantry, from the growing urban working class and from national minorities in the tsarist empire. Since almost all political activity was illegal there was no other way of expressing discontent, or of suggesting reform, than the distribution of subversive literature and underground revolutionary activity.

Any political movement which wishes to succeed must have a clearly understood programme and basis of ideas, capable leaders and popular support: these the Marxists were in time able to provide, but they were a very small minority right up to 1917. What they did then was to exploit a revolutionary situation that had been mounting to a climax with a constant stream of industrial strikes, student demonstrations, peasant outbreaks, political assassinations and illegal political activities during the previous fifty or sixty years.

The Decembrist conspiracy of 1825 was the last of the eighteenth-century Palace revolutions, but it can be regarded as the beginning of the nineteenth-century revolutionary movement that led to the events of 1917. It was an attempted revolution which had leaders, but no clear programme and no popular following. It did, however, have a great influence upon the intellectual forerunners who prepared the way for later revolutions by disseminating their philosophic and political ideas.

The Intellectual Forerunners

The rivalry between the westernizers and the Slavophils stimulated intellectual discussion and much political philosophizing took place under the guise of literary criticism, such as for example, in the work of Belinsky the critic, and Nekrasov the poet.

Alexander Herzen (1812–1870), was the son of a rich landowner who made up for an unhappy home life by finding consolation in books. He drew his inspiration from the ideas of the French Revolution and the Decembrists and became interested in socialism at the university. He inherited a large fortune from his father and spent the rest of his life abroad writing and publishing books, as well as the journal, *Kolokol* (The Bell). He advocated the emancipation of the serfs, self-government, and common ownership of the land. The narodnik movement was inspired by him.

Another influential writer was Nicholas Chernyshevsky (1829–1889), who came from a family of priests, but became a student of revolution, and spent twenty years in Siberia for his efforts. This did not prevent him writing, however, and his novel, *What is to be done?* pictured a socialist Russia. By the 1860s, the theoretical philosophizings were beginning to be translated into practical action: the Narodniks were attempting to take socialism to the peasants and Bakunin's ideas were being enthusiastically taken up by the anarchists and nihilists.

The Liberals

The chief open opposition to the tsarist government came from the liberals; a very mixed group ranging between moderate socialists and conservatives, who wanted political and social reforms and some limitations of the autocracy. Some wanted a constitutional monarchy; others a republic, but all wanted more political freedom, some kind of representative government, and more or less social reform. Their support was largely middle class, and they were active in the zemstvos, in spite of Government attempts to eliminate them. In 1902 a liberal newspaper, *Liberation*, was started, and in 1903, the 'Union of Liberation', which was the germ of the Constitutional Democratic Party (The Cadets), was founded. The leaders of the Cadets were P. Milyukov and P. Struve who sought to obtain reform through the dumas from 1906 to 1917.

The Socialists

The Socialists were able to provide the leaders and the ideas that the discontented peasants and urban workers needed, but there were many rival divisions among them until the Bolsheviks seized power, and they all had to work underground as secret societies.

The Socialist Revolutionaries (the S.R.s)

The S.R.s arose out of the failure of the Narodnik movement. There were many S.R. groups operating in Russia in the late nineteenth century, and a number of unsuccessful attempts at uniting them, until a loose organization was achieved in 1902. They were socialists who believed that the future lay with the peasants, and wanted a democratic republic with the land divided among the peasants who would own and work it in common. One of the most remarkable figures in the movement was Madame Breshko-Breshkovskaya, the 'Grandmother of the Revolution', who came from a wealthy landowning family and joined the liberal and revolutionary groups at St Petersburg University. She became a follower of Bakunin, then of the Narodniks, and later helped to found the S.R.s. She spent twenty-two years in Siberia for her revolutionary activities, and was sent there again from 1908 to 1917. She died in 1934 at the age of ninety. Another woman S.R. was Vera Zasulich, who shot the police chief, Trepov. The extremist wing of the S.R.s advocated terrorism and assassination to achieve its ends. The first revolutionary party, the 'Zemlya i Volya', (Land and Liberty) was formed in 1876. In 1879 it became the 'Narodnaya Volya' (People's Will), and was responsible for the assassination of Alexander II.

The Social Democrats

The Social Democrats were more influenced by Marxist ideas, and directed their attentions to the urban proletariat on whom they believed a successful revolution depended. The various groups were united by Plekhanov in 1898,[1] but they split in 1903 into the Bolsheviks and the Mensheviks.

The Growth of Marxist Ideas in Russia

Marx himself was at first very anti-Russian because the tsarist government was the most reactionary, imperialist, and anti-liberal régime in Europe. Furthermore Russia was still largely an agricultural, semi-feudal country, and Marxist ideas were based on the experiences of, and were directed towards, the more advanced capitalist countries of western Europe. Nevertheless Russian was the first foreign language that *Das Kapital* was translated into (1872), and Marx's ideas were taken up enthusiastically by certain of the Russian intelligentsia, long before he himself became interested in Russia.

The germ of the successful Bolshevik ideas had already been sug-

[1] See page 199. Actually, Plekhanov accepted the work of the Minsk Congress of 1898 after it had ended.

gested by P. L. Lavrov (1823–1900), who saw the need for a revolutionary minority to educate the people, and by P. N. Tkachev (1844–1885), who advocated that there should be a small group of professional revolutionaries, acting in the name of the people, who would exploit a national rising to seize power, and transform society by taking over all industry.

The greatest of the early Russian Marxists was G. V. Plekhanov (1857–1918), who came of a noble family and joined the Narodniks as a student, but the policy of terrorism that was adopted made him question the populist beliefs, especially that the revolution would come from the peasantry. He spent forty years in exile and founded the Marxist 'Liberation of Labour' in Geneva in 1883. He saw that in time the development of capitalism in Russia would produce a proletariat and it would be this class that would lead the revolution. Before this could happen there would have to be a bourgeois democratic revolution which should be the immediate aim of the revolutionaries.

Lenin was tremendously influenced by Plekhanov and together they founded *Iskra* in 1900. When the split came in the Social Democratic movement in 1903 Plekhanov at first differed from Lenin and sided with the Mensheviks, but joined with the Bolsheviks in 1910, only to become opposed to them again over the defence of Russia in 1917.[1] He returned to Russia at the revolution, but did not serve in the provisional government, although he supported it against the Bolsheviks.

Plekhanov's forecast proved to be correct, for by the late nineteenth century considerable industrial development on capitalist lines had taken place, and it was the industrial workers who took the lead in the revolutions of 1905 and 1917.

Another narodnik who tried to adapt Marxism to Russian conditions was P. B. Axelrod. He saw that in Russia there was no sizeable proletariat, that the peasants wanted land and not socialism, and that there was not the political liberty nor the middle class to carry out the necessary first stages of the proletarian revolution as laid down by Marx. His answer to the problem was that the proletariat must attract leaders to itself and then assume control.

But it must be remembered that the Marxists in Russia were confined to small underground groups, that the leaders were a handful of exiles scattered about Europe, and that the story of the development of Marxism is almost synonymous with the career of Lenin.

[1] The main point of difference between Plekhanov and Lenin arose over whether there was to be a rising of the masses or a seizure of power by a minority on their behalf.

LENIN (1870–1924)

Vladimir Ilyich Ulyanov was born at Simbirsk in the middle Volga region in 1870. He took the pseudonym Lenin, in 1902, but it is convenient to use that name from the beginning. His father was a school inspector, and as a higher official, his rank made him a member of the hereditary nobility. His mother was a doctor's daughter who had also been a teacher, so Lenin came of a thoroughly bourgeois home that was cultured and liberal in its associations. Yet the six children all grew up with revolutionary ideas, and Lenin's eldest brother Alexander was executed for his part in an attempted assassination by the Populists of Tsar Alexander III in 1887. This event had a great effect on the young Lenin, turning him not only against the tsarist system, but also against his former liberal associates who dissociated themselves from the family at this time.

Lenin showed his intellectual brilliance at school and went to the local university at Kazan to study law, but was soon expelled after a student riot, for he had been under suspicion since his brother's execution. He was sent into the country under police supervision, but eventually gained permission to continue his legal studies and take the examination as an external student at St Petersburg University. He did the four years' work in one year and passed out top with a first-class diploma in 1891.

After this he spent a short period practising law at Samara, not very successfully, for he had long been a convinced Marxist and his true interests were elsewhere. When his family moved to Moscow in 1893, Lenin returned to St Petersburg where he took up again his contacts with the Marxists he had met there when he went to take his examination.

Although he was ostensibly engaged upon legal work he was already regarded as an authority on Marx and was known for his writings as a theoretician. He had long ago determined to become a professional revolutionary and his whole life was devoted to that end with an astonishing singleness of purpose.

He was not content to remain a theoretician and busied himself with practical political activity. In 1895 he obtained permission to leave Russia for his health, and used the opportunity to learn about European socialism and to make contact with political exiles abroad in Germany and Switzerland, particularly Plekhanov, and Axelrod.

When he returned to St Petersburg later in 1895, he began working to unite the scattered Marxist groups and formed the Union for the Liberation of the Working Class. He was preparing to publish an illegal paper when he was arrested, kept in prison for a year, and then sentenced to three years exile in Siberia. While in prison, and in Siberia, he continued writing, including his *Development of Capitalism in Russia* and he was joined in exile by Nadezhda Krupskaya whom he married in 1898.

Krupskaya was a schoolteacher who had been an active revolutionary before Lenin went to St Petersburg. She shared his life completely, helping him with his writing, caring for him in exile and joining with him in the work of government after 1917.

While Lenin was in Siberia a group of Russian Marxists met in Minsk in 1898 and formed the Russian Social Democratic Workers Party. There were only nine delegates and eight of these were arrested, but it was the beginning of the Social Democrat party (the S.D.s). From the beginning there were the divisions and differences of opinion that characterized all the early revolutionary activity in Russia. Some of these Social Democrats wished to work for economic improvements for the workers rather than for direct political activities, and Lenin on his release from Siberia in 1900 took up his work again and was determined to defeat the 'Economists' as they were known, and make the party concentrate once more on revolutionary political action.

Since it was impossible to publish his newspaper in Russia, Lenin once more left for Switzerland to arrange its printing there and its smuggling into Russia. It appeared as *Iskra* (The Spark) in 1900. From the beginning it was more than a newspaper, for it was used to organize, and keep in touch with, the revolutionary movement throughout Russia. Lenin and Krupskaya spent the years between 1900 and 1905 in Switzerland, Germany, Paris and London, writing and organizing the party.

The second party congress met in Brussels in 1903, but was dispersed by the police and continued in London with the delegates arguing all the way. Marxist delegates from Russia and exile groups from abroad met to sit on bales in a rat infested warehouse to discuss the party programme and its organization. Lenin had already provided the basis for his programme in his pamphlet *What is to be done?*, published in 1902, and he was determined to have his way with the congress. A major dispute broke out over party membership: one group wanted it to be open to anyone who showed enough sympathy to wish to join, while Lenin insisted that the party should consist only of an élite of those who were prepared to work actively for it. The issue really was whether the party was to become a democratically organized and led political group or a professional revolutionary body with an authoritarian leadership. Lenin engineered a vote when some of the delegates had withdrawn and obtained a majority of two for his point of view.

Actually twenty-two voted for him, the rest either did not vote or were not there, but he seized upon it, and called his own supporters Bolsheviki (the majority), and his opponents Mensheviki (the minority). Henceforth there were two hostile groups within the Social Democrats, although the Mensheviks were numerically larger and it was they who played the greater part in the 1905 revolution and in the early part of the 1917 revolution. Lenin lost control of *Iskra* and started a Bolshevik paper, *Vpered* (Forward); this was later replaced by *Pravda* (Truth). A third congress, for the Bolsheviks, took place in London in 1905. The creation of the Bolsheviks is an illustration of Lenin's absolute conviction of his own rightness, his determination to have his own way, and his intolerance of any other leadership but his own.

In 1905, Lenin returned to St Petersburg during the revolution but played little open part in it, although he was very active in writing and propaganda work. The revolution was crushed and once more Lenin went into exile to make a fresh start on building up the Social Democrat party after the disorganization and disillusion that followed their defeat. For a time after 1906 the Bolsheviks and the Mensheviks came together, but Lenin concentrated on tightening the control of his own faction, and in 1912 they split apart again—Lenin maintaining that only his own followers were the true party, the rest were deviationists of one kind or another.

Lenin and the War

In this nine years of exile Lenin was writing ceaselessly, organizing for the coming revolution, and still finding time to study philosophy and to keep in touch with the situation in Russia. When the war broke out in 1914, Lenin was arrested as a spy by the Austrians, but he was allowed to leave for Switzerland, where he poured out a stream of anti-war propaganda. Socialist parties, he thought, should do all they could to prevent war, and to think of Russian and German socialists fighting each other in a bourgeois imperialist war was a betrayal of the cause of international socialism.

Nevertheless, if war had to come, it presented an opportunity for the socialists to hasten the downfall of capitalism. The proletariat had no fatherland to fight for, and they would only be used as cannon fodder in an imperialist struggle for markets. Their only true course lay in turning the war into civil war and European revolution. If Russia were to be defeated that would be a lesser evil than the victory of capitalism, and events in Russia could be the spark that would inflame world revolution.

In 1917, Lenin and Krupskaya were living in Zürich, when the

Germans who knew of his opposition to the war, and who believed that they could utilize him to make Russia withdraw, arranged to have them transported through Germany to Sweden, from where they could make their way to Russia and bring about the collapse of the Russian Government.

QUESTIONS

1. Trace the development of the revolutionary movement in Russia.
2. Give an account of the life and ideas of Lenin.
3. Find out what you can and make notes on the following: A. Herzen; the Narodniks; the 1903 congress of the Social Democrats; the German scheme to smuggle Lenin through Germany in 1917; the Zimmerwald Conference, 1915.

Further Reading

BERDYAEV, N. *Origins of Russian Communism.* Bles, 1937.

FISCHER, G. *Russian Liberalism.* Harvard U.P., 1958.

FOOTMAN, D. *Red Prelude, a life of A. I. Zhelyabov.* Cresset, 1944.

FOX, R. *Lenin.* Gollancz, 1933.

HARE, R. *Pioneers of Russian Social Thought.* Oxford U.P., 1951.

—— *Portraits of Russian Personalities between Reform and Revolution.* Oxford U.P., 1959.

HILL, C. *Lenin and the Russian Revolution.* English Universities Press, 1947.

LAMPERT, E. *Studies in Rebellion.* Routledge, 1957.

MALIA, M. *Alexander Herzen and the Birth of Russian Socialism, 1812–1855.* Oxford U.P., 1960.

MIRSKY, D. S. *Lenin.* Holme Press, 1931. (Makers of the Modern Age.)

STALIN, J. *Leninism*, in *Collected Works.*

TOMPKINS, S. R. *The Russian Intelligentsia.* University of Oklahoma Press, 1957.

WILSON, E. *To the Finland Station.* Secker, 1941, and Collins, 1960.

WOLFE, B. D. *Three who made a Revolution.* Thames and Hudson, 1956.

VENTURI, F., trans. F. Haskell. *Roots of Revolution*: a History of the Populist and Socialist Movements in 19th-Century Russia. Weidenfeld and Nicholson, 1960.

YARMOLINSKY, A. *Road to Revolution, a Century of Russian Radicalism.* Cassell, 1957.

CHAPTER XVII

THE TRIUMPH OF LENIN: 1917-1924

The 1917 Revolutions

By the beginning of 1917 a revolutionary situation had developed. The emperor was completely out of touch with events; the incompetent handling of the war, the disastrous meddling of the empress and Rasputin in the work of the Government, the frustration of the liberals, the growth of industrial and agricultural discontent, the activities of the revolutionary groups and the food shortages: all created a restive atmosphere and the feeling that trouble was imminent.

The February Revolution (23 February O.S., 8 March N.S.)

Food riots, strikes and spontaneous demonstrations took place in Petrograd[1] in March 1917. The troops sent to crush the outbreaks joined the demonstrators who were shouting for 'Bread and Freedom'. The Duma was closed and the members of the Government quietly disappeared. A temporary committee of the Duma stayed on to form a provisional government while the tsar was stopped on the way back to Petrograd by the revolutionaries and forced to abdicate in favour of his brother, the Grand Duke Michael. But Michael refused to accept the crown and the imperial family was arrested pending arrangements for them to be sent into exile to England.

While the temporary committee of the Duma was making plans for a provisional government the left wing groups had formed the Petrograd Soviet of Workers' and Soldiers' Deputies which acted as if it were the Government by issuing decrees. Order number one, 14 March, authorized military units to elect committees and had the effect of undermining all army discipline. Thus there were two bodies in Petrograd; the provisional government and the Soviet, both claiming the authority that had fallen from the hands of the tsar. Most of the

[1] St Petersburg was thought to be too 'German' and the name was changed to Petrograd in 1914. Petrograd became Leningrad in 1924.

members of the Soviet were Mensheviks who were willing to let the provisional government have the responsibility of governing, for they believed it was necessary to have a bourgeois parliament as a first stage towards an eventual socialist revolution, but the reality of power was with the soviets who were more in touch with the sources of discontent and who had organizational control over the workers and the troops.

The Provisional Government

The provisional government was thus established with the approval but not the participation of the Petrograd Soviet. Its members, with Prince Lvov as Premier, and Milyukov as Foreign Minister, were all middle-class liberals and conservatives, with the exception of the only socialist, Kerensky, who as Minister of Justice had the task of liaison with the Soviet.

Russia was now a monarchy without a monarch, but the army commanders recognized the provisional government and so did the United States, Britain, France and Italy. It set out to put into effect the reforms that had been promised, to restore law and order, and to prosecute the war, while trying at the same time to maintain satisfactory relations with the Petrograd Soviet.

A general amnesty for political and religious prisoners was proclaimed, and political exiles were allowed to return from abroad; the Finnish constitution was restored and the Poles were promised their independence. Civil liberties were declared and a constituent assembly and agrarian reform were promised. Unfortunately the provisional government exercised little executive power, for this increasingly fell into the hands of the soviets which were set up everywhere on the Petrograd model; its programme was not revolutionary enough for the peasants who began seizing land, nor for the workers who continued to demonstrate their discontent with strikes, and it could not satisfy the national minorities who were demanding independence in Latvia, Georgia and the Ukraine.

The First Attempt at a Bolshevik coup d'état, July 1917

In April 1917, Lenin arrived in Petrograd, and in May he was followed by Trotsky. Marx had given little practical guidance for the achievement of power. It was Lenin's task to translate theory into practice by exploiting the revolutionary situation for a seizure of power by the Bolsheviks.[1] In Russia, the proletarian revolution came before the

[1] The general Bolshevik belief in 1917 was that the Petrograd revolution would provide a base for the world revolution that would have its centre in Germany.

'correct' stage in the productive process had been reached, and Lenin had to reinterpret doctrine to meet existing conditions. His programme was expressed in the slogan, PEACE, BREAD and LAND, and consisted of attacking the provisional government, promising land to the peasants (they were in fact already taking it), demanding that an end be put to the war, and that all power should be transferred to the soviets.

In June the first All Russian Congress of Soviets was held. The Bolsheviks were still the minority, with 105 delegates; the Mensheviks had 248 and the S.R.s 285. The Congress was followed by an outbreak, of strikes, riots and uprisings organized by the soviets. The Bolshevik leaders were against the rising, but were obliged to assume the lead when it began. The provisional government was able to crush the revolt; the Bolsheviks were proscribed; Trotsky was arrested and Lenin fled across the border to Finland.

Alexander Kerensky, b. 1881

The failure of the Brusilov offensive in July (see p. 177) and the difficulties at home, which the Bolsheviks were exploiting, brought about the withdrawal of the Cadets from the Government and the resignation of Prince Lvov. It was reconstructed to include members of the soviets who were in favour of continuing the war, and Kerensky succeeded Prince Lvov as Premier.

Kerensky was a young man, vain and ambitious, who had led the moderate socialists in the 1912 Duma. Later he joined the S.R.s and was Deputy Chairman of the Petrograd Soviet, as well as Minister of Justice in the provisional government. He was patriotic, and the policy of his government was to carry on the war and delay radical reforms until a Constituent Assembly could meet. This policy the Bolsheviks were able to turn to their advantage by exploiting the demand for reform and the general war weariness of the people.

Unfortunately for Kerensky, his government exercised no authority, and in the chaos at the front the armies were dissolving as soldiers deserted to return home and join in the seizure of land by the peasants. His position and authority were undermined by the Kornilov affair in September, while a conference of representatives called to Moscow in August failed to achieve unity. The problem that faced Kerensky was either to veer left, end the war, and introduce industrial and agricultural reform; or to veer right, restore discipline in the army, and law and order in the State. He could do neither.

Kornilov's Attempted coup d'état, September 1917

General L. G. Kornilov (1870–1918), was the Petrograd Military Commander who had arrested Nicholas II and became Commander-in-Chief when the provisional government was reorganized after the resignation of Prince Lvov. He realized the danger of a Bolshevik coup and believing that the provisional government under Kerensky was not strong enough to do anything about it, determined to counter the attempt by crushing the soviets. Thinking that Kerensky would support him, Kornilov moved his troops from headquarters at the front towards Petrograd, but they deserted him and Kerensky had him arrested. The effect of the Kornilov affair was still further to weaken the provisional government and to strengthen the Bolsheviks.

The October Revolution (7 November N.S., 25 October O.S.)

Throughout the summer of 1917 labour unrest continued, with workers taking over control of factories, peasants seizing land, and soldiers deserting from the army. In September Kerensky reformed the Government and called representatives to a Democratic Conference in an effort to muster support. A republic was declared, and a Council of the Republic was formed to advise the Government until a Constituent Assembly could be called.

Meanwhile the Bolsheviks were preparing their coup. Lenin was still in control from Finland, and their numbers were growing: there were only 30,000 Bolsheviks in February; in July there were 240,000. A secret congress of Bolshevik factions of the Russian Social Democratic Labour Party was held in Petrograd in July, and an armed uprising was decided on. In September, the control of the Petrograd and Moscow soviets passed into Bolshevik hands with a programme promising peace, a Constituent Assembly, and the nationalization of land, banks and industries. In October the creation of the Military Revolutionary Committee gave the Bolsheviks effective control over the troops in Petrograd, and they already had the Red Guards (armed factory workers) at their disposal.

In October Lenin returned to Petrograd, assumed direct control over the Central Committee of the party and demanded an early date for the rising in order to benefit from the revolutionary mood that existed with the spate of food riots and strikes in the capital. An inner group of the committee, the Politburo, was formed to speed up policy-making decisions.

The provisional government could not fail to be aware of the Bolshevik plans, but decided to take action against them too late. The

Government went, 'not with a bang but a whimper'. Sailors from the Kronstadt naval base and Red Guards surrounded the Winter Palace, where Kerensky was demanding a vote of confidence, while others seized the Post Office, the railway stations and other strategic points throughout the city. Kerensky escaped, but other ministers were arrested. There was some scattered fighting in Petrograd and in Moscow for a few days after, but except for more prolonged opposition in Georgia, the Ukraine and in the cossack areas, the Bolshevik-dominated soviets assumed nominal power throughout the country with comparative ease.

The Formation of the Soviet Government

The Bolshevik rising had been timed to coincide with the second All Russian Congress of the Soviets of Workers' and Soldiers' Deputies, and on the same evening the delegates gave their approval to the Bolshevik coup, which was not surprising since the Bolsheviks dominated the Congress. The next day the new Government was authorized by the Congress to be known as the Soviet of Peoples' Commissars (Sovnarkom) with Lenin as Chairman, Trotsky as Foreign Commissar and Stalin as Commissar for Nationalities.

As yet, the Bolsheviks only had control over the Workers' and Soldiers' Soviets, but when the Peasants' Soviets met later in November, they were able to outbid their rivals, the S.R.s, for peasant support, and could now claim to represent the Russian people.

November 1917 to January 1918

The Bolsheviks had seized power by an armed insurrection: within the next three months they proceeded to carry out their programme and to consolidate their position. The whole machinery of the State had collapsed under the strain of war and revolution, and at first, effective power was confined to the cities of Petrograd and Moscow. The rest of the country had to be won over and fought for during the next three or four years. The first necessity was to put a stop to the war in order to enable the Bolsheviks to consolidate their power at home, and negotiations were begun with the Germans that led to the Treaty of Brest Litovsk, although Lenin had a struggle to get his way on this. At home, a series of decrees transformed the social and economic basis of the State, while the Bolsheviks extended their control over the machinery of government.

All the land owned by landlords, the Crown, the Church and the monasteries, together with the livestock and equipment on it, was confiscated without compensation and transferred to Peasants' Committees: all transport and communications, the banks and industries were taken over by the State.

Church and State were separated; the registration of births, marriages and deaths, was made a civil matter, as was divorce; religious education in the schools was ended.

All titles and class distinction were abolished, including ranks in the army; committees of soldiers were set up and officers were elected. The inheritance of property was abolished, the equality of the sexes was declared: a great programme to abolish illiteracy was announced; the eight-hour day was instituted; the alphabet was simplified and the Gregorian calendar was introduced. (The November Revolution is still remembered as the October Revolution by the old style.) The courts were abolished and replaced by Peoples' Tribunals, and the police system which had broken down was replaced by the Cheka, a far more ruthless organization than the Okhrana.

All bonds and Government debts to foreign powers were repudiated and there was a declaration of complete equality, including the right of secession, for all nationalities within the Russian Empire.

With the renewal of the German threat after the failure of the early negotiations at Brest-Litovsk, the Red Army was created for the defence of the socialist Fatherland.

Much of this early legislation was in the nature of declarations of intent rather than of actual practical achievement, but it was a remarkable record of three months' activity and clearly demonstrated the determination of the Bolsheviks and the pattern of future development.

The Dissolution of the Constituent Assembly

The aim of most politically-minded Russians since the abdication of the tsar had been some kind of democratically elected Constituent Assembly. The provisional government had arranged for elections just before it was overthrown, and the Bolsheviks allowed these to continue. When the Assembly met in January, the Bolsheviks were in the minority with 25 per cent of the seats, but Lenin had no intention of surrendering power, and demanded that the Assembly should recognize the authority of the Congress of Soviets. When it refused to do so, Bolshevik troops entered the hall of the Tauride Palace and the Assembly was dissolved. Henceforth there was no organized opposition that could challenge the power of the Bolsheviks.

Nevertheless there was opposition. Nearly the whole of the civil service, who were not in sympathy with the Bolsheviks, went on strike and brought the administration and the distribution of food almost to a standstill. The Church was, of course, opposed to what had happened, the cossacks resisted, and so too, did the ordinary people, particularly the peasants, as the implications of the Bolshevik coup began to affect them.

At the third All Russian Congress of Soviets four days after the dissolution of the Assembly the 'Declaration of the Rights of the Labouring and Exploited Masses' was adopted. This proclaimed that Russia was to be a 'Republic of Soviets of Workers', Soldiers' and Peasants' Deputies' and a 'free union of free nations', with the aim of suppressing all exploitation of man by man, and confirmed all that had been done in the past three months.

The Constitution

At the fifth Congress of Soviets in July 1918, the Central Executive Committee presented a draft constitution which was ratified by the congress. The Republic of Soviets of Workers', Soldiers' and Peasants' Deputies was to be known as the 'Russian Socialist Federated Soviet Republic', but it only covered part of the former tsarist empire, for large areas had asserted their independence and were opposed to the Bolsheviks.

The constitution was really a statement of principles based on the *Communist Manifesto* and a confirmation of what had been done by the Bolsheviks. It included the Declaration of the Rights of the Labouring and Exploited Peoples and proclaimed the object of establishing socialism in all countries. The obligation to work, and certain civil rights were written into the constitution including universal adult suffrage over eighteen, but priests, former tsarist officials, members of the imperial family, and businessmen and merchants were denied the vote. All authority was based on the soviets, but there was to be one delegate for every 25,000 urban voters and only one delegate for every 125,000 rural voters. The All Russian Congress of Soviets was to be the chief legislative body and the Central Committee of the party was the real government.

Thus, while there was an air of democracy and equality about the constitution, all power was in fact confined to the Bolsheviks, now known as the Communists, who dominated the soviets and all the organs of government.

The Communist Party

In March 1918 the Russian Social Democratic Labour Party (the Bolsheviks) became the Russian Communist Party. Under Lenin's guidance it had set out to gain leadership in all the workers' organizations, especially the soviets, and by 1918 it held all the chief posts in the

Government, the army, the trades unions and similar organizations. At the fifth Congress of Soviets the Bolsheviks had 66 per cent of the seats. The party was from the first a limited body, highly disciplined, and determined to exercise the role of teaching by precept and example and leading the workers towards socialism. Thus Marx's dictatorship of the proletariat became under Lenin and Stalin the dictatorship of the Communist Party, or more correctly of its Central Executive Committee.

The Period of War Communism

After the coup d'état the Bolsheviks proceeded to apply Marxist principles on a trial and error basis with disastrous results for the economy of the country. All major industries were taken over by the State without compensation, factories were handed over to the workers, and by the land decree of November 1917, all land was made over to those who worked it. Private trading was abolished, shops and banks were closed, the rights of property and inheritance were abolished, and the money economy came to an end.

The consequences of the workers being assured of their pay was that they ceased to work, or, told that the factories were now theirs, took it quite literally and looted them. Productive work ceased and the country continued to exist only on what reserves of stock could be discovered. Theoretically the peasants were to work and produce surplus food which the Government would exchange for the surplus production of the factories, but faced with the Government's demand that they should hand over their stocks without payment they simply refused to produce more than their immediate needs.

The towns were faced with starvation and people left for the countryside, yet it was upon the support of the town workers that the Bolsheviks depended, and they had given them preferential treatment in the soviet elections by making one factory worker's vote equal to those of five peasants. The population of Petrograd fell from 2,300,000 in 1917 to 700,000 in 1919, and other cities fared similarly.

The droughts of 1920 and 1921 produced a famine that was made worse by the man-made shortages. Pigeons and dogs disappeared from the markets for there was nothing to attract them, cases of cannibalism were reported, and there were probably as many as three million deaths from starvation and diseases associated with malnutrition.

Thus Russia was brought to economic ruin: internal trade practically ceased and foreign trade stopped altogether. The transport system broke down, and inflation made nonsense of money values so that barter became the only form of exchange that was possible. In 1921 there was a hundred times as much money in circulation as in 1917, and one rouble in 1913 was equal to 2,420 in 1920.

Great areas of land were lost to Russia during the war: the total amount of cultivated land was reduced by one-sixth and industrial production by one-quarter. Under the provisional government the situation got worse, and the experiments, compromises and improvizations of the period of war communism made it worse still. Industrial production in 1920 was one-sixth of the 1917 level; coal production in 1918 was 33 per cent of the pre-war figure and that of pig iron was only 3 per cent. In 1920 agricultural production was half what it was before the war, heavy industrial output was 13 per cent and light industry less than half.

Experiments with the introduction of State farms were unsuccessful, partly because they tended to be managed by party officials who were ignorant of agricultural matters, and the Government resorted to punitive foraging expeditions that toured the countryside looking for, and confiscating, stocks of food for distribution to the towns—a task that the young Stalin helped to organize.

Thus by 1921 the communists were in control, but communism was clearly not working, largely because the peasantry were not communist material—they wanted private property in land and profits for their work. The terrorist policies that were used to extract food from them produced risings and rebellions which culminated in the naval mutiny at Kronstadt in March 1921, and the many acts of social reform, including provision for education and social insurance, remained on paper.

The Civil War, 1918–1921

The Bolshevik coup d'état was followed by a second Time of Troubles when there was complete confusion of foreign and domestic affairs, with civil war between the Russians and foreign intervention from all quarters. The Bolsheviks (Reds) found themselves opposed by a very mixed group of counter revolutionaries (Whites) consisting of former officials of the tsarist régime, army officers, nobles, liberals and socialists of all kinds.

But in addition to internal opposition, the Bolsheviks, because they had withdrawn from the war, renounced the foreign debts of former governments and were preaching and fostering world revolution, aroused the alarm and opposition of their former allies. The Germans supported the Reds because they were in favour of ending the war, but at the same time opposed them in the new states of the Baltic, Poland and the Ukraine where they did not want Bolsehvik ideas to spread. Britain, France and the United States were afraid of Bolshevik ideas but wished to keep the eastern front in being against the Germans. When the war against Germany ended they were concerned to support the counter-revolutionaries against the Reds. The Japanese hoped to gain territory in the Far East at the expense of Russia while she seemed

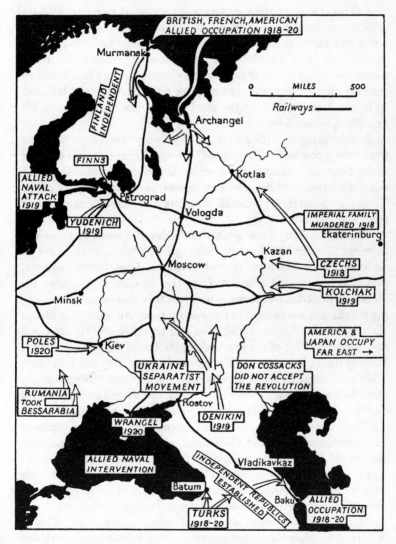

THE CIVIL WAR AND ALLIED INTERVENTION, 1918-1921
Note that the Bolsheviks had the advantage of interior lines and of control of the railways.

to be disintegrating. The Finns, Estonians and Lithuanians wanted to regain their independence from Russia, and the Poles hoped to recover the territories lost in the eighteenth-century partitions—White Russia and the Ukraine.

The Course of the Civil War

The war was characterized by savage brutality and terrorism on both sides, by confused fighting behind ill-defined fronts that moved backwards and forwards many times, by guerrilla activities and irregular warfare with much indiscipline and the pursuit of private feuds. There was no common purpose among the allies except hostility to Bolshevism and very little attempt at coordinating the activities of the anti-Bolshevist forces. A recent book on the allied intervention has with truth, the title *The Ignorant Armies*.

In the spring of 1918 a number of ex-army officers, perhaps not more than 3,000 in number, but well trained, began to group together under Generals Alekseyev and Kornilov in the south of Russia. At the same time groups of Socialist Revolutionaries were in control of the Volga region and throughout Siberia where they formed a new government and a People's Army.

The first military blow against the Bolsheviks came from an unexpected quarter. During the war against Germany an army of 30–40,000 men had been created in Russia from Czech residents, prisoners of war and deserters from the Austrian army. After the Treaty of Brest-Litovsk it was agreed that they should make their way via Siberia and Vladivostok to the western front. An attempt to disarm them by the Bolsheviks turned them into an anti-Bolshevik army and they captured most of the towns along the line of the Trans-Siberian Railway from Chelyabinsk to Vladivostok between May and June 1918. They were joined by the other anti-Bolshevist forces in Siberia; Cadets, Socialist Revolutionaries and cossacks, and, encouraged by the Japanese and the allies, they turned back from Siberia to advance upon Moscow.

There were already some British, French and American troops in Murmansk, Archangel and Vladivostok, guarding stores that had been sent to aid the Russians against the Germans, and now, encouraged by the apparently easy successes of the Czechs, the decision was made by the allies to intervene directly in support of the Czechs and the anti-Bolshevist forces generally. A large Japanese detachment, and smaller American, French, British and Italian groups were landed at Vladivostok before the end of the year. Other British forces were sent into Estonia and Baku, while the French sent military and financial help to Odessa, and later to the Poles. By the summer of 1918 all the

Russian Empire, except an area roughly corresponding to the original principality of Muscovy, was in anti-Bolshevist control. Finland had fought for and obtained her independence from Russia in 1918 and so, too, had Latvia, Estonia, the Ukraine and Georgia.

The S.R.s in Siberia formed a new government and a People's Army and moved west to join with the allied forces in the north but were checked by the Red Army. In June Denikin, who had taken over the forces in the south after the deaths of Alekseyev and Kornilov, moved north with the support of Krasnov, ataman of the Don Cossacks, but was checked at Tsaritsyn (later renamed Stalingrad, now Volgograd) by the Red Army and prevented from joining with the People's Army and the Czechs.

In September the various anti-Bolshevik groups in Siberia came together and Admiral Kolchak gained control over them by a coup d'état. With allied support, Kolchak, who had been proclaimed supreme ruler of all Russia, began an advance on Moscow in 1919 with three armies and 120,000 men, but he was driven back by the Red Army and handed over his control to Denikin in January 1920 before being betrayed to the Reds and executed.

In May 1919 Denikin again advanced north and reached Orel but was driven back to the Don and obliged to evacuate from Russia in 1920, leaving his successor, Wrangel, to continue a vain campaign with diminishing allied support. Meanwhile a campaign from Estonia was launched against Petrograd by Yudenich in October, but this too was driven back by November.

Wrangel continued his hopeless task but the French withdrew their support in April 1919 and the British left Transcaucasia, Siberia and the north in the summer while the allied blockade of Russia was ended in January 1920. Wrangel held on until he was obliged to evacuate in November.

The Poles had proclaimed a republic in 1918 and hoped to exploit the confusion of the civil war to regain for Poland the territories that had belonged to her before the partitions of the eighteenth century. They gave support to the counter-revolutionaries in the Ukraine and under Pilsudski conquered Vilna and Kiev. They were driven back by the Red Army and only saved by French support which enabled them to drive the Russians back again beyond the Curzon Line which had been suggested as a possible frontier between Russia and Poland. By the Treaty of Riga, 1920, confirmed the next year, Poland obtained the territory she had sought and about four-and-a-half million White Russians, Ukrainians and Great Russians were transferred to Polish rule.

The Bolshevik Success

Attacked from north, south, east, and west, with allied intervention on a large scale, with famine and acute discontent arising from the economic chaos of the war and the rigours of war communism imposed by the Bolsheviks, it is remarkable that they survived.

The two chief reasons for their success were the divisions and lack of coordination between the allies and the anti-Bolshevik forces and the creation of the Red Army. The soviets had the interior lines and control of the railways and could count increasingly on Russian patriotism against foreign intervention, and the vested interest they were creating among the peasants who for the first time now had land of their own. Their growing strength was enforced by ruthless terrorism after the creation of the Cheka in 1917, the new secret political police, who summarily executed thousands of real and imagined opponents of the Bolshevist régime, and by skilful and relentless propaganda that bound their supporters and divided their enemies.

But it was the Red Army that defeated the Whites in the field and the driving force behind this was Trotsky. The Workers and Peasants' Red Army was formed in January 1918, at first on a voluntary basis, but it soon became universal compulsory military service, and by 1920 it consisted of five million men although probably no more than 600,000 were available at any one time. The election of officers was abolished, discipline tightened and former tsarist officers were forced to serve by holding their families as hostages and the appointment of political commissars to watch over their activities.

Results of the Civil War

The most definite result of the war was the strengthening of the position of the Bolsheviks. They could pose as the saviours of Russia and had triumphed over all the possible opposition parties. In spite of the severities of the period of war communism and the terrorism of the Cheka, the Bolsheviks had a definite programme which they clearly intended to carry out and they had the support of all those who stood to gain economically by the transformation of Russian society.

One of the earliest casualties of the war had been the imperial family who had all been murdered by their guards when the Czechs advanced upon Moscow, but the effects on the population as a whole were staggering: the number of deaths through fighting, terrorism and even more through disease and famine, was enormous. If the population had continued its normal growth it would have numbered about 175 million in 1926: instead it was 147 million. Many thousands had emigrated or gone into permanent exile.

The material losses were also enormous, and the administration of law and order had broken down when roaming bands of desperate men, including German prisoners trying to get home, dispossessed peoples of all kinds including thousands of orphans, as well as the officially organized bands sent into the countryside to requisition food, ransacked the countryside and fomented strife between poorer and richer peasants.

Large territories formerly belonging to the Russian Empire were lost by the Treaty of Brest-Litovsk, and these included some of the most valuable food-producing and industrial areas, while the policy of self-determination that was at first applied to the subject peoples of the tsar resulted in the recognition of the independence of Latvia and Estonia in 1918, and of Lithuania and Finland in 1920. Georgia, the Ukraine, and Belorussia gained temporary 'independence', but this was short lived, and Georgia was reconquered in 1921. Belorussia, the Ukraine and Siberia were re-absorbed in 1922, while Estonia, Latvia and Lithuania were recovered in 1940.

The New Economic Policy: 1921–1924

The mutiny of the sailors at Kronstadt, who had formerly been among the chief supporters of the Bolsheviks, underlined the widespread discontent and opposition to the policies of the Soviet Government that had been mounting throughout the period of the civil war, the famine and the experiments in war communism. In particular, the resistance of the peasants forced Lenin to abandon for the time being the tactics of class warfare in an effort to produce more food and salvage the economy of the country.

The new economic policy which Lenin prevailed upon the Bolsheviks to accept, not without much criticism and heartsearching from the purists, consisted of a compromise with capitalism and a period of rule by communists that was not communism. Gosplan, a department for economic planning was set up, the land and the 'commanding heights in production' were to remain State-owned, but limited private enterprise in trade and in small scale industry were to be permitted, and in 1922 the law was re-codified to define the position of private enterprise in a socialist state. The profit motive was reintroduced with piece work rates, bonuses, preferential rations, etc., in order to encourage production, and peasants were permitted to sell their surplus production on the open market after paying a large tax in kind to the State. Foreign credit was sought, and private investment encouraged, while bourgeois experts were to be employed for their technical skills and experience. Banking and the rights of inheritance were restored, food requisitioning and forced collectivization were given up, and factories were handed over to trusts, or even to individual entrepreneurs. Trade and commercial treaties were made with other countries: with Britain in 1921, Norway and Germany in 1922, and with a number of other countries in 1924. A new class of business adventurers, the Nepmen, began to emerge.

The N.E.P. was Lenin's last service for the new soviet State. It was not of course a genuine abandonment of Marxist principles, merely a temporary expedient to restore the economy of the country by any means before proceeding with the task of building socialism. It was successful in that the economy of the country was eventually restored to something like its prewar footing, but it was above all a triumph for the peasantry and this was an affront to communist principles.

The N.E.P. covered all sides of public life except in political activity, where the authority of the party was maintained and consolidated, and many other measures were initiated in an attempt to win support for the Government: the labour code of 1922 provided for collective agreements through the trade unions[1] and there were regulations limiting working hours and the employment of women and children. The land code of the same year abolished all private property in land, but permitted free leasing if it were kept in cultivation. There were new laws for health and insurance schemes, but all these measures tended to be declarations of good intentions rather than actual achievements.

The greatest success was in the campaign against illiteracy. In 1917, 75 per cent of the inhabitants of European Russia and 85 per cent in Siberia were illiterate. The Government concentrated on the younger generation. The universities were packed with party nominees, the arts subjects were neglected and independent-minded or liberal professors expelled, and all the attention given to technical subjects and medicine.

Simultaneous with this was the attack on religion. The Church in Russia had seized the opportunity of the revolution to reform itself and to regain some of its power and freedom. The provisional government had permitted a Church congress which had restored the Patriarchate abolished by Peter the Great, and this gave the Church a degree of independence which came to a head when the patriarch excommunicated the Soviet Government for its atheism.

In 1921 the teaching of religion to anyone under the age of eighteen except at home was prohibited; the next year there were anti-religious processions at Christmastime organized by Komsomol, and the year

---

[1] The trade unions were now instruments of the State.

after that the patriarch and numbers of orthodox clergy were arrested and charged with not surrendering Church vessels to aid famine relief. Amid widespread protests from the rest of the world, the bishops were condemned to death and the persecution of all religious bodies continued.

Lenin's Contribution to Marxism

Lenin suffered a stroke in December 1922, and was able to do little active work from then until his death in January 1924. The Bolsheviks were in power and the revolution had secured most of its aims, although there was still much to do before socialism had been built out of the ruin of the tsarist empire. Thousands of ordinary Russian people had been the means and the material of the revolution, but the will-power, the ruthless single-mindedness and the leadership had been Lenin's. It was his achievement, and he received the homage due to a prophet and a saviour. His body was embalmed (against the wishes of his wife), and placed in the monstrous mausoleum that is the mecca of every communist visitor to Moscow.

Lenin was a philosopher and theorist, and at the same time, a practical organizer and tactician, with keen appreciation of political reality. He had studied not only his master, Marx, but also the art and techniques of revolution. He was never an out-of-touch emigré, but kept his finger on the pulse of the revolutionary movement inside Russia, while absorbing the lessons of the Commune in Paris in 1870, and of the 1905 revolution in Russia. He perfected the technique of the seizure and maintenance of power, and could always relate his actions to Marxist principles.

In what he did, he added to the body of Marxist thought certain modifications made necessary by the political and economic conditions within Russia.

Marx had held that the first stage in the revolutionary process would be a bourgeois revolution and that it was the duty of the socialists to work for this as a necessary preliminary to the socialist revolution. This was the belief of the Mensheviks, but Lenin claimed that the lesson of failure of the 1905 revolution was that this could not occur because Russia had no real bourgeoisie, and that, therefore, the proletariat must take the lead in the revolution. This meant that the Mensheviks and the S.R.s must be overcome, and this the Bolsheviks under Lenin's guidance succeeded in doing.

Lenin's interpretation of the meaning of the 'dictatorship of the proletariat' differed from that of Marx, for he saw no early end to the coercive power of the State, which Marx had claimed would wither away. Lenin was a bitter oponent of any form of parliamentary government for, to him, parties represented class interests, and there could only be one class, and therefore only one party, in a socialist state. True democracy he claimed lay within the soviets, with their direct elections from lower to higher bodies. From this followed Lenin's conception of the role of the party as an élite vanguard that would lead, organize, direct and fight for the people. It must be disciplined and highly centralized, with the lower organs subordinate to the higher. The State thus became synonomous with the party, and was no longer an instrument of oppression but a means for building socialism.

Lenin's ideas on the achievement of world revolution also became standard doctrine. The communist parties in all countries were to work within the existing machinery of government and the trade unions in order to seize power. While remaining true to Marxist principles, any stratagem, trick or apparent contradiction, including cooperation with bourgeois elements, was to be resorted to if it might succeed. All communist parties would be highly centralized under the control of their central executive committees, and these would get their instructions from Moscow.

Lenin also believed that the activities of the capitalist powers in investing capital abroad, and the growth of international financial institutions would inevitably lead to war, because of the inherent contradictions within the capitalist system. All countries suffering from capitalist exploitation would become ripe for revolutionary activity, and the Bolsheviks would lead the anti-imperialist crusade.

Thus communist thought today is a blend of the ideas of Marx and of Lenin as interpreted by their successors.[1] Stalin's own definition of Leninism was that it was 'Marxism of the era of imperialism and of the proletarian revolution'.

QUESTIONS

1. What were the causes of the Russian Revolution?
2. By what means did the Bolsheviks gain power in 1917?
3. Give an account of the work of the Bolsheviks, 1917–1924.
4. Give an account of the civil war in Russia, 1917–1922, and discuss its consequences.
5. Why were the Bolsheviks successful in 1917?
6. What was Lenin's contribution to the Russian Revolution?

[1] These interpretations have differed considerably, as for example in Stalin's ideas on socialism in one country, the attacks on Stalin at the Party Congresses in 1956 and 1961, the quarrels between the U.S.S.R. and Yugoslavia, and more important still, perhaps, the differences between the U.S.S.R. and China.

7. What was Lenin's contribution to Marxism?
8. Discuss the aims and achievement of the New Economic Policy.
9. Find out what you can and make notes on: Kerensky; Kornilov; Kolchak; the 1918 Constitution; allied intervention in the civil war, 1918–1922; the Red Army; the Curzon Line; the Cheka; the Kronstadt mutiny.

Further Reading

ADAMS, A. E. ed. *The Russian Revolution and Bolshevik Victory*. Problems in European Civilization. Heath. Harrap, 1960.

CARR, E. H. *History of Soviet Russia*. 5 vols. Macmillan, 1950–59.

CHAMBERLIN, W. H. *The Russian Revolution*. 2 vols. Macmillan, New York, 1952.

CURTISS, J. S. *The Russian Revolutions of 1917*. Van Nostrand, 1959.

CHURCHILL, SIR W. *The World Crisis 1914–18: Aftermath*. Butterworth, 1929.

FLEMING, P. *The Fate of Admiral Kolchak*. Hart-Davis, 1963.

FOOTMAN, D. *The Russian Revolutions*. Faber, 1962.

—— *Civil War in Russia*. Faber, 1961.

HALLIDAY, E. M. *The Ignorant Armies*. Weidenfeld and Nicolson, 1961.

HILL, C. *Lenin and the Russian Revolution*. English Universities Press, 1947.

MOORHEAD, A. *The Russian Revolution*. Hamish Hamilton and Collins, 1958.

PASTERNAK, B. *Dr Zhivago*. Collins, 1958.

PRIDHAM, SIR F. *Close of a Dynasty*. Wingate, 1956.

REED, J. *Ten Days that Shook the World*. London, Modern Books, 1928 and Lawrence and Wishart, 1961.

ROTHSTEIN, A. *A History of the U.S.S.R.* Penguin, 1950 (Pelican).

SCHAPIRO, L. *The Communist Party of the Soviet Union*. Eyre and Spottiswoode, 1960 and Methuen paperback, 1963.

WOLFE, B. D. *Three who made a Revolution*. Thames and Hudson, 1956.

CHAPTER XVIII

THE RULE OF STALIN TO 1939

Stalin's Early Life

Joseph Djugashvili was born at Gori in Georgia in 1879. His father, a freed serf, was an unsuccessful shoemaker who died when Joseph was eleven, and his mother continued working, in great poverty, as a laundrymaid to support herself and her son. Three other children had died before Joseph was born, and Ekaterina was ambitious for her only son. At the age of nine Joseph was sent to an ecclesiastical school, and in 1894, by means of a scholarship, he went to the theological seminary at Tiflis.

Smallpox had marked him and an infection in his arm had made him unfit for military service, but he was strong physically and early demonstrated his capacity to learn as well as an assertive temperament. Except in debate he was uncommunicative and learned to hide his feelings. He never showed any signs of imagination or originality but he wrote poetry and read much—mostly books that were forbidden by the seminary. Revolutionary ideas were current in the Caucasus at that time, both socialist and Georgian nationalist, and Joseph was a natural rebel with a deep feeling of class consciousness. He was expelled from the seminary in 1899, by which time he was a convinced Marxist and had joined a secret socialist organization. Although he eventually obtained a post as a clerk at the Tiflis observatory he was spending most of his time in active work for the society. In 1901, after the police had raided the first May Day procession organized by him, he went underground and became a permanent revolutionary agitator with a variety of assumed names beginning with 'Koba' and signing himself 'Stalin' (Man of Steel) for the first time in 1913.

From now on his work consisted of writing, organizing strikes, street processions, meetings, etc., and dodging the police. He was caught in Baku in 1902 and after eighteen months in jail was exiled for three years to Siberia, but in 1904 he made his way back to Tiflis and continued his revolutionary activities. Here he helped to organize raids on banks and armed hold-ups which provided funds for the party activities. In 1905 he paid his first visit to a European country outside Russia proper when he went as a delegate to the Bolshevik conference at Tammerfors in Finland, and here he met Lenin for the first time. He also attended the conferences held in Stockholm in 1906 and in London in 1907 where he met Trotsky.

The Rise of Stalin

Except for two visits to Cracow and Vienna and for his compulsory journeys to and from Siberia, most of Stalin's work was confined to revolutionary activities among the workers of the Baku oilfields. He had no knowledge or understanding of Europe, unlike the majority of the leaders of the party, who were exiles in France, Switzerland and Germany, but he recognized Lenin as his political leader and from 1909 there were growing contacts between the two men—in between his frequent arrests. In 1910 he was banished from the Caucasus region and from the cities of Russia. In 1912 Lenin, who had become aware of his value, co-opted him to the Central Committee of the Bolsheviks, and the first edition of *Pravda* appeared with Stalin as editor. For this he was arrested again and sentenced to three years exile, but escaped and returned to St Petersburg where he had an interview with Lenin who sent him to Vienna to report on the subject nationalities of the Austro-Hungarian Empire, and this was to become his special field of study. He was arrested once more on his return from Vienna and sentenced to four years' exile in Siberia. This time he did not escape and took no part in the Great War of 1914–1918.

In all this single-minded revolutionary activity Stalin seems to have had little private life, but he was married and had a son. His first wife died in 1905 and he married again in 1918.

Stalin and the 1917 Revolution

When the revolution took place Stalin returned to Petrograd from Siberia, resumed the editorship of *Pravda* and took charge of the Petrograd Soviet and the leadership of the Bolshevik Party until the arrival of Lenin three weeks later. He was elected to the new Central Committee and once more took over control during the temporary flight of Lenin following the fighting of the June Days. During this time Stalin seems to have been playing a cautious waiting game, not committing himself by openly taking part in the struggles between the factions, but when the October Revolution occurred he emerged as one of the leading Bolsheviks, together with Lenin and Trotsky, in the first

Soviet Government, with the official post of Chairman of the Commissariat for Nationalities.

The Struggle for Power within the Party

Lenin was indisputably the leader of the Bolsheviks, but already, before his death in 1924, a bitter struggle was being waged between Trotsky and Stalin for the succession. Stalin, by undertaking the less glamorous work of organization and administration, had made himself master of the machinery of the State, almost without anyone realizing it. Lenin on his deathbed did so and warned his colleagues about it, but it was too late. 'Stalin is too rude, and this fault becomes unbearable in the office of General Secretary. Therefore I propose to the comrades to find a way to remove Stalin from that position and appoint to it another man . . . more patient, more loyal, more polite, and more attentive to comrades, less capricious.' (Lenin, 4 January 1923.)

In addition to the work as Commissar of Nationalities, which in effect gave him control over half the population, Stalin was also Commissar of the Workers' and Peasants' Inspectorate, which was charged with eliminating inefficiency and corruption and thus gave him control over the whole machinery of the State. He was also a member of the Politburo, the inner cabinet of the Government. In 1922 Stalin became General Secretary of the Central Committee, which gave him control of the party and of the purges of party members carried out by the Central Control Commission. Stalin's only serious rival was Trotsky, and on the death of Lenin, he devoted all his energies to the elimination of his rival by allying for the time being with the other members of the Politburo, Kamenev and Zinoviev, against him.

Lev Davidovich Trotsky, 1879–1940

Trotsky, whose real name was Bronstein, came from a family of middle-class Jews who were farmers in the Ukraine. He was educated at the Realschule and University at Odessa where he was at first attracted to the Narodniks, and became a Marxist in the 1890s. He was ambitious and courageous, a brilliant speaker, linguist, writer and leader, and in every way his personality contrasted with that of Stalin. He had great energy and administrative ability, but his fiery tongue made him bitter enemies, and Lenin distrusted him.

In 1898 he was arrested as a revolutionary and sent to Siberia but escaped to England in 1902 where he joined other exiled social democrats, including Lenin and Plekhanov, and worked with them on the production of *Iskra*.

When the London conference of 1903 split between the Mensheviks and Bolsheviks, Trotsky sided with the Mensheviks, and only joined the Bolsheviks in 1917.

During the 1905 revolution he returned to Russia, was elected to the St Petersburg Soviet and became its chairman. When the whole Soviet was arrested and sent to Siberia Trotsky escaped, this time to Vienna.

From then on he continued the life of a professional revolutionary in exile: in 1910 he was at the Socialist International Congress in Copenhagen, in 1913 he was a war correspondent at Constantinople, in 1914 he was in Paris and Switzerland vigorously opposing the war, and in 1915 he was at the Zimmerwald conference of the anti-war socialists. In 1916 he was expelled from France, arrested in Spain, and went to America where he edited the *Novy Mir* (New World).

In 1917, after being interned on the way by the British in Canada he returned to Russia where he became chairman of the Petrograd Soviet, was arrested again by the provisional government, released and played a leading part in the Bolshevik revolution. He became Commissar for Foreign Affairs in the new Soviet Government and was responsible for the Russian negotiations over the Treaty of Brest-Litovsk. He resigned in 1918 and became Commissar for War and was chiefly responsible for creating the Red Army and reorganizing the railways. This was his most important work for the Bolsheviks, but he quarrelled with Stalin over the use of former tsarist officers. For a time he seemed to be Lenin's right hand man and his natural successor, but he was distrusted by the old guard of the Bolsheviks as a quarrelsome newcomer, and he was systematically edged out of power by Stalin. After Lenin's death Stalin succeeded in getting Trotsky dismissed as Commissar for War in 1925, expelled from the Politburo in 1926 and from the party in 1927. In 1928 he was exiled to Siberia for attacking the party and in 1929 expelled from Russia, all the time fighting a vain battle against the accumulation of power by Stalin. The great purges of the 1930s were really directed against Trotsky and his supporters, and in 1940 he was assassinated in Mexico City.

The Quarrel with Trotsky

The issues upon which Stalin and Trotsky were divided were as follows: both were Marxists and Leninists, but Trotsky believed in a general revolutionary rising and took the optimistic line that the rulers had only to follow the right socialist policy for the workers to follow; Stalin on the other hand had no faith in the popularity of socialism— it must be forced upon the people for their own good.

The difference in the personalities of the two men reflected the two main currents of Bolshevist thought about the future of the revolution;

the stages of the transition to socialism, the relative importance of the contribution of the urban workers and of the peasants to the revolution and whether there was to be a general world revolution or socialism in one country.

Stalin's Official Position

Stalin's official position was that of General Secretary of the party although he made himself Chief Minister in 1941, and was given the titles of Marshal and Generalissimo during the war. In effect he was dictator of Russia after the defeat of Trotsky and he ruled with an absoluteness that was entirely in the tsarist tradition except that it was much more effective.

The Five Year Plans: Socialism in One Country

The N.E.P. had been successful to some extent in restoring the shattered economy of the country, but at the expense of socialist principles. Stalin was determined to build up the industrial strength of Russia to equal that of the United States and to transform the Russian character in doing so. A new planning committee (Gosplan) was set up to devise means of co-ordinating all the economic activities of the State, to increase production and to eliminate private enterprise. It proposed the first Five Year Plan (1928–1932), a comprehensive programme which aimed at crushing individual enterprise in agriculture, manufacturing industry and trade, at improving living and working conditions and education, discovering and exploiting Russia's natural resources, improving the defence of the country and its economy generally. Roads and railways were to be built, productivity was to be increased by setting up definite quotas to be reached within a given time, new factories and power stations were to be set up especially in the Urals and Siberia and so on, all in a flurry of propaganda and the atmosphere of a military campaign.

In 1932 it was announced that the plan had succeeded one year ahead of schedule: the Turksib railroad connecting Turkestan and Siberia was opened in 1930 and the Dnieprostroy dam in 1932; the Stalingrad tractor works, the Gorky motor works, the steelworks at Magnitogorsk and many other new works and factories had been founded, but there was still much criticism; and because most of the investment was in heavy industry and in capital goods there did not seem to be much improvement in the conditions of life for the average Russian. Foreign capital and the help of foreign technicians had to be obtained, but it was naturally enough difficult for the Bolsheviks to obtain foreign credit except on stiff terms and for short periods. It was therefore necessary to export in order to pay for capital imports even if it meant selling the food that was needed in Russia. Productivity and the quality of the goods remained low: 40 per cent of what was produced was little better than scrap because of ignorance, lack of skill, incompetence and deliberate sabotage. Costly mistakes were made and appalling waste resulted from lack of initiative or the delays incurred by incompetent and excessive bureaucracy. Some of the foreign technicians were in fact accused of sabotage and treason and their trials caused a good deal of additional international tension.

The Second Five Year Plan

The first Five Year Plan had been largely concerned with agriculture, finance, and about fifty basic industries, and the emphasis had been on size and quantity: the second plan was devised in the light of the shortcomings of the first and it was wider in scope with more emphasis on quality and efficiency, it was more realistic in its quotas and there was more attention to decentralization.

The basic aims of increasing production and creating a classless socialist society remained but some attention was paid to raising living standards by increasing wages, extending the health and education services, and increasing the supply of consumer goods, although this remained secondary to the main task. The transport system was to be improved by the electrification of railroads and the construction of new waterways such as the White Sea–Baltic, Moscow–Volga and Volga–Don canals.[1]

It was claimed that the plan had been successfully accomplished, but only at the expense of another revision of Marxist teaching. At first the principle, 'from each according to his ability: to each according to his needs' had been the axiom, but now in the drive to increase production at all costs differential wage rates were introduced and 'socialist competition' was encouraged. A young miner named Stakhanov who greatly exceeded his quota of production at the coal face was exalted to the level of a national hero, and an extensive system of bonuses and extra privileges was built up to reward similar heroes of labour. Much of the propaganda about the Stakhanov movement was fictitious and was exposed after Stalin's death. On the other hand the labour code was tightened to punish slackers, absentees and tardy work.

The Third Five Year Plan

This plan responded to criticisms of the second plan and the needs of defence in view of the growing threat from Nazi Germany. There was

[1] Not completed until 1952.

much discontent about the wage differentials, for they tended to create a new privileged class, and the race for production led to poor quality goods and damage to machinery and tools. More attention was given to the need to produce consumer goods and to provide more housing. Labour discipline was still further tightened, and for strategic reasons, new factories were established in remote regions.

The Five Year Plans raised Soviet industry to the level that permitted the successful maintenance of war against Germany, and transformed the U.S.S.R. from an essentially agricultural country to one that was practically self-supporting for her industrial and manufacturing needs. By any measure of comparison with the countries of western Europe or the New World the standard of living of the Russian worker was low and he enjoyed little personal freedom; but nevertheless things were better than they had been and Stalin could proclaim in 1936 that 'Life is better. Life is more cheerful'—at least for large sections of Soviet society.

THE FIVE YEAR PLANS[1]

Plan	Date of Adoption	Scheduled Period of Operation	Actual Period of Operation
1	Dec. 1927	Sep. 1928–Sep. 1933	1928–1932
2	1934	1933–37	1933–37
3	1939	1937–42	1937–41
4	1946	1946–50	1946–50
5	1952	1951–55	1951–55
6	1956	1956–60	1956–Abandoned 1958

The first two were announced to have been completed before the planned date. The third plan was interrupted by the war, and replaced by a series of war economic plans. The fifth was completely revised in 1953.

Agriculture: the Second Stalinist Revolution

The changes in agriculture were as great as those in manufacturing industry, and socially and politically they were more important.[2] In

[1] (a) The plans were not meant to be precise timetables but means to an end, not the end itself. They were subject to revision in the light of experience, and there was no break in the continuity between them.

(b) The Twenty-first Party Congress adopted a Seven Year Plan for the period 1959–1965 in January 1959.

[2] The basic problem that faced the party was how to secure from a backward and unproductive agricultural society the capital that was essential for the large-scale development of heavy industry which the party had determined upon. A crash programme was necessary to strengthen the Soviet Union in face of the international situation.

1928 about 80 per cent of the Russian population were rural dwellers, and about 75 per cent of them were dependent upon agriculture for their livelihood, yet the communists, who were in power, depended upon the support of an urban proletariat. The peasants were not only the majority of the population, but since they produced the food they had the urban population at their mercy. The struggle against the peasantry to ensure adequate food supplies for the towns was one of the major problems facing the Government, and since the peasantry were by nature believers in the right to hold property and to conduct private enterprise they were the chief obstacles to the achievement of a socialist society. Furthermore the peasants expected to be able to exchange their surplus food for consumer goods manufactured in the towns; but the policy of the Government was to restrict the production of consumer goods and to concentrate on capital goods. Since the peasantry would not voluntarily work for the sake of the towns and of the Communist Party then they must be made to do so, and the decision to do this was forced upon Stalin by the persistent food shortages, particularly in 1928.

Since emancipation, the peasants had gradually acquired more land, until by 1914 they owned about 50 per cent of the arable land. From 1917 to 1918 they owned about 80 per cent of the cultivated land and rented about 10 per cent more. This was not private ownership, but held in common; only about 10 per cent of the land was privately owned. At the revolution of 1917 the peasants seized the land belonging to the Crown, the Church and the nobility, and they were encouraged to do so by the Bolsheviks, but the fundamental law of 1918 nationalized all the land although the peasants were allowed to continue working it on lease.

During the period of war communism the peasantry were systematically pillaged by forced requisitioning, and committees of poor peasants were formed with the deliberate intention of carrying class warfare into the villages. There were not very successful attempts at applying socialist principles to agriculture in the State farms (Sovkhozes), collective farms (Kolkhozes) and co-operative farms (Artels), but in 1926–1927 the State farms produced less than 2 per cent of the total grain, while the peasants produced 85 per cent. By 1927–1928 the number of collectives had increased, but they still represented less than 2 per cent of the total farm acreage and no more than one million peasant households out of about twenty-four million.

The New Economic Policy was a temporary expedient to get more food at any cost by permitting the growth of private enterprise once more in agriculture, but the food shortage of 1928 and the achievement of complete power by Stalin led to the determination to secure a planned economy and the application of socialist principles to agriculture. The Five Year Plans were designed to organize agriculture on industrial lines by increasing the size of the unit, introducing mechanization, and transforming the individual peasant into a labourer. Private enterprise and its rural symbol, the kulak or richer peasant who dabbled in the wholesale trade and moneylending, were to be exterminated and the peasants themselves were to be forced into forming collectives. The whole effort was to be organized like a military campaign with 'fronts' and 'brigades' and 'shock troops'—indeed it was in effect to be a new civil war waged against the peasants. By propaganda, by offering inducements and privileges to those who joined, and by persecuting those who did not, the Government hoped to cajole or coerce the peasants to surrender their land and stock to the collectives. In 1929 there were 57,000 collectives, but Stalin was determined to force the pace, and in 1930 there was a law providing for wholesale collectivization. Village communes were broken up and the property of the peasants confiscated so that in a short time more than half the peasantry were in collectives: but the resistance was so great, and the terror that was employed so shocking, that there was a temporary respite. In 1932 Stalin's wife, Nadia Allilujeva, protested at the treatment of the peasantry and committed suicide,[1] but the work continued. By 1933 two-thirds of all peasant households and 85 per cent of the arable land had been collectivized, although this varied according to local geographic conditions.

Results of the Forced Collectivization

In the long run the organization into large units did permit the introduction of more efficient methods, the cultivation of new crops, and increased production, but the immediate effects were appalling. The peasants resisted and had to be driven into the collectives by the use of machine-guns or by the threat of deportation and forced labour. Rather than hand over their stock to the State they slaughtered and ate it and refused to till the fields. In 1929 there were thirty-four million horses in the U.S.S.R., in 1933 there were only sixteen-and-a-half million; thirty million cattle (about 45 per cent of the total) and 100 million sheep (about two-thirds of the total) had been killed off. Once again in 1932–1933 the country was faced with one of the worst famines it had ever known.

The kulaks disappeared, about five million of them, mostly into the forced labour camps and the slow death which that meant.

[1] She may have been poisoned.

Forced Labour

The application of the Five Year Plans created tremendous opposition on the one hand and a great demand for labour on the other. These problems were made to solve each other by the use of forced labour. Opponents of the régime could be sentenced to long periods of 'corrective labour' after which, if they survived, they might be rehabilitated. At first they were sent to the north where they were put to work on lumbering and fishing supervised by the security organs;[1] after the introduction of the Five Year Plans they were employed on constructing the new towns and factories, roads, railways, canals, fortifications, mines, etc. The Moscow–Volga canal and the White Sea–Baltic canals were built by forced labour; indeed the N.K.V.D. was probably the largest single employer of labour in the U.S.S.R. in the 1930s. One estimate puts the number of workers in forced labour camps as high as thirteen million in 1940.

Social Welfare

The people were forced and bullied into the pattern required by the Communist Party line, but for those who did not oppose the régime, there were real gains. A comprehensive welfare system was ultimately built up to provide medical and health care for all, with schemes covering sickness, disability, old age, etc., and providing for convalescent and rest homes, recreational facilities, parks of rest and culture and the like for the use of all workers. Nursery schools, crèches and canteens were established at factories and communal farms partly as useful social measures, but also to enable women to work and thus increase the total labour force available for the Five Year Plans. All these schemes tended to diminish the role of the family and to bring the individual worker or peasant more fully into communal activity where he could be supervised by the party organization, but they also meant a real improvement in general living conditions.

The Great Purge: the Treason Trials

There was nothing new about purges in the Marxist parties: Marx himself had been jealous of all ideas other than his own and had waged war on his rivals; Lenin too had been determined to maintain his own leadership and had expelled dissident members of the party, but this

[1] The security organs of the Soviet State have been known under different names at different times, viz. the Cheka from 1917–1922; the G.P.U. from 1922–1934; the N.K.V.D. from 1934–1943; the N.K.G.B. from 1943–1946; the M.G.B. from 1946–1953; and the K.G.B. from 1953. Stalin used the security organs to eliminate his opponents within the party and the N.K.V.D. was responsible for all forced labour and deportations, as well as for the police.

was nothing compared with the wholesale and ruthless elimination of all opposition, real, potential or imagined, carried out by Stalin.

By 1929 he had expelled Trotsky, his chief rival, and he was securely in power, but there remained much discontent and intrigue, and indeed the situation was so critical in 1929 that Stalin tentatively offered his resignation. No one dared take up the hint that was offered, however, and in fact Stalin was indispensable. He continued to play off the factions by alternations of repression and 'liberalism' such as the 1936 constitution.

While Trotsky was alive, writing and criticizing, 'Trotskyism' was an ever-present threat to Stalin's Russia, but in the 1930s another threat became increasingly serious: the rise of Hitler in Germany, whose declared intention it was to be anti-communist and to find lebensraum for the Germans towards the east in the Russian lands. For Russia, Nazi Germany represented the final stage in capitalism and ultimate conflict was therefore inevitable. Stalin felt he must either come to terms with Hitler or fight him, and if war came the probability was that the opposition within Russia would seize the opportunity to rise against him as it had against the tsar in 1917. He must get in first and rid himself of the opposition and pose as the saviour of the country.

There had been a purge of the party membership in 1933 but the climax came with the assassination (in 1934) of Kirov, a close associate of Stalin's in the Politburo. This threw the Government into alarm and a great investigation began which claimed to have discovered evidence of counter-revolutionary plots and treason and a reign of terror began.[1]

In a wholesale wave of arrests, public and private trials, executions and deportations to slave labour, Stalin secured the elimination of almost all the old guard of the Bolsheviks along with hundreds of thousands of lesser folk. There were five main trials of senior members of the party and of the army: in August 1936, Zinoviev, Kamenev and fourteen others were tried on charges of plotting to overthrow the Government by murdering Stalin, and working with Trotsky and the Germans; in January 1937, Radek, a journalist friend of Lenin's, and sixteen others were tried as Trotskyists; then came the turn of the army officers when in June 1937 Marshal Tukhachevsky and his senior officers were tried for treason and shot; seven more party leaders were tried later that year, and in March 1938, Bukharin, Rykov and Yagoda, the head of the N.K.V.D., and seventeen others were also tried and executed as traitors.

All the accused 'confessed' their crimes but in addition to these leading figures the N.K.V.D. arrested and executed or condemned to

[1] Kirov's assassination was probably arranged by Stalin for this purpose.

the labour camps hundreds of thousands of lesser officials and non-party members. No one knows how many suffered and many thousands simply disappeared. About 20,000 army officers were arrested and several thousands shot, while about one-fifth of the party members were expelled.

The campaign of fear and hysteria proved to be damaging for Russia's prestige abroad and at home because no one dared to make any decision, and the economy of the country began to suffer. The purgers themselves were purged and the reign of terror came to an end in 1939, but by then the threat to Russia from Germany was real enough.

Significance and Results of the Great Purge

Some of the charges were fantastic; for example those of conspiring with Germany and Japan for handing over Russian territory or for the restoration of capitalism, but there was undoubtedly genuine opposition to Stalin and there was a real plot among the army officers. Equally fantastic were some of the confessions and the summary nature of the trials. What does emerge is that Stalin systematically eliminated all possible elements that could form an alternative government to his own. In doing so nearly all the old party members were removed and replaced by younger men who had a vested interest in remaining loyal to Stalin. In the army possibly 25 per cent of the officers disappeared and this may have contributed to the setbacks of the Red Army in the first years of the war that followed. For the Russian people fear and suspicion stultified all social life, for writers and artists were as likely to suffer as the politicians. Russia was cut off almost absolutely from contact with the rest of the world and the repression at home was complete —even the Moscow telephone directory was not published.

The Constitution of 1936

The horrors of the forced collectivization and the great purges of the 1930s were followed by a period of apparent and relative liberalism: in 1934 the O.G.P.U. was abolished and replaced by the N.K.V.D. which carried out the same functions but slightly less arbitrarily; in 1935 food rationing was abolished and there was an amnesty for some political prisoners; but the culminating point was reached with the proclamation of the fundamental law of the U.S.S.R.—the new constitution.

Stalin was the President of the commission which drafted the law and it was introduced with great publicity and a show of mass participation as 'the only thoroughly democratic constitution in the world'. The time, it seemed, had come to make certain political changes: socialism had been achieved, but the dictatorship of the proletariat must be retained because of encirclement by the capitalist powers; the next stage in the revolution would therefore be delayed and the withering away of the State was not yet to be.

The law was really a statement of the political situation as it was, but there were one or two important changes: election was to be by secret ballot instead of by show of hands; there was to be universal adult suffrage, and the discrimination between urban and rural workers was removed. The 'democracy' of the constitution was soon exposed when Stalin declared that 'there is no room in the U.S.S.R. for several parties or for freedom for those parties. There is room in the U.S.S.R. only for one party, the Communist party', for since it was held that the parties reflected the classes, and since there was only one class in the U.S.S.R. there could therefore only be one party. At the subsequent elections only one candidate appeared on the voting papers, and the democracy consisted in voting 'yes' or 'no'. 96 per cent of the people voted, and 98 per cent of them voted 'yes'.

Education and Social Services

The Soviet Government sought not only to create a socialist state but also the ideal type of soviet citizen. There was a genuine wish to raise the general cultural level and the educational opportunities for the Russian people combined with a determination to make them accept and conform to the Marxist philosophy. By concentrating on the education of the young and by persuading and coercing the adults they have been remarkably successful in doing this.

Like everything else in the history of the U.S.S.R., educational policy has fluctuated between indiscriminate attempts to impose communist theory and subsequent modifications in the light of what is expedient or possible in practice. In 1918 the first School Statute separated education from the Church, relaxed some of the discipline of the tsarist schools, and stressed manual rather than intellectual training. Lunacharsky was Peoples' Commissar for Education from 1917 to 1929, and during the period of the N.E.P. much experimenting went on with 'progressive' educational ideas, largely derived from the American educational thinker, John Dewey. This meant a relaxation of discipline, and control by students over their teachers in the name of democracy: and the introduction of 'projects' based on 'interest', even though the children had not mastered the most elementary techniques of learning. The result was a lowering of educational standards and a flight from the schools. In the universities, which were taken over by the Communist Party in 1922 and purged of some of the ablest men because they could not be trusted to put over the party line, preference was given to the children of working-class parents, while others were discriminated against, no matter what their abilities. This, too, led to a lowering of academic standards that were further limited by the insistence on strict ideological control.

This period of experimentation came to an end between 1925 and 1930 when the educational system was revised; there was to be less stress on political indoctrination and more on discipline and the basic skills of reading, writing and arithmetic. Physical education was given special attention, partly because communal games were socially desirable, and partly because it was a useful introduction to military training. Compulsory primary education which had been discussed since the nineteenth century became a reality. The number of children in primary schools in 1920 was nine million; in 1933 it was eighteen million; the number in secondary schools in 1922 was half a million; in 1933 it was three and a half million.

There were further changes in educational policy during the Five Year Plans: there was even more stress on the acquisition of factual knowledge and less on indoctrination; children of non-communist families were no longer excluded from higher education; and in the universities, although the stress was still on technical training, some of the traditional academic disciplines returned. Stricter discipline, and teacher control were introduced, and grading and examinations emphasized the fact that all children are not equal.

Experiment is still going on in the Soviet schools but in many ways education is one of the most successful aspects of the Russian Revolution. The achievement is indisputable. The crash programme to abolish illiteracy in the 1920s and 1930s with inadequate teachers and buildings was successful, in spite of its immediate shortcomings. In 1917 more than three-quarters of the Russian people were illiterate; by 1939 illiteracy was rare. The great programme of industrialization would not have been possible without the education that sustained it.

The campaign to capture and train the minds of youth was not confined to the schools. The official policy of limiting the functions of the family and of banning all activities of the Church meant that the State had to provide the organization of youth activities outside the schools. In 1918 Komsomol was formed to provide a comprehensive field of physical and socially useful activities as well as political indoctrination for young persons aged fourteen to twenty-three: for the ten to sixteen age group there were the Young Pioneers, and for those under the age of ten there were the Little Octobrists. For the adults there were evening classes and great importance was attached to the provision of libraries, museums, lectures, radio programmes, film shows, etc., as part of the general educational process. Literature and the arts were strictly super-vised to ensure that they conformed to official policies, but science was given every encouragement.

Religion since 1917

The Marxist is, by definition, an atheist: for him, religious ideas are class ideas and the Church is merely an ally of the capitalists and landowners in exploiting the workers. The socialist is concerned to improve his lot in this world, and beliefs about better things in the next are irrelevant. Marx had claimed that 'Religion is the opium of the people' by teaching them to accept that which they have the power to alter, but it is also true that the organized Church represents another source of authority and loyalty that cannot be tolerated in the centralized and autocratic communist State. The Church also has a wide influence outside that of doctrine and worship, for it acts in society to set the standards of public and private morality, defines the function of the family, and undertakes the education of the young. All these things the communist State denies to the Church and assumes for itself.

The 1918 constitution separated the Church from the State, the Synod was abolished and replaced by a Patriarchate, and there was a declaration of equality for all faiths. All Church property—the land and buildings, the furniture, vestments, plate, etc.—was confiscated, and individual congregations were only permitted to lease their churches from the State, and were often persecuted when they did so. The Patriarch, Tikhon, protested and excommunicated the Bolsheviks, but this did not trouble them. Many of the buildings were allowed to fall into ruin, some were turned into anti-God museums and others were put to a variety of secular uses. In 1921 public religious instruction for children under eighteen was banned and the seminaries were closed. Churchmen lost their civic rights and were discriminated against as non-useful workers and they often found it difficult to obtain food rations, accommodation or fuel. Many, including the Patriarch Tikhon, were arrested for not surrendering Church treasures to aid famine relief, and were put on trial during 1922–1923.

The Government sponsored a schism within the Church in order to weaken it, and in 1925 established the 'Friends of the Godless', whose function it was to spread anti-religious propaganda. At first there was, ostensibly, religious freedom, in the sense that a person could practise his religion privately, but only the anti-religious groups were allowed to carry out propaganda. Article 124 of the 1936 constitution states that, 'in order to ensure to citizens freedom of conscience, the Church in the U.S.S.R. is separated from the State, and the school from the Church. Freedom of religious worship and freedom of anti-religious propaganda is recognized for all citizens.'

The general line has been that religion would die out as socialism was established, but because the communist rulers knew how deeply rooted religious feeling was, especially among the peasantry, the persecution of the Church must not be so strong that the people would become more devoted to it as a result. It was done in indirect ways such as the introduction of a six-day working week so that a worker would have a day off on Sunday only once in every six weeks, and by severe punishments for absenteeism from work.

There has been no compromise in the schools where it is insisted that Marxism, not religion, is the only possible basis for education, and the teachers are expected to point out the falsities of religious faith: truth, it is claimed, lies in the study of science not religion. For example, the history teacher's task is defined as, 'to educate his pupils ideologically and politically, and of arousing in their minds a feeling of Soviet patriotism and selfless devotion to the cause of the Communist Party of the Soviet Union, and of communist construction'.

Linked with the attack on religion, but also as part of a genuine desire to bring real social equality to women came an attack on the traditional role of the family. The religious marriage service was abolished: it became a simple civil ceremony only, and divorce and abortion were made easy (1920). There were equal rights for all children, whether legitimate or illegitimate, and nurseries and communal facilities were provided to make it possible for women to go out to work and increase the available labour force. Thus by weakening the ties of the family it was hoped to strengthen those with the State.

There was some abatement of the early persecution after 1927, and some of the 'progressive' social ideas were dropped—indeed there is a curiously old-fashioned puritanism about the modern communist attitude to social morality.

Because of the need for national unity during the war Stalin allowed the restoration of the Patriarchate in 1943, the patriarch was elected again, and the Orthodox Church has regained its official position, but it must be remembered that there were large numbers of Roman Catholic, Uniate, Muslim and Jewish believers as well as many sects in the former tsarist empire. All have suffered persecution but it has been necessary for the communist government to act carefully and the application of the party line has vacillated for reasons of expediency even while theoretically it is committed to atheism, but the Roman Catholic Church, in particular, because it is an international organization that imposes a dual loyalty on its members and is opposed to communism, has always been a major object of attack by communist states.

QUESTIONS

1. Give an account of the early careers of Stalin and Trotsky and indicate the reasons for the rivalry between them and its consequences.

2. Give a critical account of the first two Five Year Plans for industry, 1928–1937.

3. Give an account of the forced collectivization of Russian agriculture in the 1930s and indicate some of the consequences.

4. Assess the significance of the great purges in the U.S.S.R. in the 1930s.

5. Give an account of either: (a) education; or (b) religion in the U.S.S.R.

6. Find out what you can and make notes on: Sovkhozes; Kolkhozes; Machine Tractor Stations; kulaks; the O.G.P.U.; the 1936 constitution; Komsomol; A. Y. Vyshinsky.

Further Reading

BASSECHES, N., trans. E. W. Dickes. *Stalin.* Staples, 1952.

DEUTSCHER, I. *Stalin, a Political Biography.* Oxford U.P., 1949.

—— *Trotsky: the prophet armed.* Oxford U.P., 1954.

—— *Trotsky: the prophet unarmed.* Oxford U.P., 1959.

KOESTLER, A. *Darkness at Noon,* (a novel about the Moscow trials). Cape, 1940.

KOLARZ, W. *Religion in the Soviet Union.* Macmillan, 1961.

LEVIN, D. *Soviet Education Today,* Staples, 1960.

ROTHSTEIN, A. *A History of the U.S.S.R.* Penguin, 1950 (Pelican).

SCHAPIRO, L. *The Communist Party of the Soviet Union.* Eyre and Spottiswoode, 1960 and Methuen, 1963.

WOLFE, B. D. *Three who made a Revolution.* Thames and Hudson, 1956. (Lenin, Stalin, Trotsky.)

The Constitution of the U.S.S.R. Foreign Languages Publishing House, Moscow.

CHAPTER XIX

FOREIGN AFFAIRS, 1917–1939

Foreign Ministers

Trotsky, 1917–1918
G. V. Chicherin, 1918–1930
M. M. Litvinov, 1930–1939
V. M. Molotov, 1939–1949

The separation of foreign and domestic affairs is one of convenience only; in fact they are closely interrelated. This is true at all times, but it was especially so for the history of Russia between the two world wars.

In 1917 the Bolshevik leaders expected that the world revolution was at hand, and the conduct of foreign relations was, for a time, determined by a degree of idealism and abstract Marxist theory. When it became clear that the world revolution was not taking place there came a return to political realism and a conflict developed between Stalin and Trotsky on the issue of building socialism in one country first, and using it as a base for the world revolution. Meanwhile there were the problems of securing the stability and defining the frontiers of the new State and of furthering the cause of international communism.

With the triumph of Stalin there came a period of ostracism and isolation, with concentration on domestic problems, and then with the threat to Russia of Nazi Germany the Soviets began to look for alliances in a system of collective security, while at the same time continuing to work for the overthrow of the capitalist system throughout the world. With the coming of the Second World War and the change in the balance of power in Europe that followed the defeat of Germany, there came a return to the traditional expansionist policies of tsarist Russia. Opportunism, conspiracy, duplicity and contradiction appear as the characteristics of Soviet foreign policy between the wars.

1917–1921

When the Bolsheviks seized power in 1917 they immediately attempted to put their Marxist theories into practice by issuing a series of decrees. Among these was a declaration of the complete equality of all nationalities and their rights of self-determination, a repudiation of all foreign loans and debts incurred by the tsarist governments, and renunciation of all imperialist treaties made by tsars. In addition there was a demand for world peace and disarmament and for a peace settlement without annexations or indemnities. All this was accompanied by a declaration that it was the mission of the Bolshevik party to lead a world-wide revolution against the capitalist and imperialist powers.

It is not surprising that the capitalist and imperialist powers; namely Britain, France and the United States, did not look with favour upon the Soviets; they disapproved of the move to make a separate peace with Germany; they had no intention of foregoing the victor's rights to enforce annexations and indemnities from the defeated State; they had large investments in Russia, and they were determined not to have Marxist risings in their territories. Consequently they refused to recognize the new Soviet Government, and later intervened in an attempt to overthrow it.

France and Britain did not respond to the Soviet demand for peace because the United States was just entering the war directly on their side; Germany, on the other hand, was anxious for peace on the eastern front so that she could concentrate on the west.

An armistice was signed in December, and Trotsky as Commissar for Foreign Affairs began negotiations with the Germans at Brest-Litovsk, but they came to nothing because the Germans were as determined to make annexations and to combat the threat of a revolution in Germany as the Bolsheviks were against annexations and for revolution. Trotsky left the negotiations with the formula, 'No peace, no war', meaning that Russia would withdraw from the war but would not make peace. The central powers, Austria and Germany, made peace with the Ukraine which had declared its independence, and then continued the war against Russia. They rapidly overran western Russia and were within reach of Petrograd, when Lenin against much opposition, persuaded the Government to accept the German terms; for peace at any price was essential if there was to be a respite for the Soviets to consolidate their position.

The Treaty of Brest-Litovsk, March 1918

This was one of the most ruthless peace treaties ever imposed: but it did give the Soviet Government the pause it needed and with the defeat

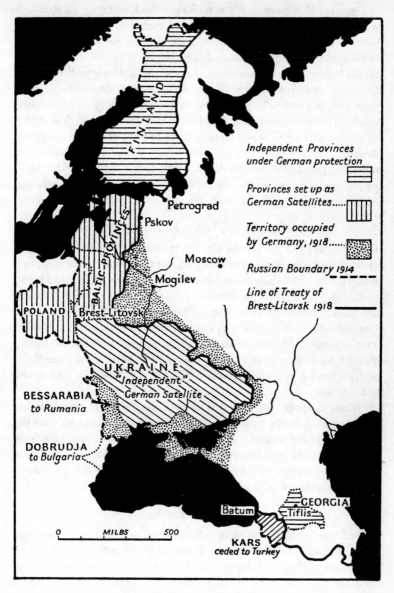

Independent Provinces
under German protection

Provinces set up as
German Satellites .....

Territory occupied
by Germany, 1918 ......

Russian Boundary 1914 - - - -

Line of Treaty of
Brest-Litovsk 1918 ——

FINLAND

Petrograd

Pskov

BALTIC PROVINCES

Moscow

Mogilev

POLAND

Brest-Litovsk

UKRAINE
"Independent"
German Satellite

BESSARABIA
to Rumania

DOBRUDJA
to Bulgaria

0   MILES   500

Batum

GEORGIA
Tiflis

KARS
ceded to Turkey

THE TREATY OF BREST-LITOVSK

of Germany that autumn it was no longer valid, so far as the Russians were concerned. Almost all the territory gained in the west since the reign of Peter the Great had to be given up; the Soviets were obliged to recognize the independence of Georgia, the Ukraine, and Finland; to hand over Poland, Lithuania, Latvia and Estonia to the care of Germany and Austria; and Kars, Ardahan and Batum to Turkey. Rumania, Russia's ally, was forced to accept similarly ruthless terms by the Treaty of Bucharest. The loss of the Ukraine, the richest part of the tsarist empire was a terrible price to pay for peace; altogether Russian territory was reduced by one and a quarter million square miles, the population by sixty-two million; 32 per cent of arable land, 75 per cent of her coal and iron mines, 33 per cent of her factories and 26 per cent of her railroads were lost.

Results of the Treaty of Brest-Litovsk

Germany was able to face the allies in the west for the final campaigns of the Great War and Lenin appeared as the German agent that, in a sense, he was. The allies refused to recognize the new régime and began to consider intervention in Russia in order to preserve their interests, and to reopen an eastern front. Thus foreign and domestic affairs merged in the chaos of the civil war and allied intervention. Meanwhile the Germans imposed their own version of law and order in the former Russian territories, gave aid to the Finnish Whites against the Reds, and imposed a one-sided commercial treaty on Russia as well as the peace treaty.

When Germany was defeated in 1918 the Treaty of Brest-Litovsk was rescinded, but because Russia had withdrawn unilaterally from the war, she was not invited to take part in the peace settlements at Versailles, nor in the establishment of the League of Nations, which Lenin regarded as 'an international organization of capitalists for the systematic exploitation of all the peoples of the earth'.

The Comintern

Cut off from normal diplomatic relations with other states and involved in the turmoil of the civil war the Bolsheviks continued to expect an immediate outbreak of world revolution and worked systematically to promote it. Lenin refused to recognize the authority of the Second Socialist International and in 1919 he set up the third Communist International or the Comintern, as it was better known. The aim was to organize all the communist parties of the world for a lasting peace through revolution. Capitalism was to be abolished everywhere and all land, and the means of production, were to be nationalized. Large funds were made available for propaganda and the encouragement of revolts in Germany, Hungary, India and China. There were regular congresses until 1928, and then there was a break until 1935, when Stalin called the last. The Comintern was most active as an international communist conspiracy between 1919 and 1924, but after the failure of the German revolution in 1923 and of the Chinese communists in 1927, it came increasingly under the control of the Russian Communist Party, and after 1928 it was little more than an instrument for promoting Russian interests as a base for some future world revolution. Most of the leaders were liquidated in the great purge, and the Comintern was dissolved in 1943.

The Problem of Nationalities

The Bolsheviks in theory recognized equal rights and self-determination for all nationalities, but in practice they discouraged it because the need for centralized control was incompatible with regional autonomy, and there were in any case great differences of cultural development between the various peoples of the former empire. At first it was not only a piece of equalitarian idealism, but was also a calculated propaganda drive to encourage revolt, especially within the multi-racial areas of the Austrian Empire. It was hoped to retain the various nationalities within the Russian Empire, but anti-Bolshevik groups, supported by the allies, declared their independence in Finland, Latvia, Estonia and Lithuania, and in 1920 the Soviets recognized the loss of the former Baltic provinces. By the Treaty of Riga in 1921, Poland secured for herself large areas of former Russian territory.

In the Caucasus three anti-Bolshevik republics were set up during the civil war in Georgia, Armenia and Azerbaydzhan, but with the withdrawal of British support, and the defeat of Denikin, the Red Army moved in and the republics were obliged to surrender their independence by 1921. A peace treaty was made with Turkey in 1921, whereby Turkey kept her acquisitions by the Treaty of Brest-Litovsk except Batum, and the frontiers between Turkey and the Trans-Caucasian republics were recognized. In 1922 the three republics were completely incorporated in the U.S.S.R. By 1922 also the Soviets had succeeded in extending their control over central Asia and Siberia.

In 1918 the Russian Soviet Federative Socialist Republic was set up for the Great Russian people (about 78 million out of a total of 147 million), and the right to equality and self-determination was reasserted. In 1922 the Union of Soviet Socialist Republics was declared which consisted of the Russian, Ukrainian, White Russian and Trans-Caucasian Republics. Although theoretically independent, each republic was in fact governed by its Communist Party, which was centrally controlled from Moscow. Thus a show of independence and self-determination was preserved above the reality of central control.

1922–1934: International Recognition

After the ending of the civil war the period of ostracism and intervention came hesitantly to an end, and in a series of treaties with European powers, commercial relations were established and recognition extended to the Soviets. The policies of the Comintern of promoting world revolution were hardly compatible with normal diplomatic intercourse and the Soviet's constant barrage of propaganda, idealism and duplicity over the need for disarmament did not gain for her a place at the Washington disarmament conference of 1921–1922, although she was admitted to the conference at Genoa in 1922. The Baltic states recognized the Soviets in 1920 and commercial treaties were made with Germany, Sweden, and Britain within the next twelve months. Official recognition and trade agreements came from Poland, Turkey and Afghanistan in 1921, Germany in 1922, Britain, France and Italy in 1924, and many other smaller countries later on, but the United States withheld recognition until 1933.

The Treaty of Rapallo

The peacemakers at Versailles, led by the French, had set up a ring of states designed to keep Bolshevism out of eastern Europe and the Soviets were ostracized and frustrated in their aims. Approaches were made at Genoa to Germany, her former enemy, but also another outcast nation, and in 1922, by the Treaty of Rapallo, Germany gave official recognition to the Soviets and entered into close political and economic collaboration. When the French occupied the Ruhr in 1923 the Soviets demonstrated their new support for Germany by protesting to the allies, as they also did when Memel was handed over to Lithuania. This growing rapprochement between Russia and Germany alarmed France and was a cause of the decision by Britain, France and Italy to extend official recognition to the Soviets in 1924.

Thus by 1925 the Soviets had secured official recognition by most of the countries of the world except the United States and had established commercial relations with them as part of the N.E.P. Since foreign trade was a State monopoly there was no separation of economic and diplomatic interests. The Soviet aim was economic self-sufficiency and only strategically necessary goods were imported. The Soviet trading agencies abroad were suspected of carrying on the conspiratorial activities of the Comintern and the hostility and suspicion of Russian

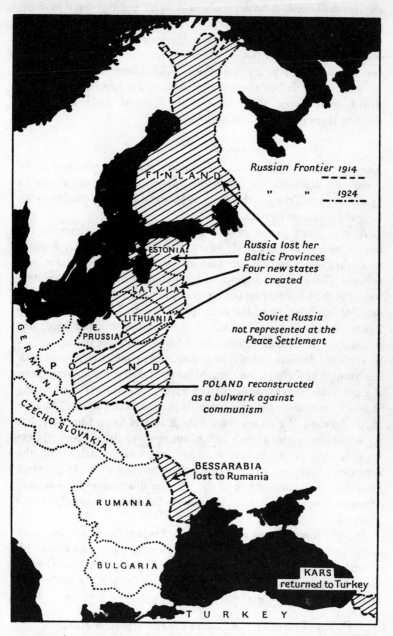

RUSSIA'S WESTERN FRONTIERS AFTER THE FIRST WORLD WAR, 1924

motives continued. A Soviet diplomatic agent was murdered in Switzerland, the Russian trade headquarters in Germany was raided by the Government and in Britain a great public outcry arose after the publication of the 'Zinoviev letter', which was later shown to be a forgery, and which seemed to indicate direct Russian interference in British domestic matters; but the attempt to form an association with the British trade unions at the time of the General Strike in 1926 by assisting them financially was unsuccessful.

The Locarno Pact, 1925

Although Germany continued her economic and non-aggression agreements with Russia she was enticed away from the close political alliance by the Locarno Treaty with France in 1925 and by her admission to the League of Nations in 1926.

After a short period of distrustful diplomatic collaboration the Soviets were once more made aware of their isolation, partly brought upon themselves by the activities of the Comintern and their own policies. There was an attempt to form an eastern bloc as a counterweight to the Locarno pact but it came to nothing because of the strong anti-Bolshevik feeling of the countries of eastern Europe, particularly Poland, which under Pilsudski, allied with Rumania and tried, unsuccessfully, to form an anti-Bolshevik alliance with the Baltic states.

With the decision to build socialism in one country that came with the triumph of Stalin, Russia retired into her shell and concentrated on the economic reconstruction of the Five Year Plans, while growing Russian nationalism replaced the early international idealism. In 1930 Stalin declared 'We do not want a single foot of foreign territory, but we will not surrender a single inch of our territory either.' Nevertheless he continued to expect that a second war was inevitable with the capitalist powers and to prepare to take advantage of it. At the same time there was constant talk of the need for disarmament, a lessening of the more open propaganda, and a move to restore normal diplomatic relations.

In 1928 Russia signed the Kellogg Pact which renounced war as an instrument of national policy and in 1929 similar pacts were made with Poland, Latvia, Estonia, Rumania and later Turkey, Persia and Danzig. Diplomatic relations were resumed with Britain in 1929 and a non-aggression pact was made with France in 1932.

Policy Towards the States on the Russian Borders

Outside Europe the Soviet policy consisted of posing as the champion of peace and disarmament and of the nations suffering from exploitation by the imperialist powers, while at the same time intriguing for the overthrow of existing governments to be replaced by communists. This served to protect the Russian State through the establishment of friendly states on the frontiers.

In 1917 the methods of the imperialists were denounced and agreements such as the Anglo-Russian division of Persia in 1907 were scrapped and the former Russian protectorates and commercial privileges over Asiatic peoples were renounced. Treaties as between equals were made with Persia, Afghanistan, Mongolia and Turkey in 1921. The Turco-Soviet agreement gave the Turks aid against the Greeks but did not result in any noticeable support for Russia, for example, over the question of the straits at the Lausanne conference in 1922. The treaty with Persia (1921), renounced all rights and privileges acquired in Persia by the tsars and gave Russia the right to send troops to Persia only if that country were invaded by a third party intending to make war on the Soviets. Afghanistan accepted Soviet aid against Britain but none of these countries gave the quid pro quo of accepting communist governments.

Georgia, Armenia and Azerbaydzhan were formed into the Trans-Caucasian Republic and incorporated in the U.S.S.R. in 1922.

The prestige and propaganda effects of these negotiations with border states were considerable and they were followed by successful trade agreements between 1924 and 1927.

The Far East

In the Far East there was less success. In Outer Mongolia the Red Army gave support in 1921 to the revolutionary Government of the Mongolian People's Republic which later declared its independence of China, but in 1924 the Soviets were obliged to recognize Chinese suzerainty over Mongolia although the communist intrigues there and in Sinkiang continued and the Government still looked to Moscow for help and guidance.

In China the Soviets pursued the double policy of negotiating with the official Government while at the same time giving aid to the Kuomintang that was in revolt against it. The Kuomintang was anti-communist but it was serving the Soviet purpose, and for four years from 1923, the Chinese revolution was given arms, money and military advice by the Comintern and the Chinese communists. This aid was one of the causes of dispute between Stalin and Trotsky: the latter wished to make the revolution communist, while Stalin counselled aiding the Kuomintang's revolutionary efforts as a first step towards an ultimate communist revolution.

The alliance with the communists was not approved in the Kuomintang, and in 1927 Chiang Kai-shek disarmed the communist troops at Shanghai and sent the Russian advisers home. The Chinese Communist Party then became the opposition to the Kuomintang as well as to the official Chinese Government.

The Chinese Government also turned against the Soviets. In 1927 it raided the Soviet embassy in Peking, arrested some of the Russian and Chinese communists there, and disclosed the negotiations between the Russians and the Kuomintang. Diplomatic relations between the countries were severed.

Another point of dispute that continued was over the formerly Russian-owned Chinese Eastern Railway that ran through Manchuria. The 1924 agreement between the U.S.S.R. and China provided that it should be jointly owned for thirty years when it would revert to China, but by 1928 the Kuomintang had gained control over most of China and was trying to force the U.S.S.R. out. In 1929 the Soviet consulate in Harbin was raided, and both sides prepared for war. A demonstration of force by the U.S.S.R. compelled the Chinese to agree to a conference in Moscow and to maintain things as they were.

The Japanese were forced out of Siberia and the independent Far East Republic came to an end in 1922. Japan recognized the U.S.S.R. in 1925, agreed not to interfere in Siberia and to give up occupation of north Sakhalin. Relations remained quiet if strained until the outbreak of the Sino-Japanese War in 1931.

The intervention of the U.S.S.R. in China helped to keep the country weak and thus ensured the security of the Soviet frontier, but when the Japanese invaded Manchuria steps had to be taken to strengthen the Far East frontier against them. The Far East army was increased, a new track was laid for the Trans-Siberian Railway, immigration was encouraged and industries developed. In order to avoid further dispute at an awkward time Russia in 1935 sold her share in the Chinese Eastern Railway to the Japanese puppet state of Manchukuo.

Relations with the United States

The United States recognized the provisional government in 1917 and continued to recognize it as the official Government until 1922, steadfastly refusing to recognize the Bolsheviks until 1933. When a Soviet envoy was sent to New York the United States refused to acknowledge him and deported him in 1920. Meanwhile American troops joined the allied expeditions to Archangel and to Vladivostok in 1918 and intervened in the civil war on the side of the Whites. They remained at

Archangel until 1919 and at Vladivostok until 1920, and trade between America and Russia was prevented by a refusal to grant licences.

Limited trading began again in 1920, the Soviets were permitted to establish an information bureau in Washington in 1922, and in 1924 'Amtorg' was set up as a single trading agency for all imports and exports between Russia and America. Trade between the countries increased as a result, but official relations remained frigid because of the activities of the Comintern, the repudiation of the tsarist debts and the inherent tensions between a Marxist and a capitalist society. Nevertheless much American aid was sent to Russia for famine relief in 1921–1923 and a large number of American engineers and technicians went to Russia to help in the Five Year Plans.

In the early 1930s there came a change in the American policy of non-recognition due to the Japanese threat to Manchuria, the rise of Hitler in Germany and the economic effects of the great depression which made it necessary to increase trade. Consequently soon after President Roosevelt took office the United States recognized the U.S.S.R., which promised to abstain from hostile propaganda in the United States. This was followed by a trade treaty in 1935, in spite of a failure to agree on the settlement of debts.

1934–1939

Until 1933, France and Britain, and to a lesser degree Poland, were regarded as the chief enemies of the Bolshevik régime in Europe, while Japan became a serious threat in the Far East after 1931. When Hitler rose to power in 1933, it was Nazi Germany that constituted the main threat to Soviet security, for fascism was regarded as the final stage of capitalism by the Marxists, and it pursued a bitterly anti-communist and anti-Russian policy; the German Communist Party was persecuted, and Hitler promised the German people a campaign in the East to find lebensraum in the Ukraine and Siberia.

In the face of the Nazi threat the U.S.S.R. abandoned its policy of isolation and sought security in a system of collective security by resuming relations with the United States in 1933, and with France, Czechoslovakia, and Rumania in 1934.[1] In 1934, also, in spite of the bitterness of her former attacks upon it, the U.S.S.R. joined the League of Nations. This was followed by conversations in Moscow with the Foreign Ministers of Britain, France and Czechoslovakia, on collective security, and alliances were made with France and Czechoslovakia in 1935.

While this open diplomacy was going on the U.S.S.R. was strength-

[1] Diplomatic relations were resumed with Britain in 1929.

ening her defences with the Five Year Plans and stepping up the activities of the Comintern.

The Popular Front, 1935

The Comintern now apparently changed its policy: its main declared theme was no longer the immediate fostering of communist revolution throughout the world, but that the fascist governments were a threat to peace, and that all progressive groups—Socialists, Liberals and the Labour parties—should form a popular anti-fascist front against them, and where this support for the security of the U.S.S.R. was forthcoming the communists would tone down their revolutionary activities and propaganda. Nevertheless the distrust of the Comintern remained, and Britain and France continued to appease Hitler and Mussolini who were very skilful in playing on their fears of Bolshevism.

Neither the entry to the League, nor the efforts to ensure collective security were very successful in lessening the apprehensions of the U.S.S.R. The League did nothing to prevent the Italian aggression against Abyssinia in 1935, the Spanish Civil War in 1936 or the Japanese attack on China in 1937. An attempt to form an eastern Locarno pact with the countries on her western borders came to nothing when Poland and Rumania refused to permit Russian troops to cross their territory in the event of war with Germany.

While attempting to build diplomatic fences against Germany, Stalin at the same time sought not to provoke her, continuing normal relations and preparations for a new trade treaty.

The Spanish Civil War

In 1936 German and Italian aid strengthened the Spanish fascists in their revolt against the republican Government. This aid was continued in spite of appeals by a non-intervention committee of other European powers including the U.S.S.R. As a result direct military intervention on the side of the republicans was undertaken by the U.S.S.R. in the form of providing food, war material and military advice, as well as permitting volunteers to serve in the International Brigade. This was the first full-scale trial of strength between the fascist and the communist camps, but since Stalin could not yet face war with Germany the aid to the Spanish republicans was discreetly reduced.

The Anti-Comintern Pact

In 1936 also Germany and Italy strengthened their new-found partnership by forming what was known as the Rome-Berlin axis, and Germany and Japan signed the anti-Comintern pact which Italy joined in

1937. This was an agreement between the three powers to fight communism in general and to oppose the U.S.S.R. in particular. The U.S.S.R. was now faced with the danger of attack from east and west and her alarm at the situation was not lessened by the apparent ineffectiveness of Britain and France in face of the fascist challenge to the peace of Europe and the security of the U.S.S.R.—indeed there were good grounds for fearing that they secretly hoped that Germany would turn against Russia and away from western Europe. These fears increased with the German annexation of Austria in 1938 and the Munich crisis arising out of the desertion of Czechoslovakia. After this Stalin seems to have given up any hope that France or Britain would take any action against Hitler.

Meanwhile the situation in the Far East was uneasy. Japan invaded China in 1937 and the Russian armies in Siberia were strengthened as a precautionary measure, while cautious support was given to China. But Stalin dare not risk doing anything that might provoke the Japanese too much, although frontier incidents instigated by the Japanese to test Russian strength were firmly checked in 1938 and 1939, and a treaty for mutual aid was made with Mongolia.

QUESTIONS

1. Find out what you can and make notes on the following: G. V. Chicherin; M. M. Litvinov; V. M. Molotov; the Rapallo Treaty; the Locarno Pact; the Zinoviev letter.
2. Give an account of the conduct of Soviet foreign affairs from 1917 to 1939.
3. Give an account of the circumstances leading to the Treaty of Brest-Litovsk and discuss its consequences for the new Russian State.
4. Discuss the Soviet handling of the problem of nationalities.
5. Discuss the Soviet efforts to build up a system of collective security between the two world wars.

Further Reading

ADAMS, A. E. *Readings in Soviet Foreign Policy*. Harrap, 1961.

BELOFF, M. *The Foreign Policy of Soviet Russia (1929–41)*. 2 vols. Oxford U.P. for R.I.I.A., 1947–49.

FISCHER, L. *The Soviets in World Affairs*. 2nd edn. Princeton U.P., 1951.

GOLDWYN, R. A. ed. *Readings in Russian Foreign Policy*. Oxford U.P. paperback, 1959.

JONES, G. J. *From Stalin to Khruschev*. Linden Press, 1960.

KENNAN, G. F. *Soviet Foreign Policy, 1917–1941*. Van Nostrand, 1960.

—— *Russia and the West under Lenin and Stalin*. Hutchinson, 1961.

SETON-WATSON, H. *The Pattern of Communist Revolution*. Methuen, 1953 and later editions.

WHEELER-BENNETT, J. W. *Brest-Litovsk: the Forgotten Peace*. Papermac., 1963.

CHAPTER XX

THE SECOND WORLD WAR, 1939–1945

The Prelude to War

In the spring of 1938 Hitler marched his troops into Austria and incorporated it into the German Reich. Within a few months it was clear that he next intended to take Czechoslovakia, which was not only rich in minerals, but was strategically important for any move which might later be made eastward. At Munich in September, Hitler made his first demands upon Czechoslovakia and Britain and France gave way without consulting the U.S.S.R. In March 1939 he occupied the whole of Czechoslovakia and at the same time took Memel from Lithuania. It seemed clear that Britain and France could not be relied upon to oppose Hitler, so Stalin began to take his own measures for the security of Russia. Litvinov who had failed to achieve collective security was replaced by Molotov as Foreign Minister in May 1939.

Britain and France, now thoroughly alarmed at Hitler's ambitions and bad faith, began negotiating with the U.S.S.R. for a military alliance, while Stalin demanded the right to send Russian troops into Poland, Finland and the Baltic states, but these countries were naturally unwilling to allow this and Britain and France were as unwilling to put pressure upon them to agree. They did, however, offer guarantees of help to Poland, Rumania and Greece in the event of attack by Germany.

The Russo-German Pact, 1939

In August 1939 the world was astonished to learn of the signing of a commercial treaty and a non-aggression pact for ten years between Nazi Germany and communist Russia. Germany provided large credits to the U.S.S.R. for the purchase of machinery, and the U.S.S.R. was to provide raw materials, but more important were the secret arrangements for the partition of Poland and the Russian acquisition of the Baltic states.[1] Thus by coming to terms with Germany Stalin

[1] Russia was to have a free hand in Estonia, Latvia, parts of Finland, Poland and Rumania: Germany was to have Lithuania and western Poland.

could claim that he was playing for time to prepare for the inevitable conflict and safeguarding his western frontiers by extending them towards his enemy.

In September, Germany invaded Poland from the west and the U.S.S.R. did so from the east: for the fourth time in her unhappy history Poland had been partitioned. So far as the U.S.S.R. was concerned German penetration further east had been checked, but the Soviet and German forces were now face to face, and Britain and France stood by their guarantees to Poland and were now at war with Germany.

At first, it seemed to have been Stalin's hope that the U.S.S.R. could stand aside while Germany, Britain and France destroyed each other, but the fall of France in May 1940, and Hitler's easy success in western Europe made it more certain that he would eventually turn east again, and it became necessary to take further measures for the security of the western frontiers of the U.S.S.R. It was essential that the route from Germany to Leningrad and Moscow via the Baltic lands must be blocked, and 'mutual assistance' agreements were forced upon Latvia, Lithuania and Estonia in October. Finland refused to co-operate in this way and Rumania refused to hand over Bessarabia when Stalin demanded it.

The Russo-Finnish War, 1939–1940

Since the Finns would not agree to grant the U.S.S.R. the military positions she demanded for her protection against the threatened German attack, it was decided to take them by force. In November 1939 the Russian attack on Finland began. The Finns held out desperately and grave shortcomings in the Russian armies were revealed. The U.S.S.R. was expelled from the League of Nations for this unprovoked aggression and Britain and France prepared to send help to the Finns.

In March 1940 the Finns, who were outnumbered, had to accept the Russian conquest and a peace treaty was made that granted the U.S.S.R. all that she wanted: the frontier was extended a further seventy-five miles from Leningrad, the U.S.S.R. gained the Finnish naval bases that protected the Baltic approaches as well as part of northern Finland. Much of the Finnish territory was incorporated in the Karelian Soviet Republic.

In June, in order to strengthen the Baltic approaches still further, ultimatums were sent to Lithuania, Latvia and Estonia demanding the creation of governments 'friendly' to the U.S.S.R.: elections were held in which only pro-communist candidates stood and the new governments applied 'voluntarily' to be incorporated in the U.S.S.R. These changes were recognized by Germany in 1941 although not of course by the other countries of Europe.

Meanwhile, and by similar methods, in order to strengthen her southern frontier, the Rumanians were forced to hand over Bessarabia and the north of Bukovina which were also incorporated in the U.S.S.R.

Last minute attempts were made to strengthen the Soviet position by securing a neutrality pact with Japan in April 1941 in spite of German attempts to forestall it, and a non-aggression treaty with Yugoslavia just before the Germans invaded that country. Stalin became Chairman of the Council of Commissars, or Chief Minister, and the army was reorganized in the light of the Finnish experiences: more men were recruited; the army was raised to five million; the authority of officers was increased and that of political commissars diminished; physical and military training for civilians and school-children was introduced. At the same time there were attempts to increase industrial production; the eight-hour day was restored, with one rest day in seven, not one in six as formerly, and regulations for directing labour were extended.

The Second Great Fatherland War, or the Great Patriotic War

The unholy alliance of communist Russia and anti-communist Germany was not likely to last long, for it was one of the more cynical marriages of convenience in history, yet for a time it worked to their mutual benefit. Hitler could concentrate his forces on western Europe for the war against Britain and France without too much fear of a Russian invasion from the east, while Stalin could consolidate his position and prepare for the war that was to come. Even so he seems to have been taken by surprise in spite of warnings that were given to him by Britain and the United States of an imminent German invasion.

There were disputes about the working of the commercial agreements after the Russo-German pact, but there was at first some real co-operation between the two countries. Hitler's successes in western Europe altered the Russian attitude, and the pact between Germany, Italy and Japan in September 1940 which was later joined by Bulgaria was even more alarming. Disputes about spheres of influence in eastern Europe and the Balkans became more bitter, for Molotov demanded that Finland, the Balkans and Turkey should lie wholly within the Russian sphere and made further demands upon Bulgaria, the Bosporus, Persia and Sakhalin. This was far more than Germany could agree to, and it was decided to make war upon Russia even before the war in the west was concluded.

Progress of the War

In June 1941, Hitler issued Directive 21 for 'Operation Barbarossa' and 200 divisions invaded the U.S.S.R. with the object of securing victory within eight weeks. Spain, Italy, Rumania, Slovakia, Finland and Hungary also joined in. The German plan was for a three-pronged attack along a 1,800-mile front: (1) via the Baltic provinces in the north assisted by the Finns to Leningrad; (2) via the traditional central invasion route to Moscow to disrupt communications, and (3) a southern thrust assisted by the Rumanians to gain control over the food and industries of the Ukraine and the oil of the Caucasus. It was expected that there would be support from the non-communist population, and Stalin had already attempted to forestall this by the great purges and by forcibly transferring suspect peoples eastwards before the invasion.

The Germans were at first very successful. The Russian armies retreated in something like chaos, and there was panic in the Government which was evacuated to Kuybyshev. Leningrad was reached in August but it held out under siege until 1944. The Moscow thrust was held up at Smolensk for a time but Smolensk was taken in August and Kiev in September and the Germans were only 100 miles from the capital. In the south they reached the Crimea. Then with the extension of the supply lines and the coming of winter the advance was checked for the time being.

The purges in the army of the 1930s had weakened its effective strength and had increased the opposition to party policy. The Russian army was not ready for the German attack and the retreat was in the nature of a rout, with a good deal of desertion, demoralization, mass surrender and panic. The blitzkreig came near to success, for in the first year of the war the Germans and their allies had occupied 580,000 square miles of former Russian territory with a peacetime population of eighty-five million, half the iron ore, half the coal, half the steel, one-third of the industries, one-third of the railway mileage, and 40 per cent of the arable land. The Finns recovered the lands lost in 1940 and the Rumanians took back Bessarabia and Bukovina. The rest was controlled by the Germans who planned to make the Russian lands a great agricultural colony and source of forced labour for the German Reich. They found a degree of collaboration from anti-soviet elements in the population, especially in the Baltic countries, the Ukraine, White Russia and from the non-Russian peoples of the Crimea and the Caucasus, but not as much as they expected, and this support was lost to a great extent because of their behaviour to the conquered peoples whom they regarded as sub-human, while about two and a half million

Jews and one and a half million suspected communists or underground fighters were ruthlessly exterminated.

The Russian answer to the German invasion was the traditional one of retreat and avoidance of encirclement until the enemy had extended his lines of communication, and then to attack these by guerilla activities while gathering forces for the counter-attack. Meanwhile a scorched earth policy of destroying everything in the way of the invader and Russia's greatest allies, her geography and her climate, could deny the enemy all supplies and force him, eventually, to retreat.

The first serious check to the German advance was the battle for Moscow which began in October 1941. They captured Mozhaisk, sixty miles west of Moscow, and Kalinin, a hundred miles to the north-west. Plans were made for street fighting in the city, but the Germans were held, and in December they gave up for the winter, and the blitzkrieg had failed. The Russians now counter-attacked and the Germans were driven back from Moscow.

In 1942 the Germans began their second main offensive: this time they planned to advance south-east to Stalingrad and towards the Caucasus for its oil, and then to swing north to attack Moscow from the south-east. Sevastopol was taken, and then Rostov, and the way was open for an advance along the Black Sea coast, but although they reached the Volga, the Germans were held up at Stalingrad[1] in September. This developed into the most crucial battle of the war, for Hitler insisted that it be taken and Stalin was determined not to let him. In November the Russians counter-attacked with a pincer movement from the north and the south; the German Sixth Army of 330,000 men was encircled, but was ordered to fight to the last man. They held out until February 1943, when the German commander, Von Paulus and twenty-four generals, surrendered with the 90,000 men that were left. The Russians then moved west but were held up for the time being by the German General Mannstein.

In July 1943, the Germans staged their final offensive near Kursk but after some initial success they were driven back by the Russian counter-offensive, and this time they kept going westwards. In January 1944 the siege of Leningrad was lifted and Russian armies crossed the 1939 frontiers with Poland and Rumania.

The Conquest of Eastern Europe

The Germans had been expelled from Russia and now Stalin exploited the new-found military strength of the Russian armies and the power vacuum left by the defeated Germans to extend the sphere of Soviet

[1] Now Volgograd.

influence and to recreate eastern Europe on the communist pattern. He had skilfully played upon the political naïvety and anti-British feelings of President Roosevelt at the wartime conferences to gain political concessions that Churchill, who foresaw the dangers, was unable to forestall, and throughout the war communist leaders from most of the countries of Europe had been training in the U.S.S.R. for the day when they could continue their political activities in the wake of the Russian armies.

With the great strength in men and equipment that had been built up, and with the prestige arising from the knowledge that they had successfully borne the brunt of the land fighting against the Germans, the Red armies swept into eastern Europe, bent upon revenge on the Germans and determined to make the U.S.S.R. safe from any further attack by the creation of a ring of satellite states on the western frontier, and the extension of communism throughout Europe.

At the Moscow conference in October 1943 it had been agreed that Britain and the United States would open a second front in the west in May 1944, and that the U.S.S.R. would simultaneously mount another offensive in the east. The landing in Normandy was made in June 1944, and the Russian offensive began by first clearing the Baltic provinces and driving Finland and then Rumania out of the war.

The Rumanian Armistice

The Rumanians hoped to save themselves by changing sides and in August 1944 they signed an armistice with the U.S.S.R., Britain and the United States, and agreed to declare war on Germany immediately.

The Finnish Armistice

In September the Finns signed an armistice with Britain and the U.S.S.R. (the United States was not at war with Finland).

Bulgaria

Bulgaria had declared war on Britain and the United States but had remained neutral towards Russia. With the reversal of Rumania's attitude, and with British troops in Greece, the Bulgarians sought to leave the war by rapidly making peace with Britain and the United States, but if they had made an armistice British troops from Greece would have occupied Bulgaria. Stalin was determined to keep eastern Europe for himself and to keep the British out, so in September Russia declared war on Bulgaria, who surrendered four days later, before any but Russian troops could enter the country.

The Red armies then joined up with the partisans under Tito in

Yugoslavia and Belgrade was freed in October. Meanwhile other Soviet armies were pressing into Hungary where the Germans set up a puppet Nazi Government after overthrowing Admiral Horthy, the regent who had been negotiating with the Russians. There was much bitter fighting and destruction before the Germans were finally driven out in April 1945.

As the Germans retreated on all fronts, it became a race between the Russians from the east and the British and Americans from the west to enter and occupy Germany. In January 1945 the Russians began a great offensive on a front stretching across eastern Europe with the object of capturing and occupying the three great capitals of Vienna, Prague and Berlin.

Budapest was taken in February, Vienna in April, and Prague in May. Meanwhile in the north the main Russian forces were moving through Poland towards Berlin. Warsaw was taken in January and in April the Russian armies crossed the River Oder. In April also the advance units of the American and Russian armies met on the River Elbe and the Russian armies entered Berlin. In May the Germans surrendered unconditionally to the allied forces.

The War against Japan

The neutrality pact between Japan and the U.S.S.R. had been honoured since 1941 because Japan needed all her forces for her war against the United States as the U.S.S.R. did for the war against Germany, but Stalin had never felt that he could trust the Japanese and had kept considerable forces in the Far East in case Japan should decide to aid her axis partner by attacking the U.S.S.R. He was pressed by the allies to enter the war against Japan in order to aid them in the Pacific war, but he had refused to divert his attention from the war against the Germans for the benefit of his allies. Nevertheless the opportunity to exploit the defeat of Japan was too tempting to be missed and at the Yalta conference in February 1945 he confirmed his intention to join in the war against Japan within three months of the ending of the war in Europe, and by a secret arrangement with the United States it was agreed that the U.S.S.R. should have the southern part of Sakhalin Island, the Kurile Islands, and Port Arthur—all that Russia had lost to Japan in 1904—as a reward.

In April 1945 Stalin denounced the treaty of neutrality with Japan and after the surrender of Germany, Russian troops were moved to the Far East. The dropping of the atom bomb on Hiroshima hastened the Japanese surrender and the Russians just had time to declare war on Japan in August and invade Manchuria, Korea, Sakhalin, the Kurile

Islands and Port Arthur before the Japanese surrendered. Thus without any serious fighting Stalin had obtained important gains in the Far East.

The Cost of the War

At terrible cost, the Russian people had emerged victorious: 17,000 towns and cities; 70,000 villages and hamlets; 98,000 collectives and about 6 million buildings were destroyed. So too, were about 40,000 miles of railway track and 30,000 shops and factories, as well as numbers of mines, bridges and dams. Perhaps about one-quarter of Soviet property was destroyed; crop production and the output of raw materials were similarly reduced, yet the U.S.S.R. still remained a major industrial power, and by a tremendous effort of reconstruction, and sacrifices by the people, the industrial production to keep up the war effort was maintained. The official figures for human losses were seven million dead, but if account were made for deaths through injury and disease incurred by the war, the figure might be nearer thirty million.

It can well be understood that the Russians were determined to make the Germans pay by reparations for the losses they had caused, and to prevent Germany from ever again being a military threat to the security of the U.S.S.R.

Wartime Diplomacy

The failure of the policy of collective security to safeguard the U.S.S.R. from the German threat led to the subordination of Marxist theory and principles to a policy of ruthless practical realism. The long-term aims of international communism were not forgotten, but for the time being the security of the Russian State came first, and Russian nationalism was stressed rather than communist internationalism. The Russo-German pact was a necessary compromise in view of the reality of the power situation and the aggression against the Baltic states and Poland was justified if the U.S.S.R. were to be defended against Germany.

When war broke out between Germany, Britain and France, the U.S.S.R. was in alliance with Germany, and took the propaganda line that it was an imperialist war; as such the communist parties in western Europe were against it. But when Germany turned against the U.S.S.R., the imperialist war became the Great Fatherland War, or the Great Patriotic War, and the communist parties supported it and agitated for the opening of a second front to relieve the pressure on the U.S.S.R. While the U.S.S.R. was hard pressed in the early years of the war there was a show of collaboration with her capitalist allies, Britain and the United States, because she needed all the help that they could send, but throughout the war Stalin consistently pursued only Russia's own interests, and with the growing military strength and the triumph over the invaders, he became more truculent and less co-operative, and extracted more and more concessions as the price of continued co-operation. He always refused to leave the U.S.S.R., except for the Teheran meeting, and there was a steady stream of British and American missions to Moscow, which all enhanced the claims that it was Stalin and the Russians who defeated Germany, practically single-handed.

In July 1941 Britain and the U.S.S.R. made a mutual aid agreement (a) to give each other aid; and (b) not to make a separate peace, and the United States offered aid. A pact was made with the Czech government-in-exile for postwar co-operation, and a military alliance was made with the Polish government-in-exile. A joint Russo-British action was undertaken in Iran to drive out the pro-German Government there. This protected Britain's oil supplies, and opened up a route for supplies of war material to the U.S.S.R. In August the Atlantic Charter set out the allied war aims and the U.S.S.R. signed it. The allies agreed not to seek any territorial aggrandizement, and to respect the wishes of the people and their right to choose their own governments and this formed the basis of the Declaration of the United Nations in January 1942. In December 1941 the British Foreign Minister visited Moscow to discuss war and peace aims, and in May 1942 a formal treaty of alliance for twenty years was signed between Britain and the U.S.S.R., by which they agreed to give each other all possible aid and undertook not to make a separate peace. They also pledged themselves to prevent further German aggression after the war, not to seek territorial gains and not to interfere in the internal affairs of other states and to work for the future security and economic well being of Europe.

In June 1943 there was a mutual aid agreement with the United States, although the U.S.S.R. had been in receipt of American Lend-Lease aid since 1941, and considerable supplies of war material were shipped from Britain and the United States at great cost in men and ships to the U.S.S.R. via Murmansk and Iran. Altogether the United States sent about eleven billion dollars worth of war material, and terrible losses were suffered by the Arctic convoys from Britain since the Germans had control of the Norwegian coast, but the allies got little thanks for their efforts, only a persistent demand for the opening of a second front in western Europe.

In May 1943 as a gesture to the western allies the Comintern was dissolved for it was inconsistent with the wartime alliance to be plotting the overthrow of their governments, but in fact the Comintern was no longer performing its original functions, and the long-term aims of the communists remained unaltered. The show of international co-operation continued, even while Stalin was clearly pursuing his own exclusive interests. Soviet representatives attended a postwar food conference at Hot Springs, in May 1943, the international monetary conference at Bretton Woods in July 1944, the security conference at Dumbarton Oaks in August 1944 and the San Francisco conference of the United Nations in April 1945, but the real bargaining was done at a series of meetings with the wartime leaders, while at the same time, in spite of previous agreements, Stalin was conducting secret peace feelers with Germany in 1943 and 1944. It may be that he did not seriously mean to make a separate peace with Germany, but by threatening to do so he extracted further concessions from the allies who wished to keep the U.S.S.R. in the war. In this he was certainly successful.

In October 1943 the foreign ministers of the United States, Britain and the U.S.S.R. met in Moscow and in November Stalin, Roosevelt and Churchill met at Teheran to discuss the second front. Stalin skilfully exploited the differences between Roosevelt and Churchill, who wanted an attack through the Balkans which would, of course, have acted as a check on Soviet expansion into eastern Europe, but he was overruled, and it was decided to make the landing in northern France.

In October 1944 Churchill met Stalin in Moscow and they agreed on spheres of influence in eastern Europe: the U.S.S.R. was to have Rumania, Bulgaria and Hungary; Britain was to have Greece, and there was to be a joint interest in Yugoslavia.

The next meeting of the Big Three was at Yalta in February 1945. By now Stalin was in a strong bargaining position, for the military superiority of the Red armies had been established, and the western allies were shaken by the critical situation produced by the German advance in the Ardennes. In a series of open agreements and secret deals plans were made for the final drive against Germany, the division of that country into zones of occupation, the destruction of nazism, and the extraction of reparations; and Stalin agreed to enter the war against Japan. The opening date of the United Nations conference was agreed upon, and a compromise on voting procedures was reached; the Ukraine and the Belorussian republics were to be admitted to the United Nations as voting members. Poland was to have an eastern frontier following the Curzon Line and was to be compensated with territory to the north and west. There was also an agreement over the form of government for Yugoslavia, and deals regarding United States air bases in Rumania and the Far East.

The final meeting of the Big Three took place at Potsdam just after the German war ended in July 1945. Truman was now President of the United States and Attlee Premier of Britain. Serious differences were now apparent between the wartime allies and the three premiers never met again, but it was agreed to establish a council for Foreign Ministers to draft the peace treaties.

Russo-Polish Relations

The most difficult diplomatic problem was that over which the war had begun—the frontiers and the government of Poland. After the division of Poland by the U.S.S.R. and Germany in 1939, Britain had stood by her guarantee to Poland and declared war on Germany, and a Polish government-in-exile was established in London that was quite naturally anti-German and anti-Russian. The Poles of course were set on recovering the lands that had been lost, but the U.S.S.R. was determined to keep the territories that had been taken from eastern Poland, partly because historically that had been part of the Russian State, and partly as a security measure against any future German attack. They were, however, prepared to compensate the Poles by offering them land in east Germany and east Prussia.

With the German attack upon Russia in 1941 the Poles and the Russians were brought together against the common enemy, and in July 1941 a Polish Soviet agreement was made which restored diplomatic relations, arranged for the release of Polish prisoners and civilians and provided for the creation of a Polish army in the U.S.S.R. and annulled the 1939 partition—or so the Poles thought. In fact, 'elections' had been held in the eastern parts of Poland in October 1939 which had chosen pro-Soviet members who had then voluntarily incorporated their lands into the White Russian and Ukrainian Soviet Socialist Republics, and there was no intention of letting these return to Poland. The Polish army was created in the U.S.S.R., but the government-in-exile maintained that 10,000 Polish officers who had been taken prisoner in 1939 had not been released, and there were disputes about the role and equipment of the army. Eventually it was arranged to let the army leave the U.S.S.R., which it did via Iran in 1942, and it assisted the British in North Africa and Italy.

In April 1943 the Germans announced the finding of a mass grave in the Katyn Forest which contained the bodies of 10,000 Polish officers whom the Germans claimed had been killed by the Russians. The Russians claimed that they had been killed by the Germans, and broke off relations with the Polish government-in-exile which wanted an enquiry by the Red Cross. Thus the temporary wartime alliance came to an end.

The bitterness aroused by the suspicions over the true nature of the Katyn Forest massacre were still further worsened by the manner of the Soviet liberation of Poland from the Germans. In July 1944 certain left wing Poles, with Russian support, organized the Polish Committee of National Liberation which moved into Poland behind the victorious Red armies, and at Lublin declared itself to be the Polish provisional government of National Unity—this at a time when Britain and the United States still recognized the government-in-exile in London as the official Polish Government.

As the Russian troops approached Warsaw the Polish underground forces in the city rose against the Germans. Perhaps they hoped to be aided by the approaching Russians, perhaps they hoped to be able to say that it was the Poles themselves and not the Russians who liberated Warsaw, but in the event it was yet another desperate tragedy in the history of a tragic country, for the Russians halted their offensive just outside the city, and the Germans crushed the rising.

There is much controversy about the refusal of the Red Army to aid the Poles: they even refused to let the western allies help them by granting the use of air bases for flying in supplies, but the effect was to make sure that no Polish leaders were left to take control of the country except the officially sponsored Russian ones.

The reality of the situation was that the Red Army was in occupation and there was nothing that anyone could do to prevent the U.S.S.R. imposing its own government and its own frontier settlement upon Poland. At the Yalta conference it was agreed that some representatives of the Polish government-in-exile should enter the provisional government, that there should be free elections for the permanent government, that the boundary should be that of June 1941 and that Poland should have Germany to the River Oder as compensation for the eastern provinces annexed to the U.S.S.R. The U.S.S.R. was also to have Königsberg, renamed Kaliningrad.

QUESTIONS

1. Discuss the circumstances leading to the Russo-German pact of 1939 and assess its consequences (*a*) for Russia; and (*b*) for the rest of Europe.
2. How did Stalin attempt to strengthen the frontiers of the U.S.S.R. before the outbreak of war in 1939?
3. Give an account of the main developments in the Great Fatherland War.
4. Discuss the aims and achievements of Soviet wartime diplomacy, 1940–1945.

5. How was the U.S.S.R. able to gain control over eastern Europe during and after the Second World War?

Further Reading

CONQUEST, R. *The Soviet Deportation of Nationalities*. Macmillan, 1960.
DALLIN, A. *German Rule in Russia, 1941–45*. Macmillan, 1957.
MACKIEWICZ, J. *Road to Nowhere*, trans. L. Sapieha. Collins/Harvill. 1963.
SETON-WATSON, H. *The East European Revolution*. 3rd edn. Methuen, 1956.
—— *The New Imperialism*. Bodley Head, 1961.

CHAPTER XXI

THE RULE OF STALIN:
THE POSTWAR PERIOD

Domestic Policy

The material losses of the war and the desire of the long-suffering Russian people for some improvement in their standards of life made the restoration and improvement of living conditions an obvious priority of postwar policy. Wartime contacts with the allies and the occupation of eastern Europe revealed to many Russians for the first time the superiority, in many ways, of the material conditions of living in the rest of Europe. Yet for Stalin, the military strength of the Red armies and the power vacuum created in Europe by the collapse of Germany provided a situation which could be exploited to strengthen the security of the U.S.S.R. and extend international communism, and this had a greater priority. It would mean conflict with his former allies and it would be necessary to maintain the Russian economy on a wartime footing.

During the war it had been necessary to depart from the pure milk of Marxist truth in a number of ways: the Government had been allied with capitalist powers and relied upon their support; the need to stimulate production by offering differential wages and by granting favours to the intelligentsia had created new privileged classes; men who had become used to the privileges of rank as officers in the army found it difficult to return to a classless society; workers had become used to evading the labour laws because of the need for labour, and collective farmers had found it profitable to appropriate collective land and property for their own use. In addition, people in large areas of the territory occupied by the Germans had been encouraged in their desire for separation from the Soviet Union. In education, thousands of schools had been destroyed and the indoctrination of many children had been interrupted, while it had been found expedient to come to terms with the Orthodox Church. The army had replaced the Communist Party in popular esteem during the war and some of the successful generals outshone Stalin. They had to be put in their places, and for all these reasons it was necessary to reassert the dominant role in the national life played by the party with Stalin as its leader.

There came a move to tighten party discipline and a purge of unreliable elements together with the development of a thorough system of training for party members at all levels in the hierarchy.

The Russian people had to be diverted from the superior attractions of the west by an intensive propaganda campaign designed to convince them of the real superiorities which they were told they enjoyed. In 1946 the so-called 'iron curtain' [1] was imposed which attempted to cut them off from all contact with the rest of the world while Russian nationalism was fostered. There were restrictions on all kinds of social contact with foreigners, rigid press and radio censorship, the death penalty for espionage was reintroduced, and a strict system of thought control over all art, science, literature and music was imposed, so that it became a matter of life or death to stray from the strict party line. In 1948 occurred the Lysenko controversy when the party adopted the line that the Mendelian theories were bourgeois frauds and that Lysenko's doctrine of acquired characteristics was the true Marxian answer to the problem of inheritance. Many writers and artists were obliged to toe the party line; Shostakovitch was one. At the same time all the credit for winning the war was attributed to Russia and in particular to the Communist Party led by Stalin, while it was discovered that most of the great scientific and technical developments had originated in Russia and that the Russian people were superior to the Americans at the same time that they were being ruthlessly driven to catch up with them.

There were large scale movements in the population during and after the war. Stalin had forcibly moved whole peoples if he suspected their loyalty. The Volga Germans were removed to Siberia, as were the Crimean Tartars, the Kalmuks and the Chechens, and the Crimean and Chechen Republics were extinguished in 1946.[2] After the war those who were suspected of having collaborated with the Germans were similarly removed. In addition to this there was the planned redistribution of industry, the movements of evacuees, demobilized soldiers, returned prisoners of war and those who had been in prison and in

[1] From Winston Churchill's speech at Fulton, Missouri, March 1946.

[2] About one-and-a-quarter million people were deported in this way, often in conditions which amounted to official extermination. See R. Conquest, *The Soviet Deportation of Nationalities.*

forced labour. These people needed not only the means of transport but also food and homes. Many of them lived for years in tents and caves and to this day the housing shortage remains one of the greatest social problems. The Government also insisted on the return of all those exiles who had fled, particularly from the Baltic states, and who did not wish to return to Soviet domination.

But great as were the needs of the people for some improvement in their living standards the main aim of the Government was to continue the policy of surpassing the production of the capitalist countries by concentrating first on the production of capital rather than of consumer goods. The fourth Five Year Plan was introduced in 1946 with the aims of reconstructing the economy, increasing production, raising the standard of living and maintaining a large army. The industries of western Russia were reconstructed, but any new construction and development was to be for the strategically safer areas in the east. The emphasis was on heavy capital goods but something was to be done for the consumer. The success of scientific and technical progress, and the directions in which greatest efforts were made, was demonstrated to the world by the first Russian atom bomb that was exploded in 1949, the first thermo-nuclear device in 1953, the first intercontinental ballistic missile and the sputnik in 1957.

The sixth Five Year Plan was influenced by the Korean war and the need to keep up industrial production of strategic materials and goods, but in general it continued along the main lines of all the plans. In 1948 Stalin announced a grandiose plan for remaking nature by belts of afforestation 3,000 miles long, the making of thousands of ponds and reservoirs for collective farms, the draining of the Pripet Marshes, and the construction of the Volga-Don canal and hydroelectric project.

The people were still driven hard: war taxes were abolished, and the eight-hour day but not the five-day week were restored; labour discipline was strictly enforced and much use was made of P.O.W. labour in the tasks of reconstruction and re-conversion. The forty-eight-hour working week was reduced to forty-six hours in 1956. Rationing was ended in 1947 and prices were reduced, but the currency reform of 1947, by drastically devaluing the rouble (one new rouble for ten old), reduced the value of peasant savings.

The need to maintain a large population to make up the losses in the war, and the social disintegration that followed the early moves to weaken the bonds of family and religion led to a renewed emphasis on the importance of the family. Grants and services for mothers were extended, and awards and honours were given to large families, while discriminatory taxation was imposed upon bachelors and small families.

The divorce and marriage regulations were tightened up and there was a move to end coeducation in schools. The wartime recognition of the Orthodox Church was continued and its efforts to reassert its supremacy over other faiths was encouraged. This did not mean any relaxation in the atheistic convictions of the Government; it was simply that it was expedient for the sake of the unity of the Russian people to tolerate the activities of the Church while at the same time concentrating on the indoctrination of young persons and hoping that the faith would die out for lack of support. This recognition of the orthodox faith was accompanied by repression of others and in particular there was a severe phase of anti-Jewish persecution from 1949. Jews were dismissed from their posts, their separate press was abolished, and thousands were deported to the 'Jewish Autonomous Province' in Siberia. Then came the Doctors' Plot in 1953, when nine men, five of them Jews, were accused of plotting to murder the Politburo and to undermine the health of leading members of the Government. It looked like the beginnings of a repetition of the great trials and purges of the 1930s.

Food production and the peasant problem remained a major concern of the Government and there came strenuous efforts to increase production and to limit the peasant's attachment to his own private plots. Discipline in the collectives was tightened up, the new lands acquired during the war were hurriedly collectivized, and in 1950 Khrushchev announced the schemes for amalgamating the collectives into larger units or agrogorods (agricultural cities) in order to make the provision of essential services such as water, electricity and sewerage more economic, but also to make it easier to extend party control and to turn the peasants into an agricultural proletariat. There was resistance, but of the 252,000 collectives in 1950, 180,000 were amalgamated into 60,000 and by 1955 they had been reduced to 85,700.

There had been no elections since 1937 and the constitution was in suspension during the war. In 1945 martial law was ended and elections on the usual pattern were held in 1946. 99.7 per cent of the people voted and of these 99 per cent voted 'yes' for their single officially sponsored candidates. 82 per cent of the new Supreme Soviet were party members and the majority of them were men of urban rather than rural origin. The Soviet approved the new fourth Five Year Plan and chose the Government but there were few changes. Stalin remained as Chairman of the Council of Ministers and Minister of the Armed Forces. Khrushchev was a member of the Politburo.

The Nineteenth Congress of the Party met in October 1952 to review the party's achievement. There was concern over the poor quality of some of the party members and leaders, and a general strengthening of the higher bodies over the lower in the party organization.

The Death of Stalin

Stalin was still in control, but it was evident to those near him that he was a sick man, and already they were looking for his successor. It seemed to be Malenkov, for he made the principal speech. There was some reorganization of the party administration, and the Politburo was replaced by a Presidium of the Central Committee with an inner group that was the true source of power.

Early in March 1953 the Russian people were told that Stalin was ill, and two days later that he was dead. They were warned not to panic and not to allow any disorder. Clearly the members of the Presidium did not know how the Russian people would take the death of the man who had been held up to them as the all-wise genius who had guided them through the perils of the past thirty years, but whom many of them could not help knowing as the ruthless terrorist of an autocratic police state.

In the event the succession was carried out smoothly by the inner group of party leaders who were determined to keep power for themselves while trying to make sure that no one of their number seized it from them. Stalin's death marked the end of a period of Russian and world history that remains to be fully assessed, but its importance is beyond question. Within the lifetime of one man Russia had risen out of revolution and civil war to withstand the greatest military machine in Europe, and to make a bid for world leadership and domination. A tremendous political and social experiment had been inaugurated and forced through with savage ruthlessness to make the U.S.S.R. a new economic model for the industrialization of a formerly backward country. The cost in human suffering was incalculable, but when the generation that paid the cost has gone, its successors will see only the real achievements: the expansion of the frontiers, the material strength, the prestige and confidence of treating on equal terms with the United States, and the belief that the future lies with them.

It is interesting to note how the traditional themes of Russian history come together in the career of Stalin. He was a product of the revolution that seemed to make a clear break with the tsarist system, and yet he continued to rule as an absolute autocrat, crushing all opposition with brutal ruthlessness; the centralization of political power in Moscow was carried to the ultimate limits, Russian nationalism was stimulated and Stalin completed the gathering in of the Russian lands begun in the fifteenth century; Russia was cut off from the west as completely as at any time in her history, and Stalin's reign continued the tradition of Byzantine intrigue and oriental bargaining that she had always known. A clean break was made with the Church but Marxism replaced the Greek Orthodox faith and Moscow was the Rome of international communism—'all roads lead to Communism' claimed Molotov. And as always in Russian history Stalin had to contend, often no more successfully than the tsars, with the peasantry and to find that his greatest allies against the invader were the geography and the climate of Mother Russia.

He was not a Marxist theorist; the writings attributed to him are dull and turgid. He followed Lenin closely until his death in 1924 and then stressed less the idea of a world revolution and concentrated on socialism in one country. In later years he posed as the great war leader, the infallible genius and saviour of his country. He became more removed from the people like the distant autocrats of tsarist times, and was surrounded by the courtiers of the Politburo and deluged with the sycophantic adulation of subservient scholars and writers.

Foreign Affairs, 1945–1953

Foreign Ministers
V. M. Molotov 1939–1949 and 1953–1956
A. Y. Vyshinsky 1949–1953

General Characteristics of Soviet Postwar Policy

The U.S.S.R. emerged from the war as one of the two great military powers in the world. With the destruction of Germany and Japan and the weakening of Britain and France, Stalin was determined to exploit the situation for the extension of Soviet influence and the furthering of the communist cause throughout the world.

It was hoped that the wartime alliance of the Big Three might continue to maintain peace through some kind of world organization to take the place of the defunct League of Nations. The Atlantic Charter had laid down general principles, and at a meeting at Dumbarton Oaks in August 1944, a draft organization for the United Nations was prepared, but the great powers could not agree on the voting procedure in the executive where the U.S.S.R. was outnumbered. At the Yalta conference in February 1945 it was agreed to permit two of the constituent republics of the U.S.S.R. (White Russia and the Ukraine) to vote as separate states, which gave the U.S.S.R. additional voting power, and at the same time the veto was introduced to the Security Council, which meant that the U.S.S.R. could obstruct any measures on which it did not have a voting majority.

The first Assembly of the United Nations met at San Francisco in April 1945, but the extent of Stalin's ambitions was revealed at the Potsdam conference in July and there were already ominous signs that the wartime unity of the allies was breaking up. The United Nations was to be used as an instrument for Soviet propaganda, for furthering communist interests whenever possible, and for obstruction of other interests whenever necessary.

The spirit in which postwar Soviet diplomacy was conducted was truculent and aggressive, and reflected Stalin's own suspicion and hostility towards his former allies as well as his conviction of his own rightness and sense of the realities of power. From the Soviet point of view, he was certainly successful, but he undoubtedly was chiefly responsible for the dissipation of the wartime goodwill towards the U.S.S.R. which had developed among the allied nations.

The Peace Treaties

With Germany, the surrender was unconditional, and there was to be no peace treaty until there was evidence of satisfactory behaviour, but for the lesser participants the Foreign Ministers were asked to prepare draft treaties by May 1946. These were delayed by disputes over the future of Trieste, which the U.S.S.R. urged should go to Yugoslavia, and over the Italian colonies in Africa which Stalin claimed, but after eight separate meetings; in London and Moscow in 1945, Paris and New York in 1946, and London, Paris, Moscow and New York in 1947, the treaties were signed.

The U.S.S.R. insisted on heavy reparations from Italy, Hungary, Rumania, Finland and Germany, and had already shifted great quantities of industrial plant from the occupied countries without waiting for the agreements. All the former enemy countries were required to dissolve their fascist and nazi organizations, while communist and pro-Soviet nationals, many of whom had spent the war years in the U.S.S.R. being groomed for the task, were introduced to the provisional governments of the 'liberated' countries.

The frontier with Poland had already been settled in August 1945; Finland confirmed the losses of 1940, plus Petsamo, and a fifty-years' lease of the naval base at Porkalla; Rumania once more handed over Bessarabia and Bukovina; Latvia, Lithuania and Estonia were reincorporated in the U.S.S.R.; Czechoslovakia was forced to cede Ruthenia; and Königsberg was taken from East Prussia. In the east, Tanna Tuva had been taken over during the war; Outer Mongolia became 'independent' but a Soviet sphere of influence; North Sakhalin and the Kurile Islands were taken from Japan; Port Arthur became a Soviet port and joint Russo-Chinese control was established over the Chinese Eastern and South Manchurian Railways.

In all, Soviet annexations amounted to about 260,000 square miles and twenty-three million people, but as important as the outright annexations was the extension of the Soviet spheres of influence through the promotion of communist governments in Poland, East Germany, Hungary, Rumania, Bulgaria, Czechoslovakia, Yugoslavia, Albania, Outer Mongolia, Manchuria and North Korea, and the activities of strong communist parties in many countries, particularly France and Italy.

Germany and Austria

It was agreed by the allies that Germany must be occupied for a considerable period to ensure that nazism was destroyed and to prevent her again becoming a military threat to the peace of Europe. In 1945 it was decided to restore Austria as a separate and independent state, to grant to Poland the eastern territories of Germany as compensation for the Polish territories ceded to the U.S.S.R., to grant the U.S.S.R. Königsberg, and to divide the rest of Germany into four zones to be occupied by the U.S.S.R., the United States, Britain and France. Berlin, which lay within the Soviet zone, was to be administered jointly by the occupying powers. An allied control commission was to be set up to co-ordinate the work of the four powers who would attempt to build up economic unity as a basis for future political unity, and reparations were to be extracted and paid to the victors for the losses inflicted upon them by Germany.

The future of Germany was the main problem in postwar diplomacy. Stalin was determined that a united Germany should remain militarily weak and under Soviet influence, if not a satellite state. He also claimed that the industrial Ruhr should be under four-power control, and that the provisional Polish occupation of East Germany should become permanent. The other governments were determined to check Soviet ambitions, for control of Germany could mean control of Europe. The signing of the Austrian peace treaty was delayed until after Stalin's death and Germany remains divided. Frustrated in his ambitions to control the whole of Germany, Stalin made sure that the eastern zone, at least, came within the Soviet sphere, by the establishment there of a People's Democracy, satellite state, in October, 1949.

The Extension of Soviet Influence in Eastern Europe

The occupation of eastern Europe by the Red Army and the change in the balance of power resulting from the destruction of Nazi Germany

Communist bloc of
peoples' democracies

Russian gains 1939–45

FINLAND

1945

1940

1940

ESTONIA 1940

LATVIA 1940

LITHUANIA 1940

EAST PRUSSIA
1945

EASTERN POLAND
1939

RUTHENIA 1945

BESSARABIA
1940

Oder-Neisse Line

Königsberg

POLAND

FEDERAL GERMAN REPUBLIC

GERMAN DEMOCRATIC REPUBLIC

CZECHO SLOVAKIA

AUSTRIA

HUNGARY

Frontier 1945

Frontier 1939

ITALY

YUGO SLAVIA

ALBANIA

BULGARIA

RUMANIA

RUSSIA'S WESTERN FRONTIERS AFTER THE SECOND WORLD WAR, 1947

gave Stalin an opportunity for the extension of Soviet influence which he exploited ruthlessly. Communist and pro-Soviet nationals from many European countries, for example, Thorez of France, and Pauker of Rumania, spent the war years in the U.S.S.R. where they were groomed for the task of entering, or forming the provisional governments of the liberated countries. Pro-communist groups were trained to make them ready to assume power in the wake of the Red Army in Poland, Yugoslavia, Albania, Greece, Hungary, Rumania and Finland. In 1943 a 'Free German Committee' and a German Officers Corps were formed from German prisoners of war with the object of forming a pro-communist nucleus in postwar Germany.

Except for Finland and Greece the provisional governments of all the countries in eastern Europe after the war contained large numbers of communists who held the key posts and who, with the presence of the Red Army behind them, eventually assumed full power. The Finns managed to resist the pressures put upon them, while the struggle in Greece developed into civil war in December 1944. British, and later American, aid to the Greek Government eventually helped it to overcome the communist threat to take over the State.

It had been conceded to Stalin during the war that he could have the right to expect to have friendly governments on his western frontiers but after 1946 these countries were drawn more and more closely into the Soviet sphere; politically, economically and militarily. Marxist social and political principles were applied, and the Soviet social and economic experiments were introduced: landowners were expropriated, collective farms set up, industries taken over by the State, and so on. The satellite countries, as they became known in western Europe, were transformed into People's Democracies on the Soviet pattern, and opponents of the communist régime were silenced or eliminated. Risings in East Germany and Czechoslovakia in 1953 were crushed. The economies of the east European countries were closely linked to that of the U.S.S.R. so that they became dependent on the Soviet for trade and credit. Treaties of mutual assistance were also made, for example with Czechoslovakia in 1943, Poland in 1945 and Rumania, Hungary, Bulgaria and Finland in 1948, which tightened the military bonds between the countries by providing for co-ordination of weapons and training, often with Russian officers in command, and in Poland a Russian Marshal, Rokossovsky, was made Minister of War.

The only serious setback to Soviet ambitions in east and south-east Europe was the defection of Yugoslavia in 1948. President Tito, the communist ruler there, refused to accept dictation from Moscow on the conduct of Yugoslav domestic and foreign policy. Yugoslavia was expelled from the Cominform[1] whose headquarters were moved from Belgrade to Bucharest, while tremendous political and economic pressure was exerted on Yugoslavia to force Tito to submit. The result of his defiance was a series of purges in the other satellite countries and a strengthening of the Soviet hold over them.

The Extension of Soviet Influence in the Middle East

Stalin was less successful in his efforts to increase the influence of the U.S.S.R. in the Middle East partly because there was more determined British and American resistance.

In Greece communist guerrillas, aided by the satellite countries to the north had involved the country in civil war in 1944. Britain and the United States gave aid to the Greek Government, and when the Greeks brought their complaint of aggression to the Security Council, the U.S.S.R. used the veto, but owing partly to the defection of Yugoslavia, and the cessation of aid to the communist rebels from that quarter, the Greek Government was able to bring the war to an end.

In Iran, where the U.S.S.R. had troops during the war, an attempt was made to use their presence to extract further concessions from the Iranian Government in 1946, but once more Britain and the United States stood firm in the Security Council, and once more the U.S.S.R. used the veto to block further action, but had to admit defeat and evacuate the troops.

An attempt to put pressure on Turkey in 1946 to force her to grant the U.S.S.R. more influence in the defence of the straits was also checked by British and American opposition, although they had promised that they would work for some change there.

The Extension of Soviet Influence in the Far East

As in Europe, with the destruction of Germany, the defeat of Japan left a power vacuum in the Far East that brought the United States and the U.S.S.R. face to face as political and military opponents.

The United States was in occupation of Japan and South Korea, and the Russians were in North Korea, as well as in the territories taken from Japan by mutual agreement with the United States. In 1946 negotiations began for the establishment of an independent Korea, but they broke down because neither side could agree on the form of government that was to be established there and both feared that it would be no more than a satellite of the other.

In Japan no agreement could be reached on a peace treaty, but since the United States occupied the country there was little that the U.S.S.R.

[1] See Glossary.

could do to get its way. In 1951 the United States made peace with Japan and was denounced by the U.S.S.R.

In China, civil war broke out between the nationalist forces supported by the United States and the communist forces supported by Russia. In 1949 the communist forces drove the nationalists from the mainland and the People's Republic of China was established in September. A year later a treaty of alliance and assistance was signed between the U.S.S.R. and China.

The Cold War: Soviet-American Rivalry

The extent of Stalin's ambitions and his success in achieving them alarmed the non-communist world. In a speech made in February 1946 Stalin returned to the anti-imperialist language of pre-war years, and in March Winston Churchill, speaking at Fulton in the United States, drew the world's attention to the communist threat and the existence of an 'iron curtain' across eastern Europe. The world was becoming divided between two great powers: the U.S.S.R. and the United States; each, with their supporters, representing two mutually hostile sets of political and economic values and interests. Instead of the peace which everyone had hoped for, international tension mounted with a series of crises and bitter rivalry in every field of international activity. The lengths to which Stalin was prepared to go were at first limited by the American monopoly of the atomic bomb, but the situation altered when the U.S.S.R. exploded her own in 1949.

Military rivalry took the form of tremendous expenditure on arms, particularly nuclear bombs and rockets as well as on 'conventional' weapons. The United States began the creation of a world-wide ring of military bases and alliances around the frontiers of the U.S.S.R. in an effort to check further expansion. The North Atlantic Treaty Organization was set up in 1949, and was followed by similar arrangements for the Middle East (C.E.N.T.O.) and for the Far East (S.E.A.T.O.). The Soviet answer was the traditional complaint of capitalist encirclement, the forcing of mutual security treaties upon the satellite countries, and a spurious propaganda drive for peace and disarmament, while at the same time retaining very large armies at home and in East Germany.

The economic difficulties of the postwar world were turned into an asset for communist propaganda, and in March 1947, President Truman of the United States announced a programme of military and economic aid to those countries threatened by Soviet intrigue and expansion; particularly Greece, Turkey, and later Iran and nationalist China. This was followed by the Marshall Plan for encouraging economic growth and co-operation between the countries of Europe by granting them United States economic aid. Those satellite countries that were tempted to join in were forbidden to do so by Stalin and a rival Molotov Plan was devised for eastern Europe in 1949.

While military and economic rivalry between the United States and the U.S.S.R. continued throughout the world, diplomatic struggles were going on at international conferences, particularly over the control of atomic energy, and within the United Nations, while the ideological contest was unceasing. Marxist propaganda was printed cheaply in Moscow and distributed throughout the world, Soviet radio transmitters poured out their message in many languages, while foreign broadcasts to the U.S.S.R. were jammed and a rigid censorship imposed. Foreign students were encouraged to study in the U.S.S.R. so that they could return to their home countries as missionaries for the communist cause. In 1947 the Comintern, which had been dissolved in the interest of wartime unity, was reorganized as the Cominform with its headquarters at Belgrade, and international espionage on a vast scale was carried on.

The Postwar Crises

Stalin's policy was to probe continuously at the perimeter of Soviet influence throughout the world in the hope of finding a weak spot where his rivals might be off guard, and then by fomenting a local crisis, to advance and consolidate his gains where possible, or to halt if the resistance was determined enough. This produced a series of international crises between 1946 and 1953 which revealed Soviet ambitions and alarmed the rest of the world.

The attempt to infiltrate into Greece from 1944 to 1946 and Iran in 1946 was checked by British and American action, but in 1948 the communists seized power in Czechoslovakia by a coup d'état. The most serious crisis, however, occurred in April 1948 when Stalin determined to force the issue over Berlin by asserting Soviet control and attempting to drive the other occupying powers out. The Soviet blockade was only overcome by flying in supplies to the city from the west and the blockade ended nine months later.

The second serious crisis occurred in 1950, when the army of the North Korean People's Democratic Republic attacked South Korea. Although it was, on the face of it, a civil war in Korea, it was in fact a trial of strength between the U.S.S.R. and the United States. One of the few postwar diplomatic blunders was made by the U.S.S.R. in quitting the meeting of the Security Council at this time, for it went on to vote for joint United Nations action to check the aggression of the North Korean forces who had the support of the U.S.S.R. and the Chinese.

QUESTIONS

1. What domestic problems faced Stalin after the war in 1945 and how did he deal with them?
2. What were the postwar aims of Stalin in foreign policy and how successful was he in achieving them?
3. Give an account of the extension of Soviet influence in eastern Europe after 1945.
4. Find out what you can and make notes on: Lysenko; Molotov; Vyshinsky; the Potsdam Conference in 1945; the Doctors' Plot, 1953; the Soviet use of the veto in the Security Council; the People's Democracies; the dispute between President Tito and Stalin; the Berlin blockade, 1949; the Korean War, 1950–53; N.A.T.O.

Further Reading

DJILAS, M. *Conversations With Stalin.* Hart-Davis, 1962 and Penguin, 1963.
LECKIE, R. *The Korean War.* Barrie and Rockliff with Pall Mall Press, 1963.
MACKINTOSH, J. M. *The Stratgey and Tactics of Soviet Foriegn Policy.* Oxford U.P., 1963.
SETON-WATSON, H. *The New Imperialism.* Bodley Head, 1961.
SOLZHENITSYN, A. *One Day in the Life of Ivan Denisovich,* trans. R. Parker. Gollancz and Penguin, 1963.
See also: *Keesing's Contemporary Archives, The Annual Register, The Statesman's Year Book,* and books recommended after chapters XVIII, XIX and XX.

CHAPTER XXII

RUSSIA AFTER STALIN

For a time, after the death of Stalin, it was maintained that Russia was being ruled by a group of leaders collectively, but behind the scenes a struggle was going on for the inheritor of Stalin's mantle. At first, G. M. Malenkov was Chairman of the Council of Ministers (i.e. Premier) and Secretary of the Central Committee of the party, but he was forced to resign and was succeeded as Party Secretary by N. S. Khrushchev in 1953, and by N. A. Bulganin as Chairman of the Council of Ministers in 1955.

Malenkov's short spell as Premier was shared by the collective leadership of L. P. Beria, V. M. Molotov, N. A. Bulganin, L. M. Kaganovich, and A. I. Mikoyan. In 1953, Beria who had control of the police and who may have made a premature bid to seize power, was arrested and shot as 'an imperialist agent'. Malenkov's efforts to provide more consumer goods for the Russian people met with party opposition and in 1955 he was forced to resign after confessing his ignorance of, and disregard for, Lenin's teaching on the priority of heavy industry over consumer demand. He was later made director of a power plant in the Urals and expelled from the Central Committee in 1957.

Meanwhile, Khrushchev, by methods similar to those used by Stalin in the early 1920s, had been consolidating his position in the party, eliminating his rivals, and packing it with his own supporters. He emerged as the first among equals, and then triumphed over them to become Premier, as well as Party Secretary in 1958.

Nikita Sergeyevich Khrushchev (born 1894)

Nikita Khrushchev was born in 1894 of a peasant family near Kursk, in the Ukraine. His father supplemented his earnings by working in the coal mines of the Don valley during the winter season. Nikita had a reputation for idleness, and received little education as a child in spite of the efforts of the village priest. He began work at the age of eleven as a shepherd boy, and was later apprenticed to a mechanic at the mines. He soon became involved in the activities of the local Bolshevik party, which he joined in 1914, becoming a full member in 1918.

He took part in the fighting of the civil war period in the Ukraine as a political commissar with the armies, and when it was over, returned to carry on full-time party activities in the Don valley and gradually worked his way up the party organization. He was educated at the workers' faculty of the Donets Industrial Institute, where he learned to read and write in one year, and got his first full-time paid post as a party organizer in 1924.

In 1926 he was demoted for exceeding the official party line towards the kulaks, but was taken under the protection of Kaganovich, who sent him to the Stalin Industrial Academy in 1929 to complete his training as a party organizer.

He remained in Moscow as a party official and with Bulganin, was responsible for housing and reconstruction in the city, including the building of the famous underground. He became First Secretary to the Moscow city party organization and a member of the Central Committee of the party in 1934, and played an important part in the organization of the great treason trials of 1936 and 1937, culminating in the execution of Marshal Tukhachevsky.

While the treason trials reached their climax Khrushchev was diplomatically moved back to the Ukraine, where in 1938 he became First Secretary to the Central Committee of the Communist Party of the Ukraine, and carried out a final purge of the kulaks. His rise up the party ladder continued with his election to the Politburo in 1939.

In the Ukraine, Khrushchev was responsible for general party administration, and this included those areas of Poland taken over by Russia after the Nazi-Soviet pact of 1939. With the German invasion, Khrushchev was given military rank and was responsible for co-ordinating political and military activities in the Ukraine throughout the war. It was his task to carry out the scorched earth policy, to arrange supplies and to keep up morale from Smolensk to Stalingrad. With the expulsion of the Germans he was faced with the problem of reconstruction, but in many ways he had been too successful, and Stalin was jealous. Khrushchev prudently resigned from the Politburo in 1946 in order to keep out of Stalin's way, and quietly consolidated his position in the party organization.

In 1949 he returned to Moscow to resume his former place as Secretary of the Moscow city party organization and as a secretary of the Central Committee. At this time, Malenkov was his great rival, but he replaced him as First Secretary of the Party, Stalin's old position, in 1953.

The other members of the Central Committee opposed the concentration of power in Khrushchev's hands and in 1957 there was a move to get rid of him, but he managed to turn the tables on them and they were dismissed. Since then, Khrushchev has ruled unchallenged, for the same year he also took over the position of Chairman of the Central Committee (Prime Minister) from Bulganin.

Domestic Policy after 1953

Stalin's last years were so repressive, and his power so absolute, that no one dared suggest change or reform, even where it was clear that mistakes had been made and errors persisted in: the excessive centralization of power was stifling economic and social development; the arbitrary rule was crushing initiative and encouraging deception; the forced socialization of agriculture was limiting production; and there was much discontent with the low standard of living because of the concentration on heavy industry at the expense of consumer goods.

There was a temporary period of uncertainty after 1953 when the Government was not sure how the people would react to the death of Stalin, and there was an attempt to win support by announcing a 'new course' which substituted the principle of collective leadership for the cult of personality and the autocratic power of one leader; there were to be more consumer goods, although the basic principle of concentrating on heavy industry was not to be abandoned; the powers of the police were to be limited, and there was to be a return to something like the rule of law that was guaranteed by the constitution; there were to be concessions to the collectives, and higher prices were to be paid to them in order to stimulate increased production. There was a degree of intellectual freedom for writers and artists that proved to be only temporary; there were limited amnesties, some political prisoners were rehabilitated and even rewarded with decorations, and the Doctors' Plot was exposed as a fabrication.

There was a general relaxation from the severities of Stalin's rule; wages and pensions were increased, prices were reduced, contacts with the world outside Russia were permitted, and there was considerable decentralization of power from Moscow to the constituent republics. It had been announced in 1952 that the fifth Five Year Plan had been in operation since 1951 and a sixth Plan was announced in 1956. This was dropped in 1958 and replaced by a Seven Year Plan.

The climax of the movement for de-Stalinization came with the

Twentieth Party Congress in 1956, which was packed with Khrushchev supporters and where, in a speech of 25,000 words, Khrushchev attacked the excessive adulation of Stalin and blamed him for mistakes in foreign and domestic policy, the conduct of the war, the arbitrary rule, the terrorism and brutality, the deliberate falsifications. Most of this was known, or suspected, outside Russia, but it represented a remarkable reversal of policy for Russia and for communist parties everywhere. Lenin's 'will' was published to further the condemnation of Stalin.[1]

The most outstanding developments have been in the field of scientific and technical education and its application especially to military needs. Russia established a lead in rocket and artificial satellite technology by sending up the first sputnik in 1957 and the first man into space in 1961. There are also vast schemes for increasing agricultural production, not only for food, but to provide raw materials for clothing and industrial needs, by developing virgin lands in Siberia and Kazakhstan.

The Russian people are undoubtedly better off materially than at any time in history and there is a justifiable pride and confidence in their achievements since 1917. The credit for all this is assumed by the party which keeps firm control of the machinery of State in spite of the relaxation of the more obnoxious elements of Stalin's rule.[2]

Foreign Affairs after 1953

The same spirit of relaxation from former severities and intransigence that marked domestic policy after 1953 seemed to be at work in foreign affairs also, but there was no giving way on fundamentals or surrender of essential interests. Talk of coexistence took the place of cold war; talk of peace took the place of hostility and the inevitability of war, but in spite of certain reductions, very large armed forces were maintained, and the supplies of rockets and submarines were increased. In fact, Khrushchev's Russia is pursuing the traditional Soviet policy of maintaining the security of Russia and furthering the cause of communism throughout the world by slightly different means. Armed conflict is no longer regarded as inevitable between the capitalist and the

[1] The attack on Stalin and his policies was carried further at the Twenty-second Party Congress in 1961, but it was, of course, still only a partial denunciation, because there remained a number of Stalinists in the Central Committee, and all of them, including Khrushchev, had risen to power under Stalin and were associated with his policies.

[2] It was felt by the party, for example, that writers and artists were getting too outspoken, and in 1963 they were firmly reminded by Khrushchev of the limits set by the party to freedom of expression.

communist societies; indeed with nuclear and rocket warfare it is not desirable, and the superiority of the communist system will, it is believed, demonstrate itself in peaceful coexistence. Meanwhile the aims of Soviet foreign policy are to make things as difficult for the capitalist world as possible while making a sustained bid to win over the so-called uncommitted nations of Asia and Africa by foreign aid and support to 'anti-colonial' political groups. The United Nations provides a convenient propaganda forum where co-operation can be practised when convenient, and obstruction when it is not.

The U.S.S.R. used its influence to put a stop to the fighting in Korea in 1953 and in Indo-China in 1954. The long-delayed peace treaty was signed with Austria after a bargain on reparations in 1955, and with Japan in 1956. Relations with Yugoslavia were taken up again in 1955 and the Cominform was dissolved. All these were, in a sense. peripheral actions which the U.S.S.R. could afford to take without any real sacrifice of her interests, but it was a different matter with Germany where there was a steadfast refusal to accept any kind of agreement for reunification except on her own terms. The 'summit' meeting at Geneva in 1955 between the U.S.S.R., the United States, Great Britain and France, which was designed to reduce international tension, was a failure because of this.

The policy of relaxing control from Moscow encouraged expressions of discontent in the satellite countries of eastern Europe and there were risings in Poland, in East Berlin in 1953, and in Hungary in 1956, that were ruthlessly crushed by the Red Army.

There has been violent opposition to the rearmament programmes in western Europe and the defensive arrangements such as N.A.T.O. and S.E.A.T.O. There has been a series of meetings between the U.S.S.R. and the western powers, and Khrushchev himself has paid a number of visits to various parts of the world. The foreign ministers met in Berlin in 1954 to discuss Germany and Austria, and in Geneva in April to discuss Korea and Indo-China. In 1955, the heads of governments met in Geneva and another meeting was arranged for Paris in 1960. Meanwhile, Khrushchev paid visits to south-east Asia in 1955, to Britain in 1956 and to the United States in 1959. These attempts to win over the so-called uncommitted nations and to play on the differences between the United States and Britain were not very successful and the Paris 'summit' meeting was wrecked before it started by Khrushchev, ostensibly because of the U2 incident, but in reality because he saw little chance of achieving his aims—viz. to disrupt the united front that was likely to be presented to him by the western powers.

The Cuban Crisis, October 1962

The most serious international incident since the Berlin blockade and the Korean war occurred in October 1962 when President Kennedy of the United States announced a naval blockade of the island of Cuba. Here a communist-led revolutionary Government had been recently established and it became known that missile bases were being built there by the Russians—ostensibly for the defence of the island, but also clearly representing a threat to the mainland of America. President Kennedy insisted on their removal and tension mounted as the Secretary of the United Nations attempted to mediate. After a week Khrushchev gave way and agreed to have the bases dismantled.

Russo-Chinese Relations

In recent years, important differences have arisen between the Russian and the Chinese Communist Parties. Although the two socialist states wish to present a united front to the rest of the world, and the U.S.S.R. has given considerable economic and technical help to their Chinese comrades, serious differences on the interpretation and application of Marxist dogma have developed, particularly over the attitude to be adopted towards the 'imperialist' countries and to the 'undeveloped' and 'uncommitted' parts of the world. How is communism to be extended and consolidated? Are there several roads to socialism or only one?

Khrushchev's policy is qualified by his awareness of the possible consequences of nuclear warfare and his belief in what he means by 'peaceful coexistence', trusting the capitalists not to attack, building up the economic strength of the U.S.S.R., and fighting them by economic means and subversion rather than by all-out war until communism triumphs through its inherent superiority.

The Chinese do not accept this and claim that they are following a more correct Marxist line in denying that capitalism and communism can coexist: they want world communism to be achieved through revolution, and in general are more 'Stalinist' and dogmatic in their policies than is Khrushchev with his pragmatism and 'revisionism'.

The contest has been carried on under the cover of verbal attacks on Yugoslavia, representing the Russian line, and on Albania, representing the Chinese line. In 1960, a conference of eighty-one communist parties meeting in Moscow papered over the cracks, but the renewed attack on Stalinism at the Twenty-second Party Conference in 1961, the humiliation of the U.S.S.R. in the Cuban crisis, and the Chinese invasion of India in 1962, sharpened the issues involved, and open attacks on China and the U.S.S.R. were made by each other's representatives at the Italian and East German Party Conferences in December 1962 and January 1963.

Other factors concerned include different appreciations of the realities of power, the different way that history and geography have influenced the course of events in Russia and China, conflicts over policy and spheres of influence in south-east Asia, Africa, and South America, and it does involve a challenge for the leadership of the communist world—ultimately, 600 million Chinese may have a better claim to that title than 200 million Russians.

QUESTIONS

1. What changes in Russian domestic and foreign policy were apparent after the death of Stalin?
2. Give an account of the rise to power of Nikita Khrushchev.
3. Find out what you can and make notes on the following: G. M. Malenkov; N. A. Bulganin; L. P. Beria; the Warsaw Pact; the Hungarian revolution, 1956; the U2 incident; the Twentieth and Twenty-second Party Congresses; the Cuban Crisis; the Sino-Soviet conflict; peaceful coexistence.

Further Reading

ABRAMOV, F. *The Dodgers*, trans. D. Floyd. Flegon Press, 1963.
CRANKSHAW, E. *Khrushchev's Russia*. Pelican, 1962.
—— *Russia without Stalin*. P. Joseph, 1956.
—— *The New Cold War*: Moscow v. Pekin. Penguin, 1963.
DEUTSCHER, I. *The Great Contest: Russia and the West*. 1960.
DUDINTSEV, V. *Not by Bread Alone*, trans. E. Bone. Hutchinson, 1957.
HASTIE, R. M. *The Life and Times of Nikita Khrushchev*. Panther Books, 1959.
KELLEN, K. *Khrushchev: a Political Portrait*. Thames and Hudson, 1961.
KHRUSHCHEV, N. *For Victory in Peaceful Competition with Capitalism*. Hutchinson, 1960.
PALOCZI-HORVATH, G. *Khrushchev: the Road to Power*. Secker and Warburg, 1960.
PISTRAK, L. *The Grand Tactician: Khrushchev's Rise to Power*. Thames and Hudson, 1961.
RUSH, M. *The Rise of Khruschchev*. Washington Public Affairs Press (1958).
Keesing's Contemporary Archives.
The Statesman's Year Book.
The Annual Register.

SOVIET POPULATION BY REPUBLICS: 1959

(in millions)

1.	*Russian Republic*	117·5
	Russians 97·8	
	Tartars 4·1	
2.	*Ukrainian Republic*	41·9
	Ukrainians 31·9	
	Russians 7·4	
3.	*Kazakh Republic*	9·3
	Kazakhs 2·8	
	Russians 4·0	
	Ukrainians 0·8	
4.	*Belorussian Republic*	8·1
	Belorussians 6·4	
	Russians 0·7	
5.	*Uzbek Republic*	8·1
	Uzbeks 5·0	
	Russians 1·1	
6.	*Georgian Republic*	4·0
	Georgians 2·6	
	Russians 0·4	
	Armenians 0·4	
7.	*Azerbaydzhan Republic*	3·7
	Azerbaydzhanis 2·5	
	Russians 0·5	
8.	*Moldavian Republic*	2·9
	Moldavians 1·9	
	Ukrainians 0·4	
9.	*Lithuanian Republic*	2·7
	Lithuanians 2·2	

10. *Latvian Republic*   2·1
     Latvians 1·3
     Russians 0·6
11. *Kirghiz Republic*   2·1
     Kirghiz 0·8
     Russians 0·6
12. *Tadzhik Republic*   2·0
     Tadzhiks 1·1
13. *Armenian Republic*   1·8
     Armenians 1·6
14. *Turkmen Republic*   1·5
     Turkmens 0·9
     Russians 0·3
15. *Estonian Republic*   1·2
     Estonians 0·9
     Russians 0·3

TOTAL   208·9 *millions*

Note: More than half the population of the U.S.S.R. is Russian, while there are considerable Russian minorities in most of the Republics. In Kazakhstan Russians outnumber Kazakhs.

THE RULERS OF RUSSIA

There have been several Russian States: the first centred on Kiev in the south-west until the Mongol invasions in the thirteenth century; the second grew around Vladimir-Suzdal in the north-east; the third, also in the north-east, was created by the Princes of Muscovy, and this developed into the Russian Empire from Peter the Great to Nicholas II, with its capital at St Petersburg. Lastly, the U.S.S.R. has continued the traditional lines of development and returned to Moscow as its centre.

The Order of Succession in Kievan Russia

Kievan Russia was not strictly speaking a State, for each prince had his own druzhina (band of followers) and there was no regular rule of succession. The towns were arranged in order of wealth and precedence: Kiev with its Grand Prince was chief, and the others, such as Novgorod, Chernigov, Pereyaslavl, Smolensk, Vladimir, etc., each had its Prince, and were nominally subject to Kiev.

Yaroslav bequeathed Kiev to his eldest living son and the other towns to his younger sons in hierarchical order. Thus a rota system of succession to Kiev developed: on the death of the eldest brother, Kiev went not to his son, but to the next eldest brother, and all the others moved up one. The sons of the Grand Prince of Kiev started at the bottom of the ladder and moved up, but sons of Princes who did not succeed to Kiev (i.e. who pre-deceased their elder brothers) were excluded from the succession.

The aim of the rota was to ensure that no prince should establish a hereditary claim to possession of territory—the princes were to act only as lieutenants of the Grand Prince, rather like departmental heads in a business firm, but inevitably conflicts broke out and the princedoms changed hands frequently.

[1] Several of the early dates are traditional and should be read with some reserve.

Period I: SW. Russia; capital, Kiev. The House of Rurik

RURIK: 862–879 A.D.; traditional founder of Novgorod

OLEG: 879–912 A.D.; cousin of Rurik; established capital at Kiev

IGOR: 912–945

OLGA (Igor's widow): 945–955

SVYATOSLAV I, Grand Prince of Kiev: 955–972

YAROPOLK I: 972–980

VLADIMIR I: 980–1015

SVIATOPOLK the Accursed: 1015–1019

YAROSLAV I (the Wise): 1019–1054

IZYASLAV I: Grand Prince of Kiev and Novgorod: 1054–1068

VSESLAV: 1068–1069

IZYASLAV II: 1069–1073

SVYATOSLAV II: 1073–1077

VSEVOLOD I: 1078–1093

SVIATOPOLK II: 1093–1113

VLADIMIR II (Monomakh): 1113–1125

MSTISLAV: 1125–1132

YAROPOLK II: 1132–1139

VSEVOLOD II: 1139–1146

IGOR II: 1146

IZYASLAV III: 1146–1154

ROSTISLAV: 1154–1155

Period II: NE. Russia; capital, Vladimir-Suzdal

YURY I (Longarm) of Suzdal: 1155–1157

ANDREW BOGOLYUBSKY: 1157–1174, Prince of Vladimir-Suzdal.
  Kiev lost its supremacy to Suzdal

MIKHAIL: 1174–1176

VSEVOLOD III (Big Nest): 1176–1212

YURY II: 1212–1216 and 1219–1238

CONSTANTIN: 1216–1219

YAROSLAV II: 1238–1246

SVYATOSLAV III: 1246–1248

ANDREW II: 1247–1252

ALEXANDER I, Nevsky: 1252–1263, Prince of Novgorod, recognized
  as Grand Duke by the Khan who later gave him Kiev and Vladimir.

YAROSLAV III: 1263–1272

VASSILY: 1272–1276

DMITRY: 1276–1294

ANDREW III: 1294–1304

MIKHAIL II: 1304–1319

YURY III: 1319–1322. Prince of Moscow from 1303. Grand Prince, 1319

DMITRY II: 1322–1326

ALEXANDER II: 1326–1328

IVAN I (Kalita): 1328–1340

SIMON (the Proud): 1340–1353

IVAN II: 1353–1359

DMITRY III: 1359–1363

DMITRY IV (Donskoy): 1363–1389

VASSILY I: 1389–1425

VASSILY II: 1425–1462

Period III: Muscovy; capital, Moscow

IVAN III (the Great): 1462–1505; Moscow the capital

VASSILY III: 1505–1533

IVAN IV (the Terrible): 1533–1584

FEODOR: 1584–1598 (End of house of Rurik)

BORIS GODUNOV: 1598–1605

FEODOR II: 1605

DMITRY V: 1605–1606, the false Dmitry

VASSILY IV: 1606–1610

VLADISLAV of Poland: 1610–1613: interregnum and period of anarchy

The Romanov Family

MICHAEL ROMANOV: 1613–1645

ALEXIS: 1645–1676

FEODOR: 1676–1682

IVAN V and PETER I: Regency of Tsarevna Sophia: 1682–1689

PETER I (the Great): 1689–1725

CATHERINE I: 1725–1727

PETER II: 1727–1730

ANNA: 1730–1740

IVAN VI: 1740–1741

ELIZABETH: 1741–1762

PETER III: 1762

CATHERINE II (the Great): 1762–1796

PAUL: 1796–1801

ALEXANDER I: 1801–1825

NICHOLAS I: 1825–1855

ALEXANDER II: 1855–1881

ALEXANDER III: 1881–1894

NICHOLAS II: 1894–1917

Period IV: Bolshevik Russia, the U.S.S.R.; capital, Moscow

LENIN: 1917–1924
STALIN: 1924–1953
KHRUSHCHEV: 1953–

THE GOVERNMENT OF THE U.S.S.R.

The constitutional movement, that is, the demand for some kind of limited monarchy, together with a representative assembly, was a product of the nineteenth century, and the first dumas were held in the reign of Nicholas II.

The attempt to rule through a constituent assembly in 1917 was foiled by the Bolshevik coup d'état and the establishment of the 'dictatorship of the proletariat', which was, in fact, the dictatorship of the Communist Party.

The first constitution of the R.S.F.S.R. in 1918 was replaced by the constitution of the U.S.S.R. in 1924. This, in turn, was replaced by the 'Stalin Constitution' of 1936, which, with amendments, remains the fundamental law of the U.S.S.R. today.

The constitution is a curious document that prescribes the machinery of the State and rights of the citizen with all the appearance of democracy, but which also includes declarations of socialist intentions presented as fact, while Article 126 confirms the dominance of the Communist Party. The constitution is a piece of window dressing and propaganda that bears little relation to the reality of the exercise of power within the U.S.S.R.

In fact, the Communist Party dominates and controls every aspect of the national life; single lists of party members are presented at elections, and the Party Secretary, who holds no official Government post, is the real ruler of the country. The way to political power is through the party, not through the Government offices.

The party is not a political party in the English sense of the word for there are no alternative parties and no official opposition. It consists of an élite minority, exercising power and leadership over the majority: only about 4 per cent of the population are party members, and of these about a quarter of a million are full-time paid officials.

The party and the Government form a dual system of 'democratic centralism' that is to say, the appearance of a democratic organization is maintained with the reality of power concentrated at the centre. It is the party's function to determine policy and to supervise its implementation by the Government.

In theory, the highest organ in the State is the Party Congress which meets at irregular intervals every two or three years: in fact it acts as little more than a rubber stamp for party decisions. In between congresses the Party Central Committee, which meets two or three times yearly, is responsible for policy, but true power lies with the Presidium (Politburo) which directs its sessions. Congresses, Central Committee and Presidium are elected by secret ballot, but at every level in the party organization from local cell to Central Committee, it is the secretary who can control elections and each secretary must be approved from above.

The rights of the citizens, particularly during Stalin's rule, are demonstrably fictitious. The U.S.S.R. is a totalitarian state with the party acting as 'the vanguard of the working people in their struggle to strengthen and develop the socialist system and is the leading core of all organizations of the working people, both public and state'.

Instead of the State withering away as the early Marxists foretold, it has intensified its functions and the central power is greater than at any time under the tsars.

Further Reading

The Constitution of the U.S.S.R.: Foreign Languages Publishing House, Moscow.

FAINSOD, M. *How Russia is Ruled*. Harvard U.P.; Oxford U.P., 1953.
SCHAPIRO, L. *The Communist Party of the Soviet Union*. Eyre and Spottiswoode, 1960 and Methuen, 1963.
SCOTT, D. J. R. *Russian Political Institutions*. Allen and Unwin, 1958.

THE DOCTRINE OF THE THIRD ROME

This idea was first advanced by a monk, Philotheus of Pskov, after the fall of Constantinople in 1453. He claimed that the first Rome, in Italy, had fallen into error in support of the Great Schism which split the early Christian Church into its eastern and western parts. Rome lost her leadership and was punished for her heresy by the barbarians who destroyed her.

Truth continued to reside at Constantinople, which was now the second Rome, but here again, error crept in, and she was punished for her sins by subjection to the Turks.

The heir to Constantinople was Moscow which was now the third Rome, entrusted with the responsibility for maintaining the faith, pure and undefiled: 'For two Romes have fallen, and the third stands, and a fourth will not be.'

Later writers were able to trace a direct link between Caesar Augustus and the House of Rurik, while others went on to claim that Moscow was responsible for all orthodox Christians and had authority over them.

The doctrine tended to inculcate an air of messianism into Russia's attitude towards other states and to give ecclesiastical sanction to the growth of the autocracy.

GLOSSARY

AGROGOROD:	Farm city—advocated by Khrushchev, 1949.
BARSHCHINA:	Compulsory labour performed by the serf for his master. Legally limited to three days per week, 1797, but often exceeded. Corvée.
BOLSHEVIKS:	Those of the majority—engineered by Lenin at the 1903 congress of the Social Democrats.
BOYAR:	Great noble.
CADETS:	The Constitutional Democratic Party.
CHEKA:	The All-Russian Extraordinary Commission for the Suppression of Counter-revolution, Sabotage and Speculation, set up as the new secret political police from 1917–1922.
CHINOVNIK:	Bureaucratic official—from chin = rank. The table of ranks set up by Peter 1 for the State officials.
CHINOVNIKI:	The bureaucracy.
COMINFORM:	The Communist Information Bureau set up in 1947 to succeed the Comintern. Abolished 1956.
COMINTERN:	The third Communist International, founded 1919.
DENSHCHICK:	Young courtier—appointed by Peter 1 as personal assistant to the tsar.
DUMA:	Assembly or council. Deliberation.
DRUZHINA:	Military followers, or company, of the early Russian princes.
DVORIANIN(sing.), DVORIANE (pl.):	Nobleman, one of the gentry, or landowner.

DVORIANSTVO:	The nobility. The non-tax-paying gentry in administrative or military service who became hereditary nobility free of all services in the eighteenth century.
GOSPLAN:	The State Planning Committee set up 1921.
G.P.U.:	The secret police set up 1922 to take the place of the Cheka. O.G.P.U. 1924.
GUBERNATOR:	Governor of a province.
GUBERNIYA:	Province.
ISKRA:	*The Spark*—Lenin's paper founded in 1900.
KULAK:	The richer peasant—a term of abuse for any peasant who opposed the party line.
KOLKHOZ:	Collective farm.
KOMSOMOL:	The League of Communist Youth, founded 1918.
MENSHEVIKS:	Those of the minority.
MIR:	The village community.
MUZHIK:	Common fellow, villein, peasant, yokel.
M.V.D.:	Ministry of Internal Affairs.
NARODNIKS:	From narod = people; those students and members of the intelligentsia who went among the people preaching socialism in the nineteenth century. Also known as the Populists.
NARODNICHESTVO:	General term for the movement involving the narodniks.
N.K.V.D.:	Peoples' Commissariat of Internal Affairs. Successor to the O.G.P.U., 1934–1943.
OBLAST:	Administrative unit; a province subdivided into rayons.
OBROK:	The annual payment by serfs in cash or in kind to the landowner.
ODNODVORTSY:	Freeholders.
OKHRANA:	The special police created in 1881 to combat revolutionaries and to protect the tsar.
OPRICHNIK:	A member of the oprichnina.
OPRICHNINA:	An entailed domain—the term given to the personal domain set up by Ivan the Terrible which was quite separate from the rest of the country, the Zemshchina, and not subject to the general administration.

OTDEL: Department.

POLITBURO: The subcommittee of the Central Committee of the Communist Party of the Soviet Union and the true centre of political power in the State—(the Cabinet).

POMESHCHIK: The possessor of a pomestie.

POMESTIE: An estate held in service tenure only, and only while the military duties were satisfactorily performed. The system extended by Ivan the Great.

POPULIST: See Narodnik.

PRAVDA: *Truth*—the Bolshevik newspaper established in 1921 with Stalin as editor.

PRIKAZ: A Government department. Order.

RASKOLNIKI: Dissidents—those who broke from the Orthodox Church in the schism of 1667. Old Believers.

RAYON: Administrative unit corresponding to English rural district, subdivided into village soviets.

RAZNOCHINTSY: Educated middle class—intelligentsia. (lit. people from various ranks, i.e. non-noble.)

SOVKHOZ: State farm.

STAROSTA: Head man of village.

STRELTSY: Body of regular infantry equipped with muskets founded by Ivan IV. Lit. = archers.

UYEZD: County or district. An administrative subdivision.

UKAZ: Decree.

ULOZHENIE: Code of Laws, 1649.

VECHE or VIECHE: Popular assembly or common council in medieval Russia.

VOEVODA: An appointed governor in medieval Russia.

VOLOST: Township—the basic unit of peasant self-government set up after 1861.

VOTCHINA: Hereditary estate, the owner of which was not obliged to render services to the ruler.

ZEMSHCHINA: The part of the realm outside the oprichnina.

ZEMSKY SOBOR: The Assembly of the Land, the representative assembly of the sixteenth and seventeenth centuries.

ZEMSTVO: Bodies for local self-government. Their organization and powers varied from time to time.

Some Measurements

One Dessiatine = 2·7 acres
One pood = 36 lb.
One verst = 0·66 mile, 1,166 yards

APPENDIX F

GENERAL HISTORIES OF RUSSIA

BEAZLEY, R., FORBES, N., and BIRKETT, G. A. *Russia from the Varangians to the Bolsheviks*. Oxford U.P., 1918.

CHARQUES, R. *A Short History of Russia*. Phoenix House, 1956. Also in an abridged version, E.U.P., 1958.

CLARKSON, J. D. *A History of Russia*. Longmans, 1962.

CROWSON, P. *A History of the Russian People*. Arnold, 1948.

FLORINSKY, M. T. *Russia, A History and an Interpretation*. 2 vols. Macmillan, New York, 1955.

HARCAVE, S. *Russia, a History*. Cleaver-Hume Press, 1954.

HOWARD, A., and NEWMAN, E. *Pictorial History of Russia*. Hutchinson, 1942.

HOWE, S. E. *A Thousand Years of Russian History*. Williams and Norgate, 1917.

KIRCHNER, W. *History of Russia*. Constable, 1959. College Outline Series. (A useful notebook.)

KOCHAN, L. *The Making of Modern Russia*. Cape, 1962 and Penguin, 1963.

LAWRENCE, J. *Russia in the Making*. Allen and Unwin, 1957 and Mentor Books, 1962.

MARTIN, J. S. *A Picture History of Russia*. Heffer, 1945.

MAZOUR, A. G. *Russia: Tsarist and Communist*. Van Nostrand, 1962.

MILYUKOV, P. N. *Outlines of Russian Culture*. University of Philadelphia, 1944.

MIRSKY, D. S. *Russia, a Social History*. Cresset Press, 1931.

MORFILL, W. R. *The Story of Russia*. Unwin, 1904.

PARES, B. *A History of Russia*. Cape, 1958.

—— *Russia*. Penguin, 1941.

PLATONOV, S. F. *History of Russia*, trans. E. Aronsberg. Macmillan, New York, 1925.

POKROVSKY, M. N. *Brief History of Russia*. 2 vols. Lawrence, 1932.

RIASANOVSKY, N. V. *A History of Russia*. Oxford U.P., 1963.

SUMNER, B. H. *A Survey of Russian History*. Methuen, 1961.

VERNADSKY, G. *A History of Russia*. Oxford U.P., 1953.

WALSH, W. B. *Russia and the Soviet Union*. Mayflower Publishing Co., 1958.

See also:

ALLEN, W. D. *The Ukraine: a History*. Cambridge U.P., 1941.

CONQUEST, R. *Common Sense about Russia*. Gollancz, 1960.

FLORINSKY, M. T. ed., *Encyclopaedia of Russia and the Soviet Union*. McGraw-Hill, 1961.

HAMILTON, G. H. *The Art and Architecture of Russia*. Pelican History of Art, 1954.

MAVOR, J. *An Economic History of Russia*. 2 vols. Dent, 1914.

RICE, T. TALBOT, *Russian Art*. Penguin, 1941. (Pelican.)

RICE, T. TALBOT, *A Concise History of Russian Art*. Thames and Hudson, 1963.
SLONIM, M. *An Outline of Russian Literature*. Oxford U.P., 1958.
UTECHIN, S. V. *Everyman's Concise Encyclopaedia of Russia*. Dent, 1961.

Comprehensive bibliographies are given in Pares, Walsh and Clarkson. See also CAREW HUNT, R. N., *Books on Communism*, Ampersand, 1959; GRIERSON, P., *Books on Soviet Russia*, Methuen, 1943; and SCHAPIRO, D., *A Select Bibliography of Books in English on Russian History, 1801–1917*. Blackwell, 1962.

Index